The
LIVING
ENERGY
UNIVERSE

The
LIVING
ENERGY
UNIVERSE

Gary E.R. Schwartz, Ph.D.
Linda G.S. Russek, Ph.D.

HAMPTON ROADS
PUBLISHING COMPANY, INC.

for the evolving human spirit

Cover design by Marjoram Productions
Cover painting by Sharon Webb

For information write:

Hampton Roads Publishing Company, Inc.
134 Burgess Lane
Charlottesville, VA 22902

Or call: 804-296-2772
FAX: 804-296-5096
e-mail: hrpc@hrpub.com
Web site: http://www.hrpub.com

If you are unable to order this book from your local
bookseller, you may order directly from the publisher.
Quantity discounts for organizations are available.
Call 1-800-766-8009, toll-free.

Library of Congress Catalog Card Number: 99-71608

ISBN 1-57174-170-4

10 9 8 7 6 5 4 3 2 1

Printed on acid-free paper in the United States

Dedication

For the living and evolving memories of our loved ones,

Our parent's parent's parents,
and our children's children's children,

Especially Shirley and Howard Schwartz,

Elayne and Henry Russek,

Dora and Louis Levin,

Carol and Frank Pearsall,

and Sam.

Time is God's way to keep things from happening all at once.
John Wheeler

The secret of life is enjoying the passage of time.
James Taylor

Time is what a life is made of.
Dr. Henry I. Russek

Table of Contents

Foreword

Children of the Night Rainbow:
An Ancient Vision of Universal Living Memory

You are a child of the universe, no less than the trees and the stars, you have a right to be here. And whether or not it is clear to you, no doubt the universe is unfolding as it should.

Anonymous note dated 1692
and found in old Saint Paul church in Baltimore

Once upon a time more than 2,000 years ago, there existed a people who lived in paradise. They believed that everything was alive, feeling, evolving, and immortal.

They believed that they were children of the night rainbow represented by the violet ring that formed around the full moon in the deep black sky.

They did not live apart from the universe but saw themselves as infinitely evolving manifestations of *manna* (energy) of a living universe. For them there was no death, only transitions to various unfolding embodiments of the vibrant energy and information that was their spirit and soul.

They relished the joy of confidence that their consciousness not only survived after death but continued to evolve forever. They felt profoundly responsible and accountable for their role in the making of universal living memories. Every chant, hula, and *pule* (prayer) represented their confidence that they and everyone and everything they loved were forever energetically connected, alive, and evolving.

These people of paradise were the Hawaiians and the other people of the islands of Polynesia. These were people who knew, and lived, the essence of what Gary Schwartz and Linda Russek have presented scientifically in this wonderful, courageous, and comforting book.

Hawaii is my home. My wife Celeste and I, my sons, my *'ohana* (family), and all my island neighbors sat together on the beach as I read this book aloud. We became an oceanic editorial board. Everyone laughed when I read Gary's question if their readers might smile, if Linda's and his carefully reasoned theory of systemic memory turned out to be right.

We had already started to smile even before I read their first question, "How would you feel if you knew *scientifically* that everything is eternal, alive, and evolving?"

When I read out loud the words, "Would you feel exhilarated, peaceful, terrified, amazed, incredulous, and inspired if you knew that everyone and everything were in a constant state of creative becoming?" one old Hawaiian woman laughed and answered, "I would feel all of those things he asks except for terrified, amazed, and incredulous. We always knew what these great scientists were saying.

"We are not frightened by this; we are comforted. We are not amazed, we are relieved that the rest of the world might be waking up to our *manna* (energy) and *mana'o* (spiritual knowledge). We're not shocked either. Actually, we're kind of bemused that it has taken 2,000 years for others to be so surprised with what we knew in our hearts all along."

This is an extremely challenging and life-altering book with the potential to revise your entire world view.

I suspect that *The Living Energy Universe* may receive some of the skeptical reaction I received when I wrote *The Heart's Code*. In that book, I suggested that theory, scientific research, and cultural mythology show that the heart literally thinks, feels, remembers, and communicates energetically with the brain, as well as the hearts and brains of others. While many scientists embraced the book, others said: The heart's just a pump and that's it.

Perhaps Schwartz and Russek can take heart in the lessons from a book I read almost twenty years ago, *The Nature of Physical Reality*, written by physicist Henry Margenau. It still influences my own life, research, writing, and clinical work.

Margenau suggested that, when we examine such serious and challenging theories as the one you will read about in this book, there are four criteria that you can use to judge which theories are worthy of serious reflection. These criteria are

- simplicity
- connectedness
- causality
- elegance

Schwartz and Russek's theory of universal living memory and living energy systems meets all four.

- Their theory is *simple* because the logic behind it is *simple*. It applies to all systems everywhere and violates no logical, scientific rule. It follows the well-known "Ockham's razor rule" of cutting out the extraneous and presenting things briefly, clearly, and concisely. Schwartz and Russek are excellent teachers and their book is a highly accessible introduction to their important new theory.
- Their theory meets the criterion of *connectivity* because it fits with other theories explaining how life and the cosmos work. Just as information, energy, complexity, and chaos theory apply to every branch of science and philosophy, their theory of living systemic memory blends well with all domains of science and philosophy.
- Their theory meets the criterion of *causality* because it provides not just relational but causal connections between many other scientific facts and long established theories.
- Perhaps most pleasing is the fact that their theory is *elegant*. It's beautiful because it appeals so strongly to the heart while not offending the skeptical sensitivity of the brain. Although some scientists may deny it, science has its own version of "style." Schwartz and Russek present exquisitely constructed logic and metaphors designed to bring a smile to your face, a glow to your heart, and an "aha!" to your brain.

As we finished reading this book at our Hawaiian *lu'au* (book party), we said a *pule* or prayer for this book and for Schwartz and Russek and their readers. As with all things Hawaiian, in keeping with our 2000-year-old indigenous science, and to connect with Schwartz and Russek's work, our *pule* too was simple, based on connection, and acknowledged the *manna,* or energy that has always been the source of everything. We were also guided to make it beautiful by offering a prayer as the bottom of the glowing red sun gently caressed the top of the blue Pacific ocean. We ended our prayer as the top of the sun blinked a brilliant green flash just before it vanished beneath the horizon—a Polynesian sign of good fortune.

Here was our prayer for these two courageous authors, their seminal book, and for you the reader as you seek to evolve your belief in science and soul:

> We *pule kakou* (pray together) that this book will help others be like the sun star that now sets out of our sight yet shines always somewhere. We *pule* that readers' hearts will be warmed by this book and that Gary will know he has answered Linda's question. We *pule* that she and their readers will know that the answer is yes. Her father, all fathers and mothers and all of their children, pets, plants, everything, are always alive and with us, in our hearts and the cosmos.

May we all be soothed by this book's scientific promise of the joy of our energetic and conscious immortality.

Paul Pearsall

Paul Pearsall, Ph.D. is Clinical Professor, Department of Nursing, University of Hawaii. His books include *The Heart's Code* and *The Pleasure Principle.*

Preface

Is Everything, Including Light Itself, Eternal, Alive, and Evolving?

*The real voyage of discovery consists not in seeking new lands
but in seeing with new eyes.*

Marcel Proust

*In this regard I would caution the reader to adhere to a maxim
once issued by Warren McCulloch:*

"Do not bite my finger; look where I am pointing."

Dr. Karl Pribram

How would you feel if you knew *scientifically* that everything is eternal, alive, and evolving?

Not just animals and plants, but rivers and clouds, planets and stars, electrons and protons, waves and particles, even light and energy itself. That every system, in some essential way, contains eternal, living, and evolving memories. That the whole universe is a living, remembering, self-revising process—a living energy universe. And therefore, in a deep sense, all things—great and small, visible and invisible, material and spiritual, past and future—are in an energetic state of creative "becoming," a universal revising process of dynamic perpetual bloom.

Would you feel exhilarated, peaceful, terrified, amazed, incredulous, inspired—all of the above? Would you smile?

Ken Wilber suggested in a footnote in his 1996 book, *A Brief History of Everything*, that maybe the universe did not begin with the big "bang" but rather began with the big "bloom." Is this the off-handed suggestion of a brilliant mind run amok, or has Wilber grasped something truly fundamental about the nature of the universe and the source of it all?

This book is about a story, a really big story, a story as big as the big bang or big bloom itself. If this story expresses a truth, it will forever change the way all of us envision both the visible and invisible aspects of nature. It will revise the way we view everything—body, mind, spirit, energy—everything.

Why Are We Writing This Story?
And Why Are We Writing It Now?

This story came to life because my coauthor, Linda, heard the core of the story from me in 1993 and said, "This story must be told."

As you will learn, I (Gary) stumbled upon this hypothesis in the early 1980s when I was a professor of Psychology and Psychiatry at Yale University, director of the Yale Psychophysiology Center, and co-director of the Yale Behavioral Medicine Clinic. At that time I was a respected young academic who had inadvertently discovered a controversial universal living memory hypothesis that potentially challenged my scientific credibility as well as my entire world view.

For many good reasons I kept the theory hidden for almost thirteen years. But as you will discover in chapter 1, I did confess it, albeit reluctantly, to Linda when we met unexpectedly. Not only did she grasp its importance, she extended the hypothesis to the process of storing energy in all systems at all levels to various degrees. With her guidance and support the story was ultimately published in those scientific journals open to new ideas.

As humankind enters the new millennium, science and society appear ready to reconsider their complex histories and revise their foundational and spiritual visions accordingly. If ever there was a time to envision the systemic memory process, it is now.

Preparing for a Paradigm Revising Story
with Appropriate Scientific Caution

When Linda and I first read Wilber's visionary words, our conscious experience of the big bang was very different from the big bloom. Whereas the big bang was violent, the big bloom seemed curiously kind—a more loving, gentle vision. It made us smile.

However, loving ideas, though obviously comforting, are not necessarily true.

True scientists are committed to pursuing the truth to the best of their ability, regardless of whether the truth is kind or not. As Chet Raymo, a professor of physics and astronomy and the author of a weekly science column in the *Boston Globe* put it in his 1998 book, *Skeptics and True Believers: The Exhilarating Connection Between Science and Religion*, we must "choose truth rather than peace of mind."

Linda and I are scientists in the deepest meaning of this word. We not only care about knowledge, we have a passion for it, whether we happen to like the knowledge or not. Though we hold certain beliefs that we hope are true, we care more about what is true than about whether our current beliefs are true. In this sense, we are true skeptics—reluctant believers at best.

Beliefs are stories all of us create to help make sense of the world around us.

Science and religion both create stories. The major difference between them is that science has an explicit responsibility to honor data more than stories, and therefore to revise and change their stories as new data are revealed. Scientific discovery, at its best, is the revealing and honoring of data and the logic that points to it, and then *revising its stories accordingly.*

The story Linda and I are about to share with you will probably stretch your mind to the limit of credibility. Personally, until quite recently, I was afraid to confess this hypothesis to anyone because of its wide-ranging predictions and its far-reaching implications. But conceptual integrity requires that science honor not only data, but the logic that leads to its collection.

If scientific logic inexorably leads to the prediction that all systems are eternal, alive, and evolving—and therefore have eternal living memories—then the logic should be communicated clearly and be put to experimental test. The systemic logic that led to the hypothesis deserves our serious consideration.

This book takes you on our personal and scientific journey to the theory of systemic memory, and beyond.

Who are We to Write a Story That Contains Extraordinary Claims?

Thanks to the gifts of our parents and teachers, Linda and I were blessed to have received the kind of academic training that enabled us to analyze and put forth this scientific story. The story told in this book is both professional and personal; it expresses our love affair with science and philosophy, as well as with each other.

Linda received her M.A. from Columbia University and her Ph.D. from the United States International University in clinical psychology. For over twenty years, in addition to her private practice, she was a research psychologist at the Harvard University Student Health Service and directed the Harvard Mastery of Stress Follow-up Study, in collaboration with her late father, Henry I. Russek, a distinguished clinical cardiologist, researcher, and educator.

I received my M.A. and Ph.D. from Harvard University and served on the faculties of both Harvard and Yale before moving to the University of Arizona.

Each of us was trained in both scientific and clinical psychology. We are aware of the myriad of mistakes that the human mind can make: self-deceptions, delusions, hallucinations, unconscious wishes, illusory correlates, confirmation biases, false memories, and so forth. We know, and honor, the late Carl Sagan's wise words, "Extraordinary claims require extraordinary evidence." Since we are about to make some extraordinary claims, we had better be aware of the need for extraordinary research to test them.

So as we offer the following predictions below, you should know that we are deeply aware of the scientific and moral responsibilities in making such controversial claims.

- Heart cells can have memory, which provides a plausible explanation for the controversial claims for cellular memory in heart transplant patients.

- Water molecules can have memory, which provides a plausible explanation for the controversial claims of homeopathy.
- Atomic systems can have memory, which provides a plausible explanation for the controversial claims for so-called "cold fusion" energy sources.
- Pure energy systems in the "vacuum" can have memory, which provides a plausible explanation for the controversial claims for out-of-body near-death experiences, survival of consciousness after death, and even communication with the Source (sometimes called the Great Spirit, the Supreme Being, the Creative One, or simply God).

As you will see, just as there are breathtaking levels of size in the universe, from the most ephemeral (pure energy and individual atoms), through the relatively large by comparison (biochemicals, cells, and organisms), to the outrageously huge (galaxies and the universe as a whole), then there should be parallel levels of universal living memories that integrate the whole.

If there are levels of universal living memories, then there should be levels of life and evolution itself, and a single organism—you, the reader—has the potential to envision all these levels of life as you explore this book and discover the systemic memory process.

Using Evocative Words to Convey Extraordinary Ideas

Physicists and mathematicians sometimes employ playful and evocative words—the "big bang," the "big bloom," "chaos," and "superstring theory" to help all of us, professionals and lay persons alike, experience the power of big theories that are inherently abstract and complex. Following their example, Linda and I use vivid words like "universal living memory," "grand organizing designer," "the natural law of circulation," and "living energy systems theory" in this book to help you both see and feel the logic of the theory and experience the vast scope of its vision.

Scientists are often taught to dress bold and creative visions in cautious, less creative clothing in order to get them published in professional journals. Our conservative choice of the systemic memory hypothesis is appropriate academic apparel.

However, what the systemic memory process envisions, in plain English, is the existence of a universal living memory process in all things, everywhere, for all time.

When you see the academic words "systemic memory process," think "universal living memory," and vice versa. Systemic memory = universal living memory. They are one and the same.

Commercial and Spiritual Implications for Abundance and Life Eternal

A true test of a big theory is that it has big implications, not only scientifically, but commercially and even spiritually.

There are many commercial implications that stem from this theory, and these commercial applications need to be considered by those of you who function in the business world. Using the same theory, some of you may make major contributions to society, and create wealth and abundance for yourself and others in the process. We will touch upon some of these commercial possibilities at the end of the book.

Finally, this theory has profound implications for our spiritual lives. If the theory is correct, the survival of consciousness—eternal, living, and evolving memories—is guaranteed.

Despite the horrors that nature has inflicted upon the human species, and the even greater horrors that we have inflicted back on nature and ourselves (all too often in the name of "God"), if the systemic memory process is correct, the living, evolving energy systems that comprise each of us, our spirits and souls, have an eternal chance to grow so we may ultimately learn from our mistakes. The capacity to revise our lives is not only built into life but into the afterlife as well. Even the concept of "survival" of consciousness after "death" is radically transformed from the perspective of the theory.

This conclusion is required by the theory. Yes, required.

The idea of living spirits will no longer fall outside of science, it will be required by science. No longer will the ancient ideas of angels and guides be interpreted solely as the wishful thinking of misguided minds.

Post-modern science has not only given us the conceptual tools to predict the existence of living, evolving info-energy systems—spirits and souls—in all material systems as well as in the "vacuum" of space, it has given us the technological tools to experimentally verify their existence, and even, potentially, the existence of the Source itself. What we experience as the physical universe may be the scaffold that helps build the evolving living energy universe.

As the late Dr. Jonas Salk wrote in *The Anatomy of Reality: The Merging of Intuition and Reason*, when intuition and reason come together to become a system—join hands and embrace to achieve a common goal—what emerges is greater than either alone.

Just as hydrogen and oxygen, when they embrace, create the miracle molecule of water, when intuition and reason embrace, the miracle of the systemic mind extends beyond even our wildest dreams. Following Salk's footsteps, we envision the merging of energy and theology, the embrace of energy theology, and the miracle of conceiving, scientifically and spiritually, the living energy universe.

Yes, all this, and more, is predicted by the theory.

When the universal living memory process is deeply understood, we stare at the light from evolving stars and see a new reflection of the remembering divine.

Like agape love, the theory extends unconditionally and integratively, from the very small to the all. If the universal living memory story is true, systems science may literally resurrect and revise the reputation of God.

Does the universe, and everything in it, remember? Decide for yourself. The story is here for your enjoyment and decision.

The
LIVING
ENERGY
UNIVERSE

Acknowledgments

If you are going to create more light for our world,
you must be willing to endure a little heat.

Frank Kawaikapuokalani "Kuma" Hewett,
a Hawaiian Kahuna author
of *The Sacred Waters*

A white page, or canvas.
The challenge, bring order to the whole.
Through design, composition, tension, balance, light, and harmony.
So many possibilities . . .

Stephen Sondheim
Sunday in the Park with George

Writing a science book about a visionary and controversial hypothesis is a complex process that requires a labor of love. The labor in birthing *The Living Energy Universe* has sometimes been painful (as mothers know), often joyous, and always challenging and life affirming.

As Dean Radin put it, "You're wacky before you succeed. Afterwards, you're a genius." If there is any genius to be discovered in this book, it reflects the knowledge and wisdom of the many people whose ideas live on in our minds and hearts. They are the guardians, we are the children. As our faithful Webster's reminds us, the word "genius" comes from the Latin *genius* which means "the guardian deity or spirit of a person, spirit, natural ability, genius, from *gignere*, to produce."

This book was written partly because of the inspiration of Dr. James Levin and Paul Pearsall. It was Jim who insisted that we take the time to tell the universal living memory story, and to be brave enough to tell the story as it really happened. Jim has understood the systemic memory hypothesis for some time, and his vision goes beyond our own. The truth is, this book would probably never have been written, and certainly not have been written this way, without Jim. Both he and Paul encouraged us to write this book from our hearts as well as our heads, and we have tried to do so. The inspiration to stay in our hearts was reinforced by Natalie Cederquist, whose playful artistic visions kept us smiling. And the inspiration to stay in our heads was reinforced by Bill Gladstone, whose knowledge of both mathematics and semantics provided essential guidance and comfort.

Though we did not know it at the time, Bill really knew his math. After Bill finished editing the book, he told us: "What convinced me that you were right was the summary formula you included in chapter 6." It turned out that Bill was a child prodigy in mathematics. He won math awards at Andover, earned advanced placement in mathematics as a Yale undergraduate, and did graduate work at Harvard University before entering the publishing world. We never expected that it would be our senior editor and agent who would convince us that the foundation of the mathematics was most likely correct.

If anyone appreciates the possibility of universal living memories it is Paul Pearsall. His book, *The Heart's Code,* provides clinical, scientific, and cultural reasons for taking the idea of info-energy systems and systemic memory seriously. We thank Paul and his *'ohana* (family) for their beautiful foreword, including Frank "Kuma" Hewett for his wise words of encouragement, and Hawaii's "Papa Henry" for his support.

I (Gary) was first introduced to the concept of feedback when as a graduate student I read Dr. Walter Cannon's *The Wisdom of the Body,* written by the distinguished Harvard physiologist and physician; this was followed by reading Norbert Weiner's *Cybernetics,* a universal theory of order and guidance in systems created by MIT's distinguished mathematician. I never recovered from these two books. My early work at Harvard on biofeedback and disregulation theory, originally inspired by these two scientists, ultimately led me to living systems theory and the discovery of the systemic memory process.

When I was at Yale University, I was further inspired by Claude Saxton Burr's *Blueprint for Immortality,* a book written by a retired Yale professor of anatomy and physiology that provided biophysical evidence consistent with the systemic memory hypothesis. It was in the process of teaching the course using James G. Miller's *Living Systems* that I came to the logic of universal living memory. Miller and colleagues pioneered the living systems vision. Richard Kraft's book, *A Reason for Hope*, provides a continued source of guidance and encouragement for learning how to apply systems thinking to matters of the heart and spirit as well as matters of the head. Dr. Jonas Salk gave me his personal copy of the book he wrote, *The Anatomy of Reality*, that continues to inspire me to this day.

Thanks to a then Yale doctoral student, Daniel Weinberger, I learned about Stephen Pepper's *World Hypothesis: A Study in Evidence*. This seminal volume profoundly influenced how I approached science and philosophy, and it set the stage not only for this book and much of our current writing, but our next two books in the trilogy as well. Rupert Sheldrake's *A New Science of Life* appeared after I stumbled upon the logic of the systemic memory process. Rupert's thesis of morphic resonance also predicts that everything is eternal, alive, and evolving.

However, Rupert's analysis began with the premise that the information storage was "non-local" and transcended space and time, whereas my analysis began with the premise that information began "local" within material systems and then extended into the "vacuum" of space. Rupert encouraged me and my students to conduct a series of controversial studies at Yale and the University of Arizona on implicit memory that could be systemic and/or morphic, and his inspiration and enthusiasm are warmly and deeply appreciated. Memory may be local and extended (the living energy systems perspective), as well as non-local (such as Sheldrake's morphic fields and Watson's enformed systems).

Many others shaped our thinking during this period, but only a few can be highlighted here. When Linda and I published our first chapter on systemic memory in Dr. Karl Pribram's *Brain and Values*, one of the persons we dedicated the chapter to was the late great physicist Heinz Pagels. His book, *The Cosmic Code*, taught me to enter the mind of the physicist, and I came to know Einstein's mind through Heinz. Thanks to Karl's openness and encouragement, systemic memory went from being a secret vision to a scientific exposition. Gary Zukav's *The Dancing Wu Li Masters* led me to my personal epiphany in Vancouver about the eternal nature of organized patterns of light energy—how we could all be "stars" and leave info-energy person prints in the sky and beyond.

Linda and I also dedicated the chapter to Dr. Larry Dossey, whose many books, including *Healing Words*, inspired us to attempt to integrate psychology, physics, medicine, and spirituality. Other major sources of inspiration and guidance came to us from Dean Radin's *The Conscious Universe*, Fred Allen Wolf's *The Spiritual Universe*, Chet Raymo's *Skeptics and True Believers*, Ervin Laszlo's *The Whispering Pond*, and Gerald L. Schroeder's *The Science of God*.

The first mention of the systemic memory process appeared in *Advances: The Journal of Mind-Body Health*. Harris Dienstfrey, the editor of this journal not only had the vision to publish our papers on "energy cardiology," the "challenge of one medicine," and "loving openness," but he brought us to William Novak who brought us to Claire Sylvia and *A Change of Heart*. Jeanne Achterberg, the senior editor of *Alternative Therapies in Health and Medicine*, along with her husband Frank Lawlis, saw the power of the logic and made it possible to publish our article on "dynamical energy systems and modern physics."

The writing of this book was also inspired by Susy Smith, presently eighty-eight years old, the author of twenty-nine published books, some of which deal with the mother of all questions (the possibility of survival of consciousness after physical death). Susy's warm and friendly style of writing is well-known to her readers. As our "adopted" grandmother (she considers us to be her "illegitimate" grandchildren), she has encouraged us to speak out about the serious implications of the systemic memory hypothesis for the continued existence of our departed loved ones, such as Henry I. Russek (Linda's father), Betty Smith (Susy's mother), and Howard and Shirley Schwartz (Gary's father and mother). She was inspired by Stewart Edward White's 1940 masterpiece, *The Unobstructed Universe*, which in turn inspired us.

We warmly thank John Steele, one of the authors of *Earthmind: Communicating with the Living World of Gaia*. Just before our book was going to the printer, John shared with us a page from his book indicating that he actually used the term "systemic memory" to describe the universal memory process at the level of the Earth (he and we are obviously on the same page). We wish to acknowledge our dear friend Lloyd Smith, who died shortly after completing his unpublished novel L'Anna about an Arizona female neurologist and healer and her Harvard Ph.D. research psychologist husband, for his encouragement and love. We also thank George Anderson, Laurie Campbell, John Edward, Anne Gehman, and Suzanne Northrop, distinguished members of our survival research "Dream Team," for their inspiration and collaboration.

We wish to honor the memories of our living and departed parents and families (including the memories of our living and departed dogs Willie, Harry, Arizona, Freudy, Freudy II, Freudy III, and Sammy), who always remain in our hearts. We also honor the memories of Dora and Louis Levin, Frank Pearsall, and Jim's friend, people we never met but know in our hearts. The writing of this book began when Louie was dying, and the first draft was read by Jim to his friend when he was dying. They are an intimate part of this book. We wish to thank the late Stanley King from the Harvard University Student Health Service, and his wife, Jane King, for their loving encouragement and support over the years.

The evolution of spirituality in medicine and society is emerging at a remarkable rate. Two recent books that have touched us deeply are Diane Goldner's reverent *Infinite Grace: Where the Worlds of Science and Spiritual Healing Meet*, and Chip Brown's irreverent *Afterwards, You're a Genius: Faith, Medicine, and the Metaphysics of Healing*. Joel Martin and Pat Romanaski's *Love Beyond Life* helped keep us focused and stay on course.

At the University of Arizona, many of our undergraduate and graduate students (who are our best teachers) have encouraged us to be strong, and tell the universal living memory story as it really is. They include (alphabetically) John Brown (who also wrote the first newspaper account of the systemic memory hypothesis, in the student newspaper *The Wildcat*), Brian Burke, Patti Harada, John Kline, Daniel Lewis, Carolyne Luna, Lonnie Nelson, Craig Santarre, Ericha Scott, Shauna Shapiro, Parmi Suchdev, and David Weinstock. Faculty who have served as especially friendly and formidable devil's advocates (FDAs) include John J.B. Allen, Lynn Nadel, and Lee Sechrest.

Dr. Iris Bell and Carol Baldwin introduced us to homeopathy, and together, we are exploring ways to test the hypothesis of systemic memory in water. They are both visionaries, and live with wonderful dogs. Iris has pushed me for almost three decades to keep reaching and growing, searching for hidden syntheses, and remembering the whole. It is Iris's vision that the next stage will be to integrate the systemic memory process with chaos and complexity theory, creating a grand revisionistic living energy systems perspective. We would not be surprised if Iris became its mother.

Dr. Andrew Weil, the editor-in-chief of the new journal *Integrative Medicine*, when he could not find a flaw in the logic, sent our paper to Richard Horton, the editor-in-chief of *The Lancet*, who could not find a flaw either. Our paper on "the plausibility of homeopathy" was published in Andrew's journal. He is a visionary and dog lover too. David Rychener of the Program in Integrative Medicine extended the book with love and perspective. Though he did not know it, his values have served as implicit guardians in this book.

Hampton Roads Publishing Company was the perfect home for a book that bridges the science of spirit and the spirit of science. The enthusiasm and guidance of Robert Friedman and Frank DeMarco are especially appreciated. The careful editing of Richard Leviton and the professional skills of Kathy Cooper, Jane Hagaman, and Rebecca Whitney were invaluable to the manifestation of this book.

The ideas expressed in this book were assisted through the support of various organizations and individuals. At Harvard, my research on biofeedback and cybernetics was funded by grants from the National Institute of Mental Health, the Advanced Research Projects Agency of the Department of Defense, and the Spenser Foundation. At Yale, my research on systems theory, emotion, and memory was funded by the National Science Foundation, the National Heart, Lung, and Blood Institute, the National Institute of Mental Health, and the Yale Behavioral Medicine Clinic. At the University of Arizona, Linda's and my research on dynamical energy systems theory and energy medicine has been funded by various sources, including the National Center for Complementary and Alternative Medicine from the National Institutes of Health, the Veteran's Administration (Iris Bell, Principle Investigator), the Canyon Ranch Foundation, and visionary donors to the Human Energy Systems Laboratory who wish to remain anonymous.

PART I

The Secret Journey to Universal Living Memory

*Imagine that you have stepped outside the whole universe,
and you are seeing it as a gigantic caterpillar of living galaxies,
slowly but surely readying to transform into a
rainbow colored butterfly universe of indescribable beauty . . .*

Sam

Chapter 1

The Reluctant Believer

How a Yale Professor Stumbled Upon the Universal Living Memory Hypothesis and Kept It Hidden for Thirteen Years

The heart knows, the thought denies, is there no other way?
Stephen Sondheim, *Pacific Overtures*

*The best and most beautiful things in the world
cannot be seen or even touched.
They must be felt with the heart.*
Helen Keller

In science it is dangerous to propose novel ideas that challenge the foundation of accepted dogma. Scientists don't like to say that they hold certain beliefs dogmatically, but they sometimes do. Although many scientists would vehemently deny this, they are sometimes as stubborn and closed-minded as two-year-old children. All of us hold beliefs that are dear to us, that define us, that make us who we are. They are stories we live by, and die by. I was certainly not ready to live by, or die by, the story that came to me one fateful morning at Yale University in the early 1980s.

Though the original discovery was made in Connecticut, the discovery came to life one evening in 1993 in Boca Raton, Florida. A woman I had known but a week asked me a question that no one had ever asked me before. Though her question reflects only one implication of the systemic memory process, I have yet to recover from her question, and I probably never will.

Our purpose in using dialogue in this book is to express not only the meaning of the conversations as we recall them, but the emotions of the conversations as well. Though this is a science book, it is being written from the heart as well as the head. And in April 1993, Linda Russek's heart asked Gary Schwartz's head a question.

"Is My Father, Henry, Still Alive?"

I was attending a family celebration in New York, and I desperately wanted to see Linda again. So both on the way to New York from Tucson, and on the way back, I stopped in Boca Raton to spend a few special hours with her. I was forty-eight then and going through a divorce. Linda was forty-four and long divorced. Linda and I spoke virtually nonstop and confessed deep secrets to each other.

Although Linda was a clinician and a scientist, she had developed deep spiritual interests following the tragic death of her father, Dr. Henry I. Russek, in 1990. Henry was beloved by his wife, children, and grandchildren, as well as by his parents. He had been a distinguished cardiologist. His family adored him, and as far as I can tell, he deserved their exceptional adoration. Henry was a family man, a devoted son, friend, and parent to his parents, and he shared fully in the diverse and challenging lives of his wife, three daughters, and their respective families.

Linda had a special relationship with her father. After she completed her Ph.D. in clinical psychology in 1978, Henry and Elayne, Linda's mother, invited her to join them in creating one of the first practices of integrative medicine in the country. Integrative medicine involves the combination of conventional and alternative approaches to medicine. Henry was the cardiologist, Elayne was the nurse, and Linda was the psychologist. In addition, Linda and Henry collaborated on a major thirty-five-year follow-up investigation to the Harvard Mastery of Stress study that demonstrated how the perception of stress in college predicted physical disease in mid-life. When Henry died, Linda lost a father, colleague, and best friend.

Henry's death launched Linda on a spiritual and scientific quest to discover if Henry's personal consciousness, after physical death, continued in some form. Was he, on some level, still alive? Could she contact him? Was there any scientific reason to believe that the essence of Henry, his spirit and soul, survived bodily death, and was evolving as well?

Linda read many books and spoke with many people.

I had, frankly, never considered this question seriously. I was a Harvard Ph.D., a former Yale professor, and in 1993 was a Professor of Psychology, Neurology, and Psychiatry at the University of Arizona. I did my research in mind-body medicine such as biofeedback, stress management, emotion, personality, and health, not parapsychology and spirituality. Sure, I had loved my parents, and when they died while I was at Yale, I assumed that my Reform Jewish upbringing was the final word: dust to dust, ashes to ashes, period.

Four A.M. that Monday morning in Boca Raton, Linda asked me, with great intensity and seriousness, "Do you think it's possible that my father is still alive?"

Taken aback I replied, "I'm not sure, but would it matter if I told you that I thought it was possible?

She said, "Yes."

I asked, "Why would it make a difference to you what I think?" .

She said, "Because you're a serious scientist, and if you think it's possible, you probably have a good reason for saying so.

I then confessed a secret.

"To tell you the truth, many years ago, when I was a professor at Yale University, I stumbled upon a hypothesis about how systems stored information that led me—in fact, forced me—to entertain the possibility of the survival of consciousness after death. However, I haven't told anyone about this hypothesis because it's so terribly controversial."

She said, "Really? What's the theory?"

I eventually explained to her how it was that I came to discover what I thought was a plausible yet seemingly outrageous memory hypothesis at the time.

I explained the logic that led to the prediction that all systems, in the process of becoming and remaining wholes, stored information dynamically. I explained that this implied not only that all systems

5

were "alive," but also that this information continued as a living, evolving system after the physical structure had deconstructed. I explained to her that I hadn't presented the theory to any scientists yet so I didn't know for certain if the logic was correct. I also explained that I didn't know if nature really worked this way even if the logic was correct.

However, I confessed that everything that I knew about physics and psychology forced me to entertain this hypothesis.

Since Linda had a very strong motivation to want to believe, her openness to the possibility of a universal living memory process was certainly understandable. However, Linda's a scientist too, and her capacity for skepticism is just as strong as mine. So she began to search for a flaw. She couldn't find one.

She said, "Gary, this idea is really important. Do you realize the implications of this hypothesis?"

I said, "I'm aware of some of the implications of this hypothesis, but I'm frankly quite afraid of them."

She coaxed me to reconsider.

"For the sake of my father and my family, we must test your hypothesis. Will you help me?"

Put yourself in my shoes.

You've just confessed a secret potential scientific bombshell to a caring and beautiful person you hardly know. You're well aware that many of your colleagues would ridicule and even attempt to destroy your academic career, if they knew that you were actually considering doing research in this area. So there I was, having fallen in love with Linda's love for her father and her dream to know, one way or the other, if Henry is still here.

I looked into her searching eyes and said, "Yes, but only if we don't tell anyone."

A Mystical-Scientific Experience in the Nude— The Light Remembers Forever

The question of eternal memory per se does not address the deep question of whether the information is dead or alive, and whether it continues to evolve or not.

What excited Linda was not just the idea that information, once created, might continue forever, but most importantly, that information could continue to live and evolve. It could do more than just maintain its personal identity; its consciousness and personality could continue to grow as well.

When we use the term "eternal memory" in this book, we are referring to eternal *living and evolving memory*, not just eternal memory. Similarly, when we use the terms "systems" and "systemic" in this book, we are referring to living and evolving systems, not just abstract systems. It is the universal living memory process, inherent in all systems at all levels, that makes the information come to life and continue to evolve, forever.

Before we discuss the logic behind the systemic memory process, we have to consider the question of information itself, and why we should seriously entertain the hypothesis that information per se is eternal. The insight that information, once created, has a kind of immortality occurred to me in the early 1980s around the time that I stumbled upon the systemic memory process. We must shift gears here and consider some basic physics about the mystery and majesty of light—the source of all life as we know it.

Ever since I was a young child, I've been fascinated by physics, especially light, and the magic of the sky at night.

When I was young, math and physics came easily to me, as if they were special gifts. As an undergraduate at Cornell University, I received the perfect grade of 100 in a course in contemporary physics. I seemed to have an intuitive understanding and feeling for light and energy. I was always in awe of the fact that with the continued development of modern technology, humankind could peer ever more deeply into space and experience the history of the universe, purportedly all the way to the beginning of the big bang itself.

If the light in the sky was to be believed, meaning that the light faithfully expressed information and energy over time in the so-called vacuum of space, then the entire universe had a memory for its creation and everything that had taken place since the beginning of time itself. It had, so to speak, a universal memory. Simply stated, the light remembered. This is what contemporary science implied. Could this really be true?

My mystical-scientific experience happened unexpectedly as I was preparing to give a distinguished Presidential Lecture at the University of British Columbia in Vancouver in the early 1980s.

At that time I was reading Gary Zukav's *The Dancing Wu Li Masters*, an inquiry into modern physics and philosophy published in 1979. *Wu Li* is the Chinese expression for physics, meaning "patterns of organic energy." I was staying in a deluxe, high-rise hotel that looked west over the English Bay, with majestic snow-capped mountains to the right, and the peninsula that ended with the University of British Columbia campus to the left. I awoke in the middle of the night around 3:00 A.M. pondering what Zukav was saying about the controversial wave-particle nature of light. I got out of bed, nude, and stood at the window looking out over the Bay and beyond.

There was a full moon that night, and the water sparkled from one end of the Bay to the other. To the right I could see thousands of houses and apartments, for miles, perched at different levels along the sides of the mountains and lit like candles of various intensities. On the left I could see, illuminated at varying distances, thousands of other flickering dwellings along the rolling peninsula.

Then it occurred to me, suddenly, that in the same way I could see all these individual homes from a distance, the people in them could potentially see me!

I imagined people simultaneously standing at their respective windows, using telescopes to look at me standing nude at my window. And I imagined my nude image simultaneously entering each and every window to the right and to the left, not only the thousands of windows that were lit, but the millions and millions of windows that were dark.

Then it hit me like a ton of conceptual bricks, and it literally took my breath away. I experienced the concept not only logically, but intuitively and physically as well. At that moment, my intuition and reasoning merged. My "heart" knew that the experience was true, I felt it deep "in my bones," and it literally reached my skin as the hair on my arms stood up. And I smiled.

I realized that as the moonlight was reaching my windows, my image was being reflected not simply into the millions of individual windows in the city of Vancouver, but out simultaneously into space as well. I not only realized, but actually experienced subjectively, that one second after I stood at the window, my image was approximately 186,000 miles into space.

Of course, the intensity of my image was relatively small—minuscule in comparison to the light of the moon (which actually is reflected light coming from the sun)—but the photons carrying my personal information and energy were out there. This simple conclusion was required by fundamental physics.

After standing for two seconds at the window, my subtle image was approximately 372,000 miles out into space. With every second, my information-energy patterns were spreading out into space, traveling at the speed of light, getting weaker and weaker, yet "larger and larger" as they fanned out into the "vacuum" of the cosmos.

I was like a star—a minuscule star of course—but a star nonetheless. My patterns of information and energy were traveling out into space, and once in the vacuum of space, there was no way to get rid of them! My information-energy patterns—the visual memory of my body—had a kind of immortality.

My light kept going, and going, and going . . .

Of course, my information-energy patterns would interact with energies and objects along the way. However, in the same way that we can see the "history" of the stars unfolding as a continuing "memory" of their information and energy when we look into the night sky from the earth, the unfolding history of my tiny photons—my image—could potentially be seen by an intelligence with a suitably sensitive telescope some distance from Earth.

Today there is solid scientific evidence that validates my unanticipated personal epiphany. Remote-sensing satellites continuously record our visible and invisible energies, including infrared and ultraviolet energies, from near space. And once in space, our personal information and energy keep traveling . . .

Do you know how many photons it takes for a retinal cell to register light by creating a neural impulse? Millions? Thousands? Hundreds? Science tells us—just one.

Do you know how many photons were reflected off my nude body every second and went back into space? Millions, and millions, and millions . . .

The first thing I decided was that if my energy continued in one form or another, then I'd better take some responsibility for what kind of information and energy I wished to leave behind. I immediately decided to lose weight.

Is the Eternally Remembered Light "Dead Light"?

I cannot express in words the profound significance this experience had on me—the realization that not only did outrageously tiny photons store the history of the universe, they achieved this feat remarkably and reliably well.

Remember, when you look up into the sky at night your eyes witness the history of literally millions, and millions, and millions of stars, extending over billions of years.

Of course, we experience consciously only a small portion of the informational history coming down from these stars, some of which have long since "died." Nonetheless, all this information is displayed on our retinal cells, each of which is much smaller than the head of a pin. How many photons can dance on a single retinal cell of the eye? Think about it.

All that memory, all that history, all that information not only within the tiny pupils of your eyes, but here and there and everywhere. This is fundamental Physics 101. Elementary astrophysics. The basic headache—and hope—for science and spirituality.

So, Linda and Henry, you and me, in the presence of light, we all create patterns of information that expand forever into space. Our energy patterns are there, ready to be read by anyone clever enough to do so.

However, the prevailing story is that these memories are "dead" memories, meaning, we presume that they reflect the history of the past and do not change with the present. For example,

- Gary the stubborn two-year-old in the 1940s, and
- Gary the very thin rock and roll guitarist in the 1950s, and
- Gary the slightly overweight Ph.D. student at Harvard in the 1960s, and
- Gary the quite overweight Yale professor in the 1970s and '80s, and
- Gary, the exercising, weight conscious, energy psychology professor in the 1990s.

All those Garys are supposedly traveling in the vacuum of space, stored in a gigantic space camcorder of sorts, every microsecond of information and energy remarkably and reliably preserved. Talk about miracles? This is, in essence, the accepted story in physics and astrophysics.

Of course, physics professors do not typically emphasize the deep philosophical implications of all this. For the most part, they do not ask is the light alive and evolving? Is light conscious? Are only neurons, especially the ten billion neurons in the human brain, conscious, or is consciousness a quality of light itself—the essence of life itself? How could we tell if a photon was conscious?

And even if a photon was conscious and evolving, who cares?

Well, Linda cares, and everyone else who has ever lost someone whom they deeply loved and adored. If light is alive, if light is conscious, if light not only stores memories but continues to grow and evolve, it would give the Lindas of the world a reason to believe, a reason to hope, a reason to dream of eternal living and eternal love.

David Chalmers, the distinguished philosopher and author of the 1996 book *The Conscious Mind*, has proposed that consciousness, like energy and mass, is a fundamental property of the universe, and exists to varying degrees in all things. According to Chalmers, consciousness is a universal phenomenon. However, Linda and I are scientists, not philosophers. Modern science tells us that light is dead, photons are merely massless "things"—waves or particles depending upon the way you look at them.

Then why was I excited that night in Vancouver, and why do I recount this story today?

The reason is that if science tells us that information, once released, continues in some form forever, we then have the critical first step in addressing the deeper questions—can something, once it comes into existence, continue to live and evolve forever?

If information is this persistent and eternal, then we need to remember this fundamental fact as we consider the logic that leads to the conclusion that all natural systems store information in an integrative and dynamic fashion that make them alive and evolving. In other words, the hypothesis that information carried by light, for example, is eternal, provides the soil that nurtures the deeper implications of the universal living memory hypothesis: that in all dynamical systems, information becomes, and stays alive, and evolves integratively. Systemic memory is universal living memory.

This is why the systemic memory hypothesis bothered me so much when I came upon it at Yale. Since science and common sense remind us that information, at least in the vacuum of space, continues forever, if some fundamental integrative process brings the information to life in a dynamic, evolving way—the systemic memory process—and this process itself continues forever, then life too continues to evolve forever! And if consciousness involves information, as Chalmers and others assert, then consciousness stays alive and evolves too. The logic is simple.

If the systemic memory process is truly 100% universal, non-specific, and non-prejudicial—meaning that the core logic applies to all systems:

- photons (visible and invisible light energy)
- atoms
- chemicals
- cells
- organs
- organisms
- consciousness
- families
- communities
- the world as a whole
- solar systems
- galaxies
- and the universe as a whole

—then the implications of the process for everything, whether physical or non-physical, being alive and continuing to evolve becomes inescapable.

No, I was not about to touch this with a ten-foot pole and put my academic career on the line. Not for thirteen years. But eventually I met Linda and we talked. It was she who gave me both a scientific and personal reason to take the thesis seriously, remove it from the secret vault within my mind, and with her inspiration and extension, bring it to the light of day.

Universal Living Energy Systems Theory and Beyond

At the present time, the systemic memory hypothesis is just what it says it is: a highly plausible scientific hypothesis ready to be understood and investigated. But the truth is, it is still a story. The scientist who tells you his theory is "fact" has confused the distinction between inference and observation, between the map and the territory.

There are various conceptual approaches in science that encourage creative and integrative thinking. One particularly powerful approach is called systems thinking, which in its more sophisticated and evolved forms includes complexity, chaos, and self-organization theory. Systems theory is so simple in its core, and so complex in its execution, that it is often misunderstood by scientists and lay persons alike. It requires that we learn how to think in circles, and appreciate circulation in all things.

For Linda and me to teach you how the systemic memory process works, we must first teach you how systems thinking works. It was in the process of teaching a new course on human psychobiology and systems theory at Yale University in the early 1980s that I came to discover the logic of a universal living memory process in all systems.

Chapter 2

Preparing for the Big Journey

A Scientific and Spiritual Guided Tour

The most beautiful emotion we can experience is the mystical. It is the power of all true art and science. He to whom this emotion is a stranger, who can no longer wonder and stand rapt in awe, is as good as dead. To know that what is impenetrable to us really exists, manifesting itself as the highest wisdom and most radiant beauty, which our dull faculties can comprehend only in their most primitive forms—this knowledge, this feeling, is at the center of true religiousness. In this sense, and in this sense only, I belong to the rank of devoutly religious men.

Albert Einstein

We will end up where we are going if we do not change direction.

Chinese Proverb, sixth century B.C.

In the preface, we initiated this journey with a simple yet profound question, "Is everything, including light itself, eternal, alive, and evolving?" We asked the question as Wilber posed it, "Did the universe begin with a big bloom, rather than, or in addition to, a big bang? Is the entire universe an eternal, living, evolving memory system?" In chapter 1, we considered how our visual information and energy travel as light in space forever, and we considered Linda's deep question, "Is Henry (her departed father) still alive?" We considered what it means to tell stories in science and religion, and whether stories themselves can evolve. We are now in chapter 2,

14

giving you the blueprint for the rest of the journey. The guided tour ends Part I of the journey.

In Part II, "A Brief History of Time, God, and Memory," we explore the history of the evolution of ideas about memory, science, and religion. In chapter 3, we again ask the question, "Are photons really dead?" We initiate the discussion of thinking about simple systems composed of "A's and B's"—such as Albert's (A's) and Betty's (B's), or electrons (A's) and protons (B's)—interacting with each other, circulating their information and energy repeatedly, and storing info-energy in the process. And we prepare ourselves for envisioning the universal living memory theory by using a model or map of four stages in the evolution of religion, and four similar stages in the evolution of science.

What are these four stages? Though they are complex and cover thousands of years of history, we use a friendly acronym to help remember them. The four stages (S) use the words multiple (M), integrative (I), living (L), and evolving (E): SMILE.

In the case of religion, the four stages are:

- from the ancient concept of **multiple** independent gods (Stage M),
- to the idea of one, **integrative** God (Stage I),
- to the vision of a loving God, manifested and **living** on earth in the form of a person(s), who potentially could live on inside us (Stage L),
- to envisioning a dynamic, becoming God who could be **evolving** too (the emerging Stage E).

In the case of science, the four similar stages are:

- from the ancient idea of **multiple** independent laws (Stage M),
- to the general concept of a unified **integrative** system of laws (Stage I),
- to the hypothesis of **living** systems being a special class of complex systems (Stage L),
- to the thesis that all systems, from the micro to the macro, including the "laws" of science themselves, are in a state of constant **evolution** (the emerging Stage E).

Interestingly, the four stages in science seem to be lagging behind the four stages in religion. Is scientific knowledge continually attempting to catch up with evolving spiritual wisdom?

The four stages (S) are summarized in Table 1 below:

Table 1: Four Stages in Religion and Science			
	Basic Concept	Religion	Science
Stage M	Multiple	Multiple gods	Multiple independent laws
Stage I	Integrative	The integrative God	Integrative systems of laws
Stage L	Living	Living "Christ(s)"	Living systems
Stage E	Evolving	Evolving God	Evolving systems of laws

We can picture the four stages in many ways. One picture is on the facing page.

We can summarize the journey this way:

From multiple independent gods (Stage M), to one integrative God (Stage I), to a living God on earth (Stage L), to an evolving God, everywhere and in everything (Stage E), this is the big spiritual journey. From multiple independent laws (Stage M), to general integrative systems (Stage I), to living systems (Stage L), to evolving systems and laws (Stage E), this is the parallel big scientific journey.

Note that each stage (S) incorporates and extends the ones preceding it. Each step is a monumental leap along the way of becoming. To help us keep it straight, we need only remember to SMILE.

In chapter 4, we consider the first step from multiple independent laws (Stage M) to integrative system laws (Stage I) from the "Old Testament," first in religion, then in science. In chapter 5, we consider the step to living systems (Stage L) in some depth, and then envision the emerging step of evolving systems (Stage E), the "New Testament," first in religion, then in science, including what are sometimes called the new spirituality (creation, process, and quantum theologies) and the new science.

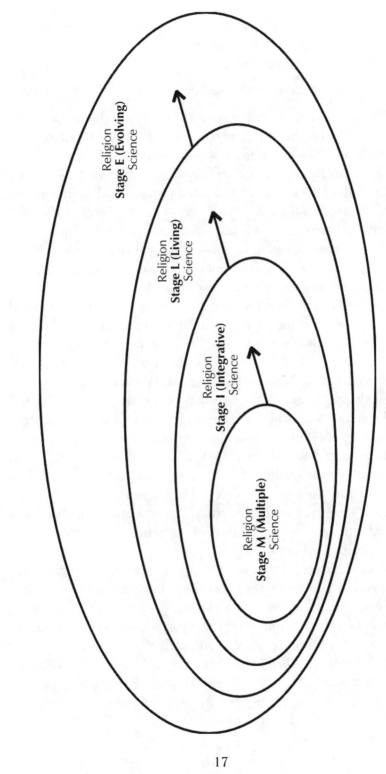

Religion
Stage E (Evolving)
Science

Religion
Stage L (Living)
Science

Religion
Stage I (Integrative)
Science

Religion
Stage M (Multiple)
Science

In chapter 6, we enter the land of the universal living memory process through what Linda calls the "natural law of circulation." We use the mathematical metaphor,

Evolution = Memory multiplied by Circulation^{Repeating} ($E = mc^R$)

to help you summarize and remember the model. This chapter contains the heart of the story, and it includes the actual scientific proof for the existence of what many would call God.

With this proof and the discovery of universal living memory we end Part III of the journey. If you cannot wait to read the theory and its exciting applications, feel free to skip to chapter 6 and return to the history (chapters 3 to 5) later (even after you have finished the book!). As you will see, in this book it's okay to go from A to B and back again. Nature seems to work this way, and memories appear to be made this way too, what Linda calls the A-B circuit.

In Part IV of the journey, we explore many possibilities predicted by universal living memory. As the Harvard physician/psychologist William James said a century ago, "In order to disprove the law that all crows are black, you need only find one white crow." In Part IV we consider many "white crows" in modern science.

In chapter 7, we ask the question "Does the heart remember?" and consider some amazing stories of transplant patients and the plausibility of cellular memory in every cell in the body.

In chapter 8, we ask the question "Does water remember?" and consider the plausibility of homeopathy and other memory like anomalies in physics, chemistry, and medicine.

In chapter 9, we ask the question "Does the soul remember?" and consider the plausibility of out-of-body consciousness and survival of consciousness after death.

And in chapter 10, we ask the question "Does the universe remember?" and consider the plausibility of universal memory everywhere in the quantum vacuum of space.

Part IV considers some of the many implications of universal living memory for science, society, and each of us.

In chapter 11, called "The Living Energy Universe," we consider implications for twenty-first-century science, including physics, chemistry, biology, and psychology, as well as education, business, healthcare, spirituality, and more.

In chapter 12, "Searching for Invisible Rainbows," we take a variety of side trips and consider a host of far-reaching questions, from levels of life and the life of evil to the plausibility of "ghosts" and "spirit-assisted" medicine, as possible places to visit in the future. Topics range from energy zoology to energy theology.

In chapter 13, we consider "what's next?," including the evolution of visionary scientific theories that extend the living energy universe to the loving energy universe. As you will see, there are reasons to hope and to dream. New voyages are being readied.

In chapter 14, we return to Linda's question "Is my father still alive?" and consider whether it is scientifically possible to resurrect the reputation of God.

In the afterword, we explore "what's wrong with the hypothesis" addressing nine categories of possible criticism, and we explain why systemic memory theory is both "interesting" and "amusing."

For those of you who are especially adventuresome, we offer two technical side trips in the appendices. Appendix A presents a sample of what universal living memory reads like when it is written for the scientific community. Appendix B presents a sample experimental paradigm for exploring systemic memory in physical chemistry.

New visions require that we see old words in new ways, that we revise our visions as we evolve. Besides the word SMILE, you will meet a few other friendly acronyms, sometimes expressed in two ways to reflect a more complete picture of their evolving meanings. Their evolving meanings, summarized below, will bloom before your eyes as you take the journey with us.

Alphabetical Listing

DNA	**D**ynamic **N**oetic **A**ntenna
	Divine **N**oetic **A**ntenna
$E=mc^R$	**E**volution = **m**emory * **c**irculation^{Repeating}
GOD	**G**rand **O**rganizing **D**esigner
	Giving **O**pen **D**esigner
LIFE	**L**oving **I**ntentions **F**aithfully **E**xpressed
LOVE	**L**isten **O**bserve **V**alue **E**mpower

ONE	**O**mniscient **N**urturing **E**nergy
SAM	**S**upreme **A**gape **M**emory
	Spirit-**A**ssisted **M**ind
SOUL	**S**ystemic **O**rganization of **U**niversal **L**ove
SMILE	**S**tages—**M**ultiple **I**ntegrative **L**iving **E**volving
	Systemic **M**anifestation of **I**ntelligent **L**oving **E**nergy
SYSTEM	**SY**nchronized **S**toring of **T**ime, **E**nergy, and **M**otion
	SYmpathetic **S**toring of **T**ime, **E**nergy, and **M**otion
TEST	**T**ransformational **E**volving **S**ystems **T**heory
	Transformational **E**nergy **S**ystems **T**heory
WEIRD	**W**onderful **E**ntertaining **I**nspiring **R**emarkable **D**ivine
	Wonderful **E**ntertaining **I**nspiring **R**evisable **D**esigned

For Linda and me, this journey has been more than scientific; it has been spiritual, not only in Einstein's "mystical" way but in a deeply personal way as well. My science "awakening" at Yale, as Linda terms it, occurred simultaneously with a spiritual "awakening" as I read books on religion and spirituality in addition to systems theory and quantum physics. One could say that my Vancouver transcendent nude image experience had both a scientific and spiritual side, and the two sides continue to evolve to this day.

As this book evolved, revision by revision, the inherent spiritual side of the journey became clearer. For Linda and I, science and spirituality are like two sides of a universal coin. We ultimately cannot have one without the other. Hence, this scientific and spiritual guide reflects more completely the whole of the journey.

For the latest discoveries added just before the book was going to print—including how you can see systemic memory with your own eyes—read the Authors' Note at the end of the book.

PART II

A Brief History of Time, God, and Memory

The reception of a new paradigm often necessitates redefinition of the corresponding science. Some old problems may be relegated to another science or declared entirely 'unscientific.' Others that were previously non-existent or trivial may, with a new paradigm, become the very archetypes of significant scientific achievement.

Thomas Kuhn

Chapter 3

SMILE

Four Stages in the
Evolution of Science and Religion

*Life is infinitely stranger than anything which the mind of man
could invent. We would not dare to conceive the things which are
really merely commonplaces of existence.*
Sherlock Holmes to Dr. Watson

*There are more things in heaven and earth
than are dreamt of in your worldview.*
Ken Wilber paraphrasing William Shakespeare

Photons do not learn, they do not grow with experience, they do
not age. They do not have minds, they are not conscious. Though
photons may be eternal, they are unchanging, un-evolving. Simply
put, photons are said to be dead.

One of the most fundamental distinctions in all of science is animate versus inanimate, living versus dead. Very complex, higher order systems, beginning with cells, are considered to be living; simple,
lower order systems such as the molecules comprising cells are typically considered to be dead. Though ancient so-called "pagan" religions believed otherwise—that life was universal—modern science
presumably "knows" better. Science has the "true" story. Period.

This is how I was raised.

Of course, I had watched rivers flow and clouds grow, and I wondered if there was more to nature than physics claimed. But I was a good science student and learned the stories as if they were "facts." As an undergraduate at Cornell, studying electrical engineering and pre-medicine, I took courses in classical and quantum physics. There, I learned that matter and energy were not quite as inanimate and dead as science had once believed.

Quantum physics tells us, in no uncertain terms, that everything is, in fact, uncertain. According to quantum physics, subatomic systems like photons and electrons exist more like distributed waves or fuzzy clouds than discrete objects or particles; that is, until they're observed or measured.

Depending upon how they're measured, electrons and photons will appear either like waves, distributed in space, or like particles, localized in space. They are, relatively speaking, here *and* there *and* everywhere to various degrees, waiting to "materialize" in a specific form. Quantum phenomena are weird to say the least. Physicists even refer to this as quantum weirdness. If we were looking for a place in science to find spirits and life, the quantum level would be the place to look. As Gary Zukav wrote in *The Dancing Wu Li Masters*, at the quantum level everything seems to be dancing all the time.

However, though the quantum world may be weird and wonderful, it is still, according to current dogma, dead. This is because the quantum world is said not to learn; it purportedly does not grow with experience; it does not have memory; and it does not evolve. Again, I was a good science student, and I learned this story as if it were "fact."

What Is a System? From Dead "Facts" to Living "Feedback"

One day, in preparation for my new course on human psychobiology and systems theory at Yale University, I wanted to give my students both the logic and the feeling for how feedback in a system works. Feedback is fundamental to systems. Feedback means that information, energy, and matter return to a component in the system. The information, energy, and matter go out, and then return. What goes around, comes around. In a word, that's feedback.

Consider a system that has only two components, A and B—we'll call them Albert and Betty—and the two components are in constant communication with each other. Imagine that after Albert speaks to Betty, Betty responds (feeds) back to Albert with information relative to what Albert just said to her. In the language of symbols, A sends information to B, and B returns (feeds back) information to A. The information from B to A is called feedback.

Albert Einstein was a hero of mine, and I saw him as a remarkable model to learn from and emulate. I had been taught that the inspiration, the intuition, the big "aha" that led him to the theory of relativity occurred when Einstein imagined that he was riding along a light beam, and he looked out at the universe around him. What he saw when he became one with the light beam gave him a new, profound vision that forever changed how he, and ultimately the rest of us, looked at the universe. His new vision integrated space and time, and beyond.

I wondered, "What would I see if I did what Einstein did?"

What if I made believe that I was an electron in the system between A and B, and I went on the ride the electron took from A to B and back again. What would I experience? Would this help me explain to students how feedback in systems worked?

Boy, was that a ride! As I took the ride, round and round, and wrote down what I saw in simple mathematical language, what unfolded was not at all what I expected.

After the electron and I had gone from A to B and back again just once, I realized something that was absolutely amazing.

What returned to A was the history of A as interpreted by B and returned to A in revised form.

I am going to repeat this because it is essential to remember: *what returned to A was the history of A as interpreted by B and returned to A in revised form.*

This, in a word, is the foundation of the systemic memory process, the basis of universal living memory.

The combined semantics and intonation that Albert heard coming from Betty reflected her "interpretation" of what she had heard Albert say to her, from the immediate past. Even if Betty simply repeated word for word what Albert had said, the energy of her response (frequencies and tone of voice) would be different from

Albert's. In plain English, in a system not only does the present contain the past, but the past is interpreted and revised along the way and subsequently integrated with the present.

B has revised what was sent by A. Betty has not merely repeated what Albert had said, she has responded to what Albert had said with her own intonation and interpretation. In organized systems, the truth is, what goes around evolves around—over and over and over, changing with every cycle. The details of this process are explained in chapter 6.

One way to remember this Einsteinian-like insight is to revise his famous summary formula as a mathematical metaphor:

$$\text{Evolution} = \text{Memory multiplied by Circulation}^{\text{Repeating}},$$

or simply,

$$E = mc^R.$$

To fully appreciate the impact of what I observed, we need to give you some background information about what a system is, what a living system is, and what feedback is. We need you to appreciate the difference between systemic and non-systemic thinking, so you can see how systemic thinking leads to a dynamic, integrative, and universal vision of life and the cosmos.

Three Previous Stages of Religion and Science, and an Emerging Fourth— Preparing for the Big Journey, from the Big Bang to the Big Bloom, and Beyond

To help give you a powerful feeling for the distinction between non-systemic versus systemic thinking, and general systems versus living systems thinking, we'll draw a map illustrating parallels between three major stages of beliefs and an emerging, evolving fourth, and three similar stages of scientific beliefs, and an emerging, evolving fourth.

As we previewed in chapter 2, the four stages are as follows:

Table 1: Four Stages in Religion and Science			
	Basic Concept	Religion	Science
Stage M	Multiple	Multiple gods	Multiple independent laws
Stage I	Integrative	The integrative God	Integrative systems of laws
Stage L	Living	Living "Christ(s)"	Living systems
Stage E	Evolving	Evolving God	Evolving systems of laws

We can picture the four stages in many ways. Here is one picture, redrawn to refresh your memory.

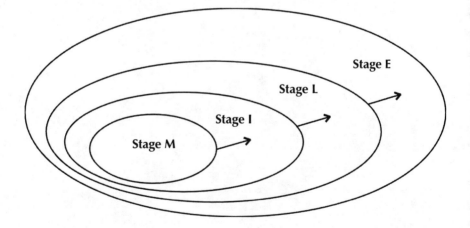

In Raymo's *Skeptics and True Believers*, he suggested that one of the great differences between religion and science is that while there are many competing religious dogmas that claim to know the truth, there is only one science. The fact that religious "truths" are often at odds with one another has had tremendous physical, emotional, social, and spiritual consequences.

Raymo suggests that science is unique because scientists all follow the same set of beliefs, they hold the same dogmas, and follow the same story. However, as we describe in the next two chapters, Linda and I demarcate four important classes, and clashes, of evolving conceptual dogmas in science that curiously parallel four important classes, and clashes of evolving conceptual dogmas in religion.

Two sides of the same coin? A universal process?

Chapter 4

From Dead Laws to Living Science

The Shift from Many Gods
and Many Laws (Stage M), to One God
and One Integrative System (Stage I)

A great anatomist used to close his opening lecture to beginning medical students with words that apply to our own undertaking as well. "In this course," he would say, "we shall be dealing with flesh and bones and cells and sinews, and there are going to be times when it's all going to seem terribly cold-blooded. But never forget: It's alive!"

Huston Smith

In the Old Testament, we are told that people once believed that the universe was ruled by a diverse set of independent gods with different temperaments, values, and goals. These independent gods could be examined individually, prayed to individually, and so forth. The multiple gods competed for power, fame, and glory. The universe contained a seeming cacophony of capricious entities that made human life chaotic and challenging.

This was Stage M (multiple) of religion.

Then the Jews came along, and as the story is often told, they were "chosen" to know that there really weren't multiple independent gods, but a single, integrative God instead. The multiple forces were reinterpreted as different manifestations of one great integrating power.

Actually, history suggests that the one integrative God hypothesis was received and/or conceived by many diverse groups during the same time period. For various reasons, most of these groups did not "resonate" with the single God idea, and they rapidly reverted to their independent, multiple smaller gods hypothesis.

Chaim Potok, in his book, *Wanderings*, makes the point that what defined the Jews as a people was the fact that they resonated with what we are calling the single integrative God hypothesis. According to Potok, they were less "chosen by God" to believe, than they "chose" to believe in one God. With the help of great and persistent leaders, they were encouraged to choose consciously to believe in a universal, integrative, God. They were the "Choosing People."

This was Stage I (integrative) of religion.

However, it is worth remembering that early on, even the Jews tended to "forget" this new choice, this new belief. We should recall, for example, the Moses story, and his frustration with the Jews' inconsistent acceptance of the single integrative God hypothesis. It apparently took great effort for the Jews to grow beyond their old memories of independent gods and evolve a consistent new "meta" memory of a unified, and unifying, God.

The pervasive conflicts and battles that ensued in the Old Testament between the champions of the many gods versus the one God stories testify to man's willingness to live for, and die for, certain huge stories. A curious parallel to Stage M and Stage I, with their associated wars, is occurring in modern science and medicine today.

From Multiple Laws to a Single System—Stages M and I in Science and Medicine

Stage M in science is called the reductionistic paradigm. A paradigm is a grand story or dogma that scientists hold at a given time. Paradigms in science are like dogmas in religion. Champions will protect their respective paradigms, virtually at all costs.

Clearly, in religion the multiple independent gods hypothesis and the one integrative God hypothesis were each huge stories that resulted, among other things, in great wars. We might call them "meta-stories" since they affected almost everything people thought, felt, and did.

Similarly, in science, the reductionistic paradigm and the systems paradigm are each huge stories or hypotheses. We might call them meta-hypotheses, since they affect virtually everything scientists think, feel, and do in research. The strife between these two paradigms continues to this day. Stephen Pepper, a philosopher of science in the 1940s, called these meta-hypotheses *world hypotheses* in his book of the same title.

Briefly, the reductionistic world hypothesis assumes that events in nature are independent, they can be studied in isolation, and they can be broken into ever finer pieces. The source of everything is to be found by getting smaller and smaller. If we could get to the bottom of it all, we would presumably know it all. This is why the modern priests and priestesses of science are the theoretical physicists because they deal with the very small, the core. Their "gods" are the "independent" parts, rather than the integral whole. The multiple independent gods hypothesis in religion is paralleled by the multiple independent laws hypothesis in reductionistic science.

Though the reductionistic method derived from this paradigm is very powerful, it is not all-powerful. Though it has served science well, it reflects only part of the story, not the whole story; especially not the living and evolving story.

As a prelude to understanding the restricted power and vision of Stage M, reductionistic science and the integrative power and vision of Stage I, general system science, let us consider something truly fundamental that the reductionistic story can't explain and that the general system story can potentially explain—the "miracle" that makes the molecule of life—water.

The "Miracle" of Water: Gaining a Feeling for Integrative Systems Thinking Through the Uniqueness of Waterness

Why do we call this section the miracle of water and the uniqueness of waterness?

Imagine that I have a large number of hydrogen atoms in my left hand, and a similar number of oxygen atoms in my right hand. At room temperature, can you see, feel, taste, touch, smell the purported atoms of hydrogen and oxygen in my left and right hands respectively? Of course not. At room temperature, hydrogen and oxygen are gases and completely invisible to our senses.

So how do we know they are there? Simple. Some priest or priestess of science, a physicist or a chemist, tells us they are there, and we believe him or her. We accept their story, typically on faith.

Next, imagine that I am a gifted juggler. I can juggle the atoms of hydrogen and oxygen, and as I juggle them, they mix. Imagine that I am really good at juggling, and I hardly drop any. After a while, I have in each hand a collection of hydrogen and oxygen atoms. Again, can you see, feel, taste, touch, smell these atoms? No, they are still gases—you'll have to take my word for this.

But should you take my word for this? Yes and no.

Yes, because I was a chemistry minor in college, and my father was a Columbia University trained chemical engineer and pharmacist. We could say I became a lay preacher of chemistry. I learned the story of invisible gases as the story was handed down from the senior bishops of Cornell's distinguished chemistry department and my dad, and I accepted their story on faith.

No, because just like many priests who've never seen Christ or the Buddha with their own eyes, I've never witnessed, with my own eyes, an atom of either hydrogen or oxygen.

What I'm about to demonstrate to you now is an experiment that's been replicated in chemistry laboratories around the world, thousands and thousands of times. This is an experiment that all of us can experience with our naked senses. We need not take it on faith.

What happens if, in my left hand, I take the hydrogen and oxygen atoms and through what science terms a chemical reaction we enable them to combine and form a more complex system, a molecule, which science calls H_2O. We ignite them—with a simple flame—and the resulting "ash" is water.

Can you see, feel, taste, touch, smell this new set of molecules? Of course, it's liquid water. The invisible has become manifest. The imagined is now material. And it is absolutely all wet. Now, here is the deep question: Where did the new integrative properties of water—its waterness—come from? How could two invisible gases, when combined, create the unique set of properties that make water one of the most miraculous of all molecules? As the imaginary becomes "real," the result seems inconceivable. It is a fact that no other combination of atoms produces a molecule with the identical properties of water. Water is absolutely, 100% unique. Only water has waterness. Water has what systems theorists term "emergent" properties.

When the individual components, in this case atoms of hydrogen and oxygen, come together and join forces, they can create something larger than themselves; they can, in this case, create waterness. And through their dynamic relationship, magic metaphorically can and does happen. Such is the mystery of systemic integration. It is called by different names: dynamic self-organization, emergent properties, wholeness.

Water is especially magical. For example, below 32 degrees Fahrenheit, liquid water becomes a complex crystal called ice, and ice floats. Most "solids" sink when placed into their liquid forms, yet this is not the case for ice.

Another example: Can you picture in your mind a book containing hundreds of photographs of snowflakes displayed page, after page, after page? I have such a book. The beauty, complexity, and novelty of each and every flake is breathtaking. How can all this, and so much more, come from two invisible gases?

Let's be clear. By miracles and magic we do not mean supernatural, as all of this is obviously "natural." Moreover, science can describe the new properties with great accuracy. However, the mysterious appearance of new properties is amazing. The unique emergent properties of waterness cannot be predicted ahead of time by attempting to study hydrogen and oxygen by themselves. Hydrogen and oxygen must be studied as an integrative system. This is Stage I.

Reductionistic science (Stage M) cannot predict, from studying hydrogen and oxygen as if they were "independent little gods," what "new bigger god" will emerge or what it will look like. Reductionistic science cannot explain why it is the case that when hydrogen and oxygen join forces, dance together, and make an eternal commitment to transcend their individual identities, they become something far greater than, and uniquely different from, their individual selves. Reductionism does not predict emergent properties. Reductionism does not predict the everyday wholistic miracles of nature.

Systems theory, on the other hand, *assumes* emergent integrative properties.

The whole is greater than the sum of its parts. You may wonder, "How often is this the case?" According to general system theory, if something is indeed a dynamic integrative system, the answer must be, "always."

When you appreciate the miracle of water, and you appreciate that water is a common prototype of emergent phenomena at all levels of nature, you have a deeper feeling for the shift from reductionistic to systemic thinking, the profound transformation from Stage M to Stage I in science and medicine. In medicine, this emerging integrative field is called integrative medicine. Integrative medicine fosters the unique systemic healing outcomes that can occur when conventional and alternative medicine dance together and become "one medicine."

As you will discover as we reach Stage E in the next chapter, the logic of systemic memory provides us with a scientifically plausible means for understanding and studying how the miracle of waterness, and "emergent-ness" properties in general, take place.

Linda and I propose that the key to explaining emergence, the heart and soul of all systems great and small, is the universal living memory process.

General System Theory as Stage I—Competition or Evolution?

What we are calling Stage I in science is the "organismic" paradigm in Stephen Pepper's terms, or the "general system" paradigm as coined by Ludwig von Bertalanffy, in his book, *General System Theory.* The idea of a general integrative system that exists from the micro to the macro, that is recapitulated at every level in nature, can be likened to the one integrative God hypothesis. General system principles reflect universal principles that supposedly apply to all things at all levels in nature. Hence the use of the term "universal" in universal living memory.

Everything, from the simplest to the most complex, is a manifestation of this abstract integrative system. Therefore, to understand nature we must understand the nature of the general or universal integrative system from which all material systems are an expression. This is the heart of general system theory.

Sounds a lot like an invisible, inferred, mystical God, doesn't it? Parallels between general system thinking and the one God hypothesis are described in detail in Richard Kraft's 1983, *A Reason for Hope: A Synthesis of Teilhard de Chardin's Vision and Systems Thinking*.

However, let's be concrete here. In practical terms:

- Whereas reductionistic science assumes that things are *independent*, general systems science assumes that things are *interdependent* and hence *integrative*.
- Whereas reductionistic science assumes that things are *disconnected*, general systems science assumes that things are *interconnected* to various degrees.
- Whereas reductionistic science assumes that things can be understood in *isolation*, general systems science assumes that things can only be understood when they are *allowed to interact freely*.

How are we to comprehend the relationship between the many independent/many gods hypothesis of reductionistic thinking (Stage M) and the one integrative system/one God hypothesis of general system thinking (Stage I)? Are they competing stories that must engage in war, or are they evolving stories?

Just as quantum physics ultimately incorporated and integrated classical Newtonian physics, the general systems vision ultimately incorporates and integrates classical reductionism.

Reductionistic thinkers tend to emphasize antagonism to ideas, since reductionistic thinking encourages "us *versus* them" thinking. Systems thinkers tend to emphasize friendliness to ideas, since systems thinking encourages "us *and* them" thinking. Systems thinking is fundamentally integrative, which is why we term it Stage I. Whereas traditional reductionistic science was prototypically best expressed by classical Newtonian physics, the evolution of systems science was prototypically best expressed by quantum physics and the evolution of biology as an expression of complex systems.

35

From a reductionistic perspective, the universe is viewed as basically dead except for the "accident" of life. The story is that life presumably occurred as an accident, by chance, in a universe of random, independent laws that followed the big bang. From an integrative systems perspective, the universe is seen as being fundamentally dynamic and creative, and with enough complexity that biological life as we normally know it must unfold (using Wilber's term, the big bloom).

Consider this question:

Does the caterpillar die when it is replaced *by* the butterfly? Or, is the caterpillar "transformed" as it "evolves" *into* the butterfly? Your answer depends on the way you look at it—reductionistically (Stage M, "*by*") or systemically (Stage I, "*into*"). Die and be replaced, or transform and evolve? The continued evolution of systems thinking, like the continued evolution of religion, reframes these questions, and gives us a new universal vision of "death," life, everything.

To summarize, in science Stage M is reductionistic theory, Stage I is general system theory. From multiple independent gods to a single integrative God in religion, and from multiple independent laws to a single, integrative Grand Organizing Design (G.O.D.) in science, a general, universal system is hypothesized.

The transition from "dead" to "living" systems is like the transition from a "clockwork" God of an imagined mechanical universe to a living God of a "participatory" universe. As F. David Peat writes in his foreword to John David Ebert's book, *Twilight of the Clockwork God*:

> "Today we are no longer passive observers of a cosmos created by a Clockwork God but full members of a participatory universe." Peat goes on to warn us: "We now know that only those systems which are open and responsive to their environments will, in the long run, survive. . . . In this new world we are all responsible, are participators. And so the rest is up to us."

Hence, if systems are ultimately self-revising (the premise of systemic memory), then humans not only participate in the revision of science, but even the revision of the Source.

We are now ready to move to Stage L—living systems thinking—and the emerging Stage E—which is heralded by the systemic memory hypothesis.

However, before we consider Stages L and E in science, we will continue our parallel with the evolution of religion and describe the shift from the Old Testament, which included Stages M and I, to the New Testament, which includes Stage L, and expresses the evolution to Stage E.

It turns out that it is possible to argue that the great historical religious figure called Christ, and other monumental religious figures before him, such as Buddha, implicitly modeled what science now terms living systems theory (Stage L). Moreover, with the aid of the logic of the systemic memory process (Stage E), we find scientific support for the controversial spiritual hypothesis that Christ himself may not only be eternal and alive, but be evolving as a living energy system as well.

Can science and religion ultimately be moving toward the same conclusion, that everything is eternal, alive, and evolving?

Chapter 5

Are Ideas Themselves Alive and Evolving?

How Living Systems Theory Predicts the Living (Stage L) and Evolving (Stage E) Nature of Scientific and Spiritual Ideas

It is Jesus' real concerns, which were threatened with eternal oblivion, that can celebrate genuine "resurrection" at present. Now we can recognize that in Jesus the same heart beats, touched by the same love for humanity and determined by the same feeling of compassion for all beings, as in the life and teachings of Guatama Buddha, the Awakened One.
                                        Elmer Gruber and Holger Kersten

Everything is alive.
                                        Dr. James Levin

Are ideas themselves alive and evolving?

Can the spirits and souls of others literally live on inside of us? Is it scientifically possible, as claimed by certain religions, that Jesus' ideas can live on and continue to grow in us? Moreover, is it scientifically possible that Buddha's ideas, which preceded Christ by six centuries, lived on and evolved in Jesus many centuries after the Awakened One died? Jesus, Buddha, Moses, and others before them—is it possible that they are intimately related in some deeply systemic way? Is science leading us to the conclusion that these metaphysical and psychospiritual beliefs not only have a serious basis in theory, but are even predicted by contemporary theory?

38

The shift from "dead" science to "living" science has many consequences that were seemingly unanticipated by the pioneers who originated the theories.

The shift from general systems theory (Stage I) to living systems theory (Stage L) has a profound, unanticipated consequence—that ideas themselves can be alive. Moreover, systemic memory (Stage E) indicates how ideas, as living systems, can be evolving as well. Most scientists are not aware of this consequence, yet. But they will become aware as they read this chapter—and shift from the "old" to the "new" testaments of religion and science. It is time for us, all of us, to awaken to this scientific possibility.

Let us look first at the New Testament in religion, and recall the profound paradigm shift that took place in consciousness with the teachings of Jesus, one of humankind's most revered beings.

As you attempt to experience the idea of an eternal "living Jesus" functioning as an eternal "living Christ" in the next few pages, remember, you're reading this in preparation for learning how to experience the parallel idea of a "living idea" as a natural manifestation of a "living system." To understand universal living memory, you should first understand "aliveness" as envisioned and experienced by humankind's two greatest and most controversial institutions, religion and science.

They Are the Pillars, We Are the Children

Sir Isaac Newton is quoted as saying he "sat upon the shoulders of giants." As Linda and I write these words, we too sit metaphorically on the shoulders of giants as we once sat, literally, upon the shoulders of our own departed fathers, and we look from this great height with new eyes. When Linda's father passed, he was honored by the American College of Cardiology as being a "gentle giant."

Everything you've read, and will read in this book reflects the evolving vision that comes from sitting on the shoulders of those who've come before us, the scientists and mystics we honor in this book. They are the pillars, we are the children. Their memories are part of the storehouse of our personal memories, hence they are literally "part" of our individual consciousness and provide the foundation for our minds.

39

However, is it possible that their unique memories are, to various degrees, functioning as dynamic systems of ideas (Stage I), literally living (Stage L) and evolving (Stage E) inside Linda and me? Or, are they basically independent of us, and dead (Stage M)? Moreover, can their memories potentially be alive and evolve inside all of us, and therefore in you too?

As you read about their systems of ideas in the next few pages, and if you find yourself thinking about them, will their ideas become alive and evolve in your own mind too? Living systems theory (Stage L) and the systemic memory hypothesis (Stage E) say "most definitely maybe."

Are Ideas Themselves Alive and Evolving?
A Prelude to Stage L and Living Systems Theory

When Jesus was executed, his physical body died. The prevailing story in religion is not only that his soul was resurrected, but that his physical presence was purportedly witnessed briefly after he died.

For thousands of years, people from all corners of the earth and all walks of life have claimed they have reexperienced Jesus in one way or another. As G. Scott Sparrow shared in his 1995 book *I Am With You Always*, are all these *"True Stories of Encounters with Jesus,"* as the subtitle reads, merely self-deceptions or mistakes of the mind? Are all these people simply suggestible? Or, is it possible that the essence of Jesus, even "his" ideas themselves (remember, Jesus claimed that "his" ideas actually came from the "Father"), are not only alive (Stage L), but are evolving (Stage E) to this day?

Most of us presume that our ideas come from "our" mind, and that we are in control of "them." This presumption, however, doesn't fit with all the data. Consider a common example that most of us know first hand, sometimes all too well:

Have you ever tried to go to sleep and discovered, to your dismay, that "your" mind was racing with uncontrollable thoughts? That when this happened, "you" felt somehow separate from "your" thoughts? That "your" thoughts seemed to have a "mind of their own"? That "they" sometimes jumped around and around despite "your" best efforts to make "them" stop?

Here is the theoretical question: When these wayward thoughts are jumping around and around in your head, are they creating feedback loops, and becoming a "system of ideas" living inside your mind? Can such thoughts be said to function as living systems? Can such thoughts be thought of as literally "being alive"?

Obviously, most of us do not typically think about thinking this way. Thoughts are thought to be like photons, or rocks. Thoughts are "things," they are "dead." However, according to contemporary science, it may be time for our minds to evolve. Remember the fundamental question we are asking in this book is, "Is everything—even thoughts themselves—eternal, alive and evolving?" What does it mean to say that an idea is "alive"? You may wonder, how could something as seemingly ephemeral as an idea exist in the first place, and then, secondarily, be alive?

Consider the following question:

Can an idea be envisioned as being a "conceptual system," composed of parts, "little" ideas, so to speak joining, dancing, and resonating together, making up "bigger" integrative ideas? Can idea "A" literally interact with idea "B" and become an integrative "A-B" idea system? Moreover, do certain ideas have an affinity for each other, just like certain molecules, such as hydrogen and oxygen, or people, such as Linda and me?

Stage M science would say "of course not." Thoughts are independent ephemeral things. However, Stage I science would say "of course." Thoughts are highly interconnected, mental structures in the mind, part of a complex dynamic mental network, and therefore function as integrative thought systems.

What about stories? Are stories simply multiple ideas existing independently (Stage M), or do stories represent complex collections of ideas organized into an integrative whole (Stage I)? Most people would agree that stories and theories seem to be complex collections or systems of integrated ideas.

Now the deep question becomes, what happens when we add Stage L to Stage I?

Can such "systems of ideas" function as "living" systems in people's minds, and therefore live on in the minds of others? Can systems of ideas have a "life of their own"?

41

Can systems of ideas be born, grow, and evolve in the mind, just as plants and animals do on earth?

Here's the train of logic:

1. If ideas can be integrative systems (Stage I),
2. and systems can be alive (Stage L),
3. then ideas can be alive too (Stage L).

Following this train of logic, we must first ask the deep question, what does it mean to be a "living" system? Once we can answer this question, we can address the truly challenging question, can a system of ideas function as a living system, and therefore "have a life of its own"? According to James G. Miller, the father of living systems theory, the answer is, theoretically, yes. But first, let's consider Stage L in religion, and review the history of Jesus.

Jesus Consciousness and the New Testament—The Shift from Dead (Stage I) to Living (Stage L) Religion

As the story is told, there was a monumental shift in human consciousness from the Old to the New Testament with the birth, life, death, and resurrection of a man named Jesus. History tells us that Jesus had been born a Jew, and as a young boy he was educated by Jewish scholars and mystics. He may have been educated by other scholars and mystics as well, including Buddhists, according to Gruber and Kersten. Apparently, Jesus was unique for his time. His vision of the one God went beyond the "one God to be feared" to the "one God to be loved."

Jesus saw everyone, and everything, as an expression of one loving God. Moreover, Jesus believed that the capacity to see and experience the world in this way was a gift given to all human beings. This gift of gifts, properly nourished, could enable anyone, if they adopted Jesus's ideas, to experience love as well. Note that Jesus didn't claim that these were "his" ideas. "They" were gifts, given to him by his ancestors and his God, the Father, who was, in fact, everyone's God.

Here is the really controversial part.

In the New Testament, the claim is made that Jesus can live on within all of us if we choose to incorporate his ideas into our minds and hearts. This is key, especially when we explain the striking parallel between Stage L of religion and Stage L of science.

Note that in Stage L of religion, whereas God was invisible and presumably "perfect," and therefore incapable of evolving, mankind was visible and presumably "imperfect" and therefore capable of evolving.

One of the key points in Stage L is as follows: just as God lives eternally, we could live eternally too, and by following Jesus's lead, we could become more perfect like him.

Jesus was viewed as the most visible and perfect expression of a God that listened to, observed, valued, and empowered the poor and downtrodden as well as the rich and the downtrodding. This God of LOVE (what Linda and I refer to as "Listening, Observing, Valuing, and Empowering") was expressed in the flesh by a young man consumed with the experience of God as a loving parent.

We are told in the New Testament that Jesus could live on in all of us. Moreover, we are repeatedly told that if we wish to become like Jesus, and we invite him to live within us, we can be resurrected like Jesus too. Stage L was the evolution of humankind's ideas of love and life and the possibility of eternal life in a universe that was potentially alive, eternal, and by inference, evolving, the emerging Stage E.

We still had the idea then of a presumably perfect and unchanging God, but at least concerning the established imperfect and dynamic minds of humankind, we could remain alive, be eternal, and evolve; that is, if we listened to Jesus and other similar visionaries throughout recorded history.

Only recently did Linda and I realize, after reading books about the history of God, like Jack Mile's God: A Biography, that the idea of God was evolving throughout the course of the Old and New Testament, and therefore might actually be an evolving divinity, at least in the human mind (Stage E). This possibility is recognized in contemporary philosophy and religion. It is called "Process Theology" in the academic literature. As you will see, the key concept is "process," and process implies energy.

Living Systems Theory as New Testament—The Theory Itself Is Alive, and Evolving

In 1978, James G. Miller published *Living Systems*. When Miller's book was published it was acclaimed as a monumental integrative achievement of human thought, reflecting the collective work of many brilliant scientists and philosophers, and the active collaboration of a large interdisciplinary team that, at various times, was housed at Harvard University, the University of Chicago, and the University of Michigan.

It is sad to say that I do not know anyone personally who has read this book cover to cover, nor do I believe that most living scientists, if given a fair and comprehensive test on it, would pass. The text is difficult, the material is comprehensive, and the work spans too many fields for most modern specialists to appreciate. In addition, many scientists still function at Stage M, whereas *Living Systems* explicitly covers Stages M, I, and L, and implicitly introduces Stage E.

Living Systems can be likened to a "bible" of old and new science combined. If reductionism and general systems theory can be likened to the Old Testament (Stages M and I), and living systems theory and the evolving new paradigm, heralded by concepts like systemic memory, can be likened to the New Testament (Stages L and E), then Miller's bible of science can be said to contain both testaments. Like the bible of religion, Miller's bible of science is exhaustive, and exhausting. If ever there was a grand story in science on a scale matching the grand story in religion, it is *Living Systems*.

Miller and his colleagues outlined in exquisite and excruciating detail how all well-known living systems shared nineteen *"functional subsystems."* By "functional," they meant "behave" or "do"; by "subsystem," they meant "component" or "part." Notice that Miller's theory does not focus on specific "structures" such as physical objects—the theory is devoted to "functions," about how a system behaves. The theory is therefore, first and foremost, about process.

What this means is that all living things have to be able to "do" certain things and achieve certain goals in order to be said to be alive. Hence, for Miller, living is a process of being and becoming. Three of the nineteen functions or processes are particularly relevant to our discussion about ideas in the mind. They were termed by Miller and colleagues "memory, decoder, and reproducer subsystems."

What this means is that *all* living systems, *all* cells, tissues, organs, organisms, and so on, according to Miller and his colleagues

- have the capability to store information and energy: they have a "memory" process,
- they can process information and uncover its meaning: they can "think,"
- they can replicate themselves in some form: they can "reproduce."

These three statements are not terribly original or controversial per se. Even the idea that ideas can reproduce, function as little "replicators," is not controversial. Some contemporary evolutionary biologists and psychologists use the term "menes" to suggest that information can function as little "genes," have "agency," and therefore evolve just like cells and organisms do. As Susan Blakemore recently suggested, the brain can be thought of as functioning as a "mene" machine, providing the means for "menes" to evolve.

However, are "menes" truly alive? Can the theory of menes itself be alive? Miller's theory suggests yes.

What is novel and hugely controversial is the realization that the complex theory that Miller and his colleagues created theoretically meets all nineteen formal criteria for functioning as a living system itself. In fact, when we read *Living Systems* from the perspective of a living systemic process, we discover that living systems theory can be said to function as a complex living system in the minds of people who take the time to learn the theory!

Simply stated, living systems theory is itself a living system because living systems theory meets all of its very own criteria for being alive (Stage L), and moreover, for evolving (Stage E) as well. Moreover, to the extent that living systems theory is alive to various degrees, other theories can be alive too.

Is mental life really "life"? Is it really "alive"? Are ideas, as systems, actually "living"? And can ideas, as systems, have a systemic living memory process too?

What occurred to me upon reading *Living Systems* in the early 1980s was that theories themselves, and hence ideas, could be said to meet the complete set of formal criteria for functioning, and therefore, could be alive.

Inspired by Houston Smith's *The Religions of Man*, I had the realization that not only does Jesus and his teachings sound a lot like integrative systems theory (Stage I), but that living systems theory (Stage L) provides the scientific rationale for the belief that people, including Jesus himself, could literally continue to live on inside us if we appropriately nourished their ideas! Though I smiled about the scientific and spiritual possibilities of this combined integrative and universal living vision, I feared the potential academic and religious consequences.

Were people ready to hear this thesis? Were their minds ready to evolve?

I wrote a paper, titled "Ideas Alive? Implications of Living Systems Theory for an Integrative Vision of Mind and Religion," and didn't show it to a soul. In fact, in a state of momentary academic panic, I filed the "Ideas Alive?" paper in the circular file cabinet under my desk.

Try to put yourself in my shoes. It was the early 1980s. I realized the possibility that living systems theory had profound implications for concepts of life that extended beyond our current appreciation. I realized that such ideas, on first hearing, sounded a bit crazy, and the implications sounded even crazier.

I realized that some of my colleagues in psychology and psychiatry would "rush to judgement" and accuse me of having too many loose associations—loose conceptual screws. Though they hadn't read, and would likely never read, the monumental integrative work that provided the logic for Stage L, which in turn leads to Stage E, they might still condemn me out of hand.

Remember, I was well-trained in clinical psychology at Harvard, and was then co-director of the Yale Behavioral Medicine Clinic. I knew I was not suffering from a thought disorder, but it was not safe to share the logic of living systems theory with virtually anyone in the academic world certainly then, and still somewhat today.

As I envisioned the inherent logic, and turned it around and around in my head, I realized that it, in fact, flowed seamlessly from the logic and research of some of the most intelligent and integrative minds in the history of science and philosophy. So I knew I was not alone, yet I felt very alone.

I had become aware that living systems theory provides a critical key for understanding what makes traditional "animate" systems come alive (cells, organs, people) and by extension "ideas themselves," (Stage L). I had stumbled upon the logic of a potentially universal living memory process that all systems at all levels, from the miniscule to the monumental, engage in a process essential to their very being. The process involves the natural integration and dynamic storage of information over time, and therefore it is, by definition "evolving" as well as "alive" (Stage E).

My thoughts were racing, "What have I gotten into now? And where am I going?"

Is everything really eternal, alive, and evolving? Is nature a creative-unfolding process rather than a purely random process? Is the hypothesis that ideas are alive, and that ideas continue after death, really required by the theory? Do some of the seemingly inconceivable stories attributed to psychics and mediums have a foundation in contemporary science? Do all cells really have memory? Is energy itself alive and evolving? If there is a God, is God alive? Is He, She, It, Them, in a deep way, evolving?

And do I have to take all this into account in my professional and personal life?

I tried various things to distract me from these ideas, to attempt to put them out of my mind. And I was fairly successful, until I met Linda.

The Evolving Stage E in Religion and Science

At this moment in history, Stage E of religion is being informed by Stage E of science, and Stage E of science is being informed by Stage E of religion.

As the new millennium begins, science is on the verge of establishing the rationale and providing data that curiously support some ancient religious beliefs. In addition, contemporary science, through its bold theories and innovative technology, is extending our spiritual experience beyond anything written about or even imagined in the Old and New Testaments combined.

Remember, the stories in science and the stories in religion are ultimately just that—stories. They are tools of the mind, helping us understand nature and appreciate her majesty and mystery. Though these stories may have a life of their own, and even literally be "alive" (Stage L), the stories do not necessarily express the essence of what makes nature who she is. The map is not the territory.

When one reads new science books such as *The Science of God*, or *God: The Evidence*, or *Nature's Destiny*, our capacity to experience wonder and reverence for life and the universe does more than return. It transcends anything experienced in the time of Moses or the Buddha or Jesus. Modern technology, driven by a profound curiosity and desire to know, becomes ever more spiritual as it addresses ideas like energy, the quantum "vacuum," and "enformy." Paraphrasing Einstein, science becomes mystical, or more precisely, it becomes scientifically mystical.

Yes, when all is said and done it appears that religion will have to "change" (evolve) or "die." However, the same can be said about science. Science too must "change" (evolve) or "die."

The major difference between science and religion is that science is supposed to change. Its capacity for change is its ethical imperative, its reason for being, the basis of its integrity. Science is supposed to be alive (Stage L). It is supposed to evolve as a function of experience, through logic and data, through inference and observation. It is supposed to engage in a process of self-revision through theory and research.

If the emerging data and theory require it, reductionistic theory (stage M) should evolve into integrative systems theory (Stage I), which should evolve into living systems theory (Stage L), which should then evolve into "it" (Stage E). "It" doesn't officially have a name yet. One of our graduate students, Craig Santarre, suggested adding the term "Transformational" which leads us to "Transformational Evolving Systems Theory" (or TEST). As long as science keeps expanding its horizons, testing and retesting its stories, opening its tools to new phenomena and new ideas, it will be alive and evolve.

As you learn the logic of the universal living memory process and the implications that stem from this logic, you will understand why we say that systemic memory may herald the emerging Stage E in both science and religion. Systemic memory revises our vision of general systems theory (Stage I) and living systems theory (including chaos and complexity theory, Stage L). It becomes a transformational/evolving/revisionistic/energy systems theory (Stage E) at all levels, everywhere.

Linda and I are, so to speak, revising the three R's of learning—reading, writing, and arithmetic—adding the evolving three R's of transformational systemic thinking—revising, resonating, and remembering. Science is the process of "re-searching," which is a combination of revising, resonating, and remembering. The universe, in all of its richness and beauty, may involve the same process as well.

For the Record—How the Universal Living Memory Story Came to Life

Linda and I recounted the history of the scientific birth of the systemic memory hypothesis in our foreword to Paul Pearsall's 1998 book, *The Heart's Code.* There we summarized three of the specific fears that I experienced when I first discovered the logic of universal living memory.

The first fear was that to determine whether the logic was correct, I would have to write a paper outlining the logic and share it with my colleagues. Once my colleagues knew the implications of the logic—for example, that hearts could learn and carry one's personal code—they might question my credibility.

The second fear was that if the logic turned out to be wrong, I would be ridiculed and my academic prestige tarnished irreparably.

But the third fear was the worst of all: the logic might actually be correct. If this were true, then I would dramatically have to change my cherished beliefs about how nature worked.

How I handled these three fears was typical of the "sane" scientist. I didn't share the logic with anyone and kept it quiet for thirteen years! Unlike the "Ideas Alive" concept, which I put to paper and then "filed" to some distant dump site, I never attempted to write a formal paper about universal living memory when I was at Yale. The three fears got the better of me.

But in 1993 I shared the secret logic with Linda and she proposed, "Gary, it's time to put the fears aside and communicate the logic. If your theory is correct, it could be of great benefit to others, if not the world. Besides, the logic of storing information can be extended to storing energy, which provides a key to understanding the deep implications of the work we're doing now in energy cardiology." Energy cardiology is a new field that views the heart as a biophysical energy generating system. We decided it was time to share the logic with those in the scientific and clinical community who were open to changing their minds.

When Linda and I were about to publish our paper in 1996 titled "Energy Cardiology: A Dynamical Energy Systems Approach for Integrating Conventional and Alternative Medicine," Linda insisted that we mention the systemic memory hypothesis, since it predicted that certain cardiac transplant patients might connect with the personal memories of the donor stored within the heart's cells. I told her, "Linda, if we include this, most cardiologists will do more than smile. They will laugh us out of science and dismiss the whole energy cardiology paper, period." But Linda persisted, and we included a few, very brief sentences about the prediction.

Meanwhile, Harris Dienstfrey, the editor of *Advances: The Journal of Mind-Body Health* (recently renamed *Advances in Mind-Body Medicine*) received a phone call from a writer named William Novak asking whether he knew of any scientists who might have a theory for how a woman named Claire Sylvia could have retrieved stored personal memories from the new heart and lungs she had received. Ironically, though I didn't know it at the time, her heart and lung transplant operation occurred at the Yale University School of Medicine in the summer of 1988 just as I was leaving Yale to move to the University of Arizona. Harris suggested that Bill call us.

When Bill told us Claire Sylvia's remarkable story, published in 1997 in *A Change of Heart*, I was, frankly, shocked! It's one thing when logic leads you in an unusual direction; it's another when you learn that the logic might actually be useful—that is, it might be predictive and productive in a novel and important way.

Claire Sylvia, of course, was just one person. Many could, and would, view her story as an amusing anecdote, and attempt to explain her seemingly retrieved memories as a statistical coincidence, a side effect of all the drugs she was taking, or the stress of her condition. These are all traditional and plausible reductionistic explanations that must be entertained as part of responsible science. However, when we learned from Bill about a psychoneuroimmunologist, Paul Pearsall, who at the time had collected 73 documented cases of apparent cellular memory, Claire Sylvia's story took on greater importance to us.

When our energy cardiology paper appeared, and we mentioned the Claire Sylvia story in the published commentary that followed the article, the distinguished neuroscientist Dr. Karl Pribram, a former professor at Stanford University who was then the James P. and Anna King Distinguished Professor and Eminent Scholar, Commonwealth of Virginia, and Director of the Center for Brain Research and Informational Sciences at Radford University, heard a brief outline of the systemic memory hypothesis. Much to our surprise, since we had not yet shared the logic with any major scientist, when we explained the logic to Pribram, he found the logic compelling, though he didn't like some of the predictions.

The logic of integrative systemic memory is consistent with much of Pribram's theoretical writing about "holographic" and "holonomic" theories of memory storage in the brain. What Pribram had not apparently realized is that the logic that science uses to explain memory in the brain is universal (systemic), and it applies equally forcefully and unconditionally to all systems at all levels.

Pribram was planning to hold the fifth conference on neurodynamics at Radford University in Virginia, and he invited us to prepare a formal paper about the theory and present it at the conference. Linda and I were simultaneously honored and horrified. It was, as they say, time to "put up or shut up." Obviously, conceptual integrity required that we face our fears, and put the ideas to paper.

In the process of writing our chapter titled "Do All Dynamical Systems Have Memory? Implications of the Systemic Memory Hypothesis for Science and Society," which was published in 1998 in Pribram's edited book *Brain and Values* (a version of this chapter is included here in appendix A), we had the chapter read and reread by multiple skeptical scientists.

Four people helped tremendously by serving in the role of "devil's advocates." We frankly begged them to try and find a flaw in the logic that had persistently escaped me since the early 1980s and Linda since 1993. The four of them spanned four generations of friendly devils, so to speak (they included the head of the Department of Psychology of the University of Arizona). They too could not find a flaw in the logic. They became what we affectionately call our FDA (friendly devil's advocates).

We ultimately presented the paper at Pribram's conference in the fall of 1996. It was received with great interest and ambivalence. No one at the conference discovered a flaw in the logic, but a number of scientists hated the implications and thought the whole exercise was ridiculous. Other scientists saw the implications as inspired and encouraged us to continue the work. The rest, as they say, is history, and it continues to evolve as many other scientists are now studying the mathematical logic and still none have found a flaw.

Ready for the Logic?

Now that you

- have some historical background concerning the origin of universal living memory and can place it in the broad context of the evolution of scientific and religious thought (using the four-stage SMILE framework as a friendly conceptual guide),
- realize that all systems have emergent properties (remember the uniqueness of "waterness") and can function as living systems, and that theoretically, "mental" systems (ideas) may be just as alive as "material" systems,
- know the curious route by which the scientific theory, called the systemic memory hypothesis, ultimately came to be published in the literature,

you are ready to join us in the next chapter as we return to a classroom at Yale University and explore the logic of feedback that predicts, apparently inexorably, that everything, including light and energy itself, is alive, eternal, and evolving.

Chapter 6

Does Everything Remember?

The Universal Living Memory Process and the Natural Law of Circulation: $E = mc^R$

A vision's just a vision if it's only in your head.
If no one gets to see it, it's as good as dead.
It has to come to light.

Stephen Sondheim
Sunday in the Park with George

If I hadn't believed it, I wouldn't have seen it.

Yogi Berra

The logic that describes the universal living memory process is not itself controversial. In fact, as you learn the logic in this chapter, you will probably say what I said when I first learned the logic. "Of course! It's obvious." You may even wonder, as I did, "Why didn't I see it before?"

Momentarily, we will proceed to swing a small child in a playground, and then using the same physical strength and the very same swinging procedure, proceed to knock down a gigantic skyscraper. We will also review how Nikola Tesla, using the same logic, predicted that it was even possible, in principle, to "split the earth."

Swinging a little child and a huge building (or even a planet) involve what are termed "positive feedback" loops in systems theory. As you'll see, these positive feedback loops create integrative systemic memories in all systems of every conceivable shape and size because they engage in the process of circulation. Simply put, the systemic memory process creates universal living memories of information and energy.

Many scientists over the past 100 years have grasped the essence of the logic of feedback. They include such luminaries in the history of science as:

- The father of psychology, William James
- The distinguished neuroscientist and systems theorist, Warren McCulloch
- The brilliant anthropologist, Gregory Bateson
- The pioneering neuroscientist, Karl Pribram
- The great visionary physicist, David Bohm

They have each, in their own way, used the logic of circular feedback to explain, for example, how the brain stores memories. Bohm has used the logic of circular feedback to speculate how the "vacuum" of space may store memories that transcend space and time. We will discuss his vision in chapter 10. You may wonder, isn't it strange that these brilliant scientists failed to see that the basic logic was universal and applied unconditionally to all systems—general systems, living systems—everything?

Was their vision simply limited by their specialties? Or, were they afraid, implicitly if not explicitly, to face the controversial paradigm-changing implications of the logic of circulation?

We'll return to this deep question after you learn the logic of the systemic memory process and have come to understand the extensive implications of the theory for science, spirituality, and life in general.

How to Swing a Small Child and Knock Down a Gigantic Building—Prelude to the Systemic Memory Process

Most of us have swung a small child in a playground, and even been swung as young children. However, most of us have never knocked down a building using the motion of a swing, and we've never thought about the possibility of knocking down a gigantic skyscraper using the same swinging procedure, employing the same swinging logic.

Nikola Tesla, the brilliant, eccentric inventor, who among other things invented AC current and AC generators that empower humankind worldwide, actually envisioned collapsing buildings through the gentle power of what is sometimes called sympathetic vibration or resonance, or what Tesla called "mechanical resonance." I remember reading about Tesla's vision of mechanical resonance in 1994, and I shared the story with Linda. In her inimitable way she said, "Gary, Tesla was creating living systemic memory! We must remember that." As you'll see, she was right.

First, let's review how we swing a child, and then we'll learn how to swing a building. We can swing a child in two fundamental ways:

One way is through brute force. If we are strong enough, we can pull the child way back or push the child way forward, and begin each swing with a bang. We could call this the big bang approach to swinging.

The other way is through gentle force. Here what we do is apply a soft force, and as the child swings slightly back and forth, we add a gentle push with each cycle of the swing. We "sympathize" with the cycle (vibration) of the child, and little by little, the child swings out further and further. We could call this the big bloom approach to swinging.

The key to gentle, blooming swinging is to synchronize one's swinging with the cycle of the swing. Since the swing "remembers" the previous push, the child will increasingly swing out further and further with each addition of the gentle, sympathetic force.

A friendly way to think about systems is the acronym SYSTEM Synchronized (or Sympathetic—both apply) Storing of Time, Energy, and Motion.

What Tesla realized was that everything—yes, everything—was vibrating. Therefore, theoretically, if we added sympathetic information and energy to each vibration, we could gently but surely accentuate the natural vibrations that the system naturally expressed. Since Tesla's mind functioned integratively and systemically, he envisioned applying this sympathetic vibration or resonance model to everything that vibrated. This included skyscrapers.

Let's say your goal was to knock down the Empire State Building. What you would do is measure the subtle, spontaneous swaying of the Empire State Building, and you would begin to shift your weight gently and consistently in synchrony with the building. Each time the building swayed in the designated direction, you would add your gentle force. Since your force would continually add, slowly but surely, to the vibration of the building, the building would continue to swing, slowly but surely, in the direction nudged by your gentle force.

If you were to function sympathetically with the building, you would flexibly adjust each push to occur with the sway of the building, back and forth, over and over again. You would "go with the flow." According to Tesla, if you did this repetitively (recurrently), you and the Empire State Building would slowly but surely swing even more. The big bloom of your swing, if continued sympathetically for a long enough period, could potentially result in the big bang of the building falling over!

Most buildings are designed to withstand the sporadic big bangs of winds and rain, earthquakes, and the like. However, most buildings are not designed to resist synchronized sympathetic vibrations that can be achieved through the big bloom. Buildings are top heavy. Furthermore, they are built in pieces. Hence, if gentle sympathetic vibrations are consistently added through positive feedback for weeks and weeks, it's statistically possible that certain buildings could collapse.

Gentle sympathetic vibrations will not be sufficient to knock down something sturdy, at least not in a brief period of time. But, if the mechanical resonance principle is implemented with sufficient energy over a long enough period of time, Tesla reasoned, even very sturdy things can be led to vibrate out of control.

Experiencing Tesla's Own Story—
Honoring the Inspired "Mad Inventor"

How did Tesla come to the conclusion that mechanical resonance, sympathetically applied, could have such powerful consequences? Whereas Linda and I initially came to the conclusion conceptually, Tesla apparently came to it empirically.

Here is how Margaret Cheney tells Tesla's story in her book, *Tesla: Man out of Time.* We recite this section in its entirety not only to honor the "mad inventor" (Cheney's phrase), but also to enable you to appreciate how powerful this phenomenon can be, as purportedly witnessed by Tesla.

> One day in 1898 while testing a tiny electromechanical oscillator, he [Tesla] attached it with innocent intent to an iron pillar that went down through the center of his left building at 46 East Houston Street, to the sandy floor of the basement.
>
> Flipping on the switch, he settled into a straight-backed chair to watch and make notes of everything that happened. Such machines always fascinated him because, as the tempo built higher and higher, they would establish resonance with first one object in his workshop and then another. For example, a piece of equipment or furniture would suddenly begin to shimmy and dance. As he stepped up the frequency, it would halt but another more in tune would take up the frantic jig and, later on, yet another.
>
> At police headquarters on Mulberry Street, where Tesla was already regarded with suspicion, it soon became apparent that no other part of the city was having an earthquake. Two officers were dispatched posthaste to check on the mad inventor. The latter, unaware of the shambles occurring all around his building, had just begun to sense an ominous vibration in the floor and walls. Knowing that he must quickly put a stop to it, he seized a sledgehammer and smashed the little oscillator in a single blow.
>
> With perfect timing the two policemen rushed through the door, allowing him to turn with a courteous nod.
>
> "Gentlemen, I am sorry," he said. "You are just a trifle late to witness my experiment. I found it necessary to stop it suddenly and unexpectedly and in an unusual way. However, if you will come around this evening I will have another oscillator attached to this platform and each of you can stand on it. You will, I am sure, find it a most interesting and pleasurable experience. Now you must leave, for I have many things to do. Good day, gentlemen."
>
> Years later he told Allan L. Benson of other experiments he had made with an oscillator no larger than an alarm clock. He described attaching the vibrator to a steel link two feet long

and two inches thick. "For a long time nothing happened . . . But at last . . . the great steel link began to tremble, increased its trembling until it dilated and contracted like a beating heart . . . and finally broke!

"Sledgehammers could not have done it," he told the reporter; "crowbars could not have done it, but a fusillade of taps, not one of which would have harmed a baby, did it."

Pleased with this beginning, he put the little vibrator in his coat pocket and went out to hunt a half-built steel building. Finding one in the Wall Street district, ten stories high, with nothing up but the steelwork, he clamped the vibrator to one of the beams.

"In a few minutes," he told the reporter, "I could feel the beam trembling. Gradually the trembling increased in intensity and extended throughout the whole great mass of steel. Finally, the structure began to creak and wave, and the steelworkers came to the ground panic-stricken, believing that there had been an earthquake. Rumors spread that the building was about to fall, and the police reserves were called out. Before anything serious happened, I took off the vibrator, put it in my pocket, and went away. But if I had kept on ten minutes more, I could have laid that building flat in the street. And, with the same vibrator, I could drop Brooklyn Bridge in less than an hour."

Tesla's mind went from the sweet to the scary, and he was not playing games. Here is how he proposed applying the same mechanical resonance principle to potentially destroying the Earth:

Nor was this all. He boasted to Benson that he could split the Earth in the same way—split it as a boy would split an apple—and forever end the career of man. "Earth's vibrations," he went on, "have a periodicity of about one hour and forty-nine minutes. That is to say, if I strike the Earth this instant, a wave of contraction goes through it that will come back in one hour and forty-nine minutes in the form of expansion. As a matter of fact, the earth, like everything else, is in a constant state of vibration. It is constantly contracting and expanding.

"Now, suppose that at the precise moment when it begins to contract, I explode a ton of dynamite. That accelerates the contraction, and in one hour and forty-nine minutes, there comes an equally accelerated wave of expansion. When the wave of expansions ebbs, suppose I explode another ton of dynamite, thus further increasing the wave of contraction. Is there any doubt as to what would happen? There is no doubt in my mind. The Earth would be split in two. For the first time in man's history, he has the knowledge with which he may interfere with cosmic processes!"

When Benson asked how long it might take him to split the Earth, he answered modestly, "Months might be required; perhaps a year or two." But in only a few weeks, he said, he could set the Earth's crust in such a state of vibration that it would rise and fall hundreds of feet, throwing rivers out of their beds, wrecking buildings, and practically destroying civilization.

No wonder they called Tesla the mad inventor. Though Tesla was not known for his humility (to put it mildly), he was nonetheless a serious scientist and revised his hypotheses as new information presented itself. As the following quote indicates, Tesla understood the need to qualify his predictions about splitting the Earth:

> To the relief of ordinary citizens, Tesla later qualified his claim. The *principle* could not fail, he said, but it would be impossible to obtain perfect mechanical resonance of the Earth. (Cheney's italics.)

Hopefully, the Earth is a sufficiently complex system so that no simple pattern of sympathetic vibrations could achieve "perfect mechanical resonance." However, is Tesla's strong intuition that the "*principle* could not fail" correct? Below you will be able to decide for yourself as you learn the step-by-step reasoning of the systemic memory process. As you will see, Tesla's purported observations and intuitions about the accumulation of information and energy through mechanical resonance are remarkably consistent with modern scientific models of positive feedback loops in systems of all shapes and sizes.

Now that you've gained an intuitive sense for how gentle pushes can have significant consequences when they're administered sympathetically and persistently, you're ready to enter the abstract world of systems logic, positive feedback loops, and the apparently inexorable creation of integrative and universal systemic memories.

For those of you who are still skeptical and see this as a puzzle, we hope you will say to yourself what Linda and I have said to ourselves time and time again: "If there's a flaw here, I'm going to find it!"

We will speak of A's and B's, interactions and emergents, recurrent feedback loops and circular causality. The logic will become abstract for a few pages, and you may need to reread some of the sentences. However, the gift you'll receive for paying close attention will be that you'll finally understand why many consider the mathematical logic of systemic memory to be a scientific proof for the existence of living memories in all things in the universe, including remembering the divine.

What Is Positive Feedback?
Linda's "Natural Law of Circulation"

Consider the simplest of systems—the two-component system, A and B. Using the swing example mentioned above, A would be the swinging child and B would be you.

A moves or vibrates and sends something to B, and B returns information back to A.

If the information is added to what A is doing (which is the meaning of the term positive in positive feedback—remember, this is what you did when you added synchronized information and energy to the child swinging or the building swinging), then A's behavior will be augmented by the presence of the information coming from B.

With each A-B cycle, A sends information to B and B then sends information back to A that augments what A is doing. This is the abstract representation of the concrete description of the swinging child or the building.

Now, consider what happens to the relationship of A and B as this additive, positive feedback process continues over time. As A continues to behave, its behavior is augmented, over and over, by the history of itself as it was interpreted by B and returned to A in revised form.

This is because each time A behaves, its behavior is passed on to B, and B sends A's behavior back so that A is augmented by what it just did. So in a single "cycle" between A and B, A's behavior gets to B, is then interpreted by B, and finally returns to A. This takes place over the time course of a single cycle.

With each "A to B and back to A" cycle, what A does represents the accumulated history of what it had done before because in a positive feedback loop, each cycle augments the "new" with the "previous," and the previous is actually the history of all the cycles preceding it. Hence, A's behavior is augmented by the history of itself as A has been perceived by B.

When a system is constructed with a positive feedback loop, the system's behavior grows over time. This "learning" unfolds dynamically and potentially explosively. If a positive feedback loop continues indefinitely, the system may not be able to withstand physically the accumulating sympathetic vibrations, and it will ultimately "explode" (the child may fall off of the swing, the building may fall down, the nuclear reactor may explode). At one point in the history of science, this was called "catastrophe theory."

According to *Webster's Second Edition Unabridged Dictionary*, the word integrate comes from the Latin *integrare* which means "to make whole, renew." With each cycle, a system is renewed, joining the present with the past in a dynamic wholistic fashion. However, positive feedback, carried to an extreme, ultimately destroys the wholeness of the system. Does this imply too much systemic memory?

We're ready to take you through the simplest of math from A to B and back again. You'll take the electron ride that I took that fateful day at Yale, and you'll witness the accumulation of history—the creation of integrative systemic memories—first hand.

After our electron ride together, you'll see how the logic of feedback slowly but surely augments itself like a positive feedback loop, and ultimately explodes with new predictions and possibilities. You may want to take a piece of paper, and write down the A's and B's as you go through the story, and draw out the logic for yourself. That's what I did almost twenty years ago.

Prelude to the Logic—A Completely Optional Formula to Ponder, If You Wish

We have said that systemic memory can be envisioned as Evolution = **memory** * circulation[Repeating]. However, if you are among the few who like actual summary formulas, you may choose to examine and remember a mathematical description of the meta-phorical "mc[R]." Otherwise, simply skim the words and skip to the next section, the merry-go-round of the circular feedback logic.

In the oversimplified formula outlined below:

- A and B stand for "A" and "B"
- t stands for time (t+ stands for the time it takes information to travel from A to reach B, or B to A)
- r stands for recurrent (repeating in circular fashion)
- "aba . . ." represents the evolving systemic (interactive) memory ($a_1b_2a_3$, etc.)

$$(A_t + B_{t+})^r = (a_{t+}b_{t++}a_{t+++}. . .)^r$$

As the song goes, from an integrative and universal systems perspective, "memories are made of this." And we are made of memories that live and evolve with time.

Taking the Ride from A to B and Back Again

The key to understanding the journey we are about to take is to realize that we are going from A to B and back again, and the journey takes time to go around the circle.

Let's connect A and B for the very first time. Remember, A and B can be anything. They can be:

- two photons interacting in a laser
- an electron and a proton interacting in an atom
- hydrogen and oxygen interacting in water
- two interacting tuning forks
- two neurons interacting in the brain, or two cells interacting in the heart
- two minds interacting (Albert and Betty)
- a person interacting with a building (from Tesla)

- the earth interacting with the moon
- the sun interacting with the earth
- two interacting stars (curiously, stars often exist in pairs)
- two interacting galaxies

The logic does not care what A and B are. A and B can interact *between* levels. For example, electron to cell, cell to person, or person to planet. What the logic cares about is that A and B are ready to be connected for the first time, and once they are connected, they will function as a circular positive feedback loop.

When I first imagined this super simple system, I imagined an electronic oscillating circuit. A and B were two electronic components, and electrons were traveling in a circuit from A to B and back again.

The simplest way to segment the journey is to break the journey into four time periods:

Time 1—The time we leave A, on our way to B

A   B

A   B

Time 2—The time we reach B

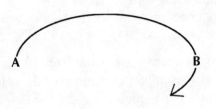

Time 3—The time we leave B, on our way back to A

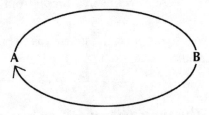

Time 4—The time we return to A.

Now, what happens at each of these time points?

At time 1, A is vibrating. Even if A is a simple tuning fork, seemingly at rest, it is actually "vibrating"—creating tiny sub-audible sounds that can be recorded by sensitive microphones. *Remember, the quantum world is never still.* A is always vibrating, always dancing as the book, *The Dancing Wu Li Masters* reminds us.

We call this information at time 1, a_1. In other words, the information of A at time 1 = a_1.

Time 1

A   B

Now we travel from time 1 to time 2, and reach B.

At time 2, what reaches B is the history of A from time 1.

For the simplest (abstract) case, let's imagine that the information traveling from A at time 1 (a_1) has not changed its form from time 1 to time 2. Therefore, the information from A at time 2 (a_2) carries the pure information from A at time 1 (a_1). Hence, the information from A at time 2—called a_2—equals a_1. In the language of mathematics, $a_2 = a_1$. Even if the "energy" happens to be decreasing, the form or pattern is kept the same.

Time 2

At this point (time 2), B begins to respond to the information from A. Remember, we are imagining that this is the first time that A and B have begun their communication. They are becoming an integrative system for the very first time.

We must remember that at time 2, just before B begins to respond to the information coming from A, B is also vibrating. Therefore, the information of B at time 2 = b_2.

Now, here is the first big conceptual realization—the first big "aha."

At time 3, after B has responded to A, what is leaving B and readying to return to A? Well, the information coming from B at time 3 could be called b_3. However, what does b_3 *actually contain?* The logic tells us that what has happened to B at time 3 reflects some kind of interaction between the information of a_1 and the state of B at time 2, which we called b_2. Therefore, b_3 at time 3 actually equals a_1b_2. Mathematically, $b_3 = a_1b_2$.

For convenience, Linda and I use the letters "a_1b_2" to express any kind of complex interaction that can occur between a_1 and b_2. For example, a_1b_2 could reflect a_1 times b_2 (multiplication). a_1b_2 can

Time 3

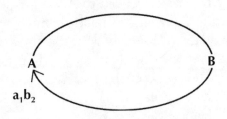

reflect any form of integration, simple or complex, linear or nonlinear. The key is to remind ourselves that at time 3, b_3 actually $= a_1b_2$.

The term a_1b_2 reminds us that b_3 is reflecting the integrative history of the interaction of a_1 and b_2. So, what begins to return at time 3 is the history of A at time 1 (a_1) as perceived and by B at time 2 (b_2). The history of A as perceived and revised by B (a_1b_2) is readying to return to A. The integrative systemic memory is forming.

Now, it takes additional time for the a_1b_2 information at time 3 to return to A. We call this time 4. At time 4, A has in all likelihood changed. Any number of other factors could have led A to be in a different state. Even its own vibrational state could be different. For simplicity, in the abstract, we can say that the state of A at time 4 $=$ a_4. However, the state of A at time 4 is about to be influenced by the arrival of the information returning from B.

Let's imagine for the sake of simplicity that the information coming back from B (which is a_1b_2) has not changed in form from time 3 to time 4. Therefore, the state of A at time 4 will begin to interact with the information returning.

Time 4

Hence, A at time 4 (a_4) will begin to be revised by a_1b_2.

Now, here is the 64 trillion dollar question: What will A be doing at time 5?

Well, if A had not been connected in a circular feedback loop relationship to B, at time 5, A would be going along its merry way. A at time 5 would simply equal a_5 (ignoring all other possible interactions, for the moment). A5 would $= a_5$.

However, if A was connected in a circular feedback loop relationship to B, $a_1 b_2$ would have returned to A at time 4. Hence, at time 5, a_5 would reflect the interaction of A at time 4 (a_4) with the returning information from B at time 3 ($a_1 b_2$). Therefore, a_5 would become $a_1 b_2 a_4$, a complex integration of historical information.

Time 5

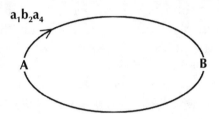

$a_1 b_2 a_4$

A   B

At time 5, A would actually reflect a history of itself at time 1 (a_1), interpreted by B at time 2 (b_2), resulting in $a_1 b_2$ at time 3, which interacted with A at time 4 (a_4), becoming $a_1 b_2 a_4$. The conclusion is unavoidable.

When B is connected to A, as time goes by, A is continually bathed in a history of itself as interpreted and revised by B. And as long as A and B are connected, this circulating and integrating systemic process continues, ever more complexly, over and over and over again. In technical terms, the feedback process is "recursive," meaning "reoccurring." This is the heart of recurrent feedback interaction. It is the basis of dynamic systemic memory.

In Appendix A, the math is described in a more complex way (using slightly different language and symbols), but the essence of the logic is the same. What returns to A, over time, is a history of itself as interpreted and revised by B. And the same thing happens to B when A and B are connected and become a dynamic recursive system. B begins to send information and energy to A just as A begins to send information and energy to B. What returns to B, over time, is a history of itself as interpreted and revised by A!

Yes, it all gets very complicated, very fast. And mathematical magic can happen.

One expression of this evolving complexity is termed "chaos" (an unfolding order whose details are often impossible to predict ahead of time). The other is called "self-organization." In fact, Peter Coveney and Roger Highfield in their 1995 book, *Frontiers of Complexity*, define complexity as "units endowed with the potential to evolve in time."

Curiously, contemporary chaos and complexity theory is primarily modeled at Stage L—the revising, resonating, remembering feedback process is typically presumed to begin at cellular levels rather than to function at all levels. However, the systemic memory hypothesis revises this limited vision by illustrating how the fundamental logic equally applies to all systems that engage in recurrent resonance. Systemic memory extends self-organization to become self-revision; self-organizing systems become self-revising systems, and the process is hypothesized to occur at all levels to various degrees.

The universal living memory process—an expression of evolution in time—is a systemic potential in all systems of recursive/circulating A's and B's.

A's and B's can even be two pendulum clocks on a wall. When set into motion, they will engage in spontaneous resonance, revising their inter-clock relationship, and emerging into a remembered synchrony of swings. The clocks will, so to speak, "self-organize" and become a two-clock, self-revised system. They will ultimately beat as one.

The basic logic is simple and straightforward. Positive feedback is a scientific fact. Sympathetic vibration is a scientific fact. The accumulation of information in a circulating positive feedback loop, as expressed in the system's behavior, is a scientific fact.

However, the actual math is incredibly complex. In complex systems theory the field is called non-linear dynamics, and the modeling and calculation of the ever more complex accumulating interactions is daunting. Only the very simplest systems have been modeled with any success to date.

For example, no one has yet taken the core logic of the systemic memory process, and modeled how hydrogen and oxygen, when they connect, develop a systemic resonance (sympathetic vibration) relationship history, over time, which establishes the wholistic memories that lead to the emergence of what we experience as water.

For example, how many A-B recursive cycles does it take for hydrogen and oxygen as gases to develop and express the emergent properties of water? One? Ten? Thousands? Millions? A question for future research.

Let's repeat this conclusion using slightly different words.

In the same way that the complex relationship between the abstract identities A and B unfold over time, the very much more complex relationship between the actual entities hydrogen and oxygen should unfold over time too. The concept is the same.

The principle is identical. It's the particulars that are different.

In our technical scientific papers, we used the term "recurrent feedback interaction" to express the complex accumulation of information and energy that naturally occurs in systems when feedback processes interact, and they do so over and over and over. We also described the process as being a process of "circular causality." A causes an effect in B, B then causes an effect in A, A then causes an effect in B, and the process of mutual causality occurs in a circular fashion.

Let's be clear here. Positive feedback processes are so well documented, so well appreciated, that scientists often take them for granted. Reductionist (Stage M) scientists do not like circular logic but recursive feedback requires circular thinking and circular mathematics. Hence the systems shift to Stages I, L, and E. Positive feedback systems function as if they have memory, meaning their history unfolds in complex ways as a function of the process of feedback.

Note that the term "positive" in positive feedback means that the dynamic interactive information is, by definition, added to A. A is influenced by an unfolding history of itself, as revised by B, in such a way that A continues changing (evolving) in the direction it was previously going. This is "positive" circulation.

If this was a "negative" feedback loop instead, the circulating information would be subtracted from A. A would still be influenced by the unfolding history of itself, as revised by B—only now, in such a way, as to reverse the direction A was previously going. The systemic memory process applies to all kinds of feedback, the simplest to understand is positive feedback. In nature, complex systems involve various combinations of positive and negative feedback loop processes occurring in parallel.

The challenge for scientists and nonscientists alike is to come to realize that the logic of feedback, which predicts the systemic memory process, leads us to discover a remarkable universal living memory that is inherent in the nature of all systems in the universe. Most scientists, including contemporary chaos and complexity scientists, haven't recognized the fact that the logic that justifies the systemic memory creation and storage process is completely and totally universal. It applies to all systems at all levels. This is why Linda calls it the "Natural Law of Circulation."

In subsequent chapters, we will apply the logic to cells, water, energy systems, and even the nature of consciousness itself. We will consider what memory means and what aliveness means in light of the systemic memory process. We will consider the distinction between storing information and energy versus retrieving information and energy. We will consider material implications and spiritual implications of universal living memory. We will consider the idea that if matter evolves, then it follows logically that energy evolves too.

The challenge for each of us is to remember that whenever and wherever circular positive feedback processes are found to occur in nature, the logic of the systemic memory process must apply.

It turns out that positive feedback processes are ubiquitous in nature. This means that all things that engage in circular causality should change and grow over time to various degrees. Whatever the system is, if it engages in recurrent positive feedback, it engages in the systemic memory process to some degree. Hence, everything should be constantly evolving and unfolding, revising itself along the way, and everything stores systemic relationship memories within its own process.

The logic is curiously unconditional. Once you understand the general case, and if you haven't found a flaw in the logic, then you are scientifically obliged to accept the general case as plausible and potentially universal. Specific predictions abound in all directions that can be put to empirical test.

The logic even applies to the vacuum of space. In chapters 9 and 10, we will explain how modern physics requires that we seriously entertain the possibility that "virtual" info-energy systems are created in the "vacuum" between the atoms of matter themselves. Remember, between every A and B is a space, the "vacuum" and the information and energy going from A to B can connect and circulate with the information and energy coming back from B to A.

Clearly, the "space" between A and B is not "empty." It is "filled" with the ongoing stream of information and energy that continuously flows between A and B. This stream of information and energy can potentially become an info-energy system between A and B. These info-energy systems in the vacuum should precisely replicate the dynamic organization of the A's and B's between them. As you will read in chapter 9, the logic actually requires the hypothesis that out-of-body consciousness is plausible, as is the survival of consciousness and personality after physical death.

The logic continues, unconditionally from the material to the spiritual and beyond.

The Simple/Mundane and the Complex/Profound—Preparing for the New World of Predictions and Possibilities

As we have said, once you "get it" you realize that the core of the logic is simple. However, the implications are complex, exceptionally broad in scope, and profound.

This kind of thing—simple logic, complex implications, vast applications—happens in science every once in a while. Probably the best known example is $E=mc^2$. If ever there was a simple and mundane formula for a complex and profound idea, it is Einstein's famous formula.

The existence of a universal living memory process requires that we expand our vision of nature, science, spirituality—in essence, everything. In this sense, the idea of universal living memory is a huge idea, and is a virtual conceptual proof for the existence of a living, evolving God.

The size of an idea, its depth and breadth, is proportional to the number of ideas and phenomena it addresses. Since the idea of integrative systemic memory is so unconditional and universal—it potentially applies to everything—it is potentially as big as the universe itself. Like the previous ideas of systems and feedback, which are prototypic huge ideas because they apply potentially to everything, the new idea of the systemic memory process is similarly huge.

Having witnessed the logic described above, you should be able to imagine how the following predictions can be derived from the theory:

- Photons, and even energy itself, can be eternal, alive, and evolving.
- Electrons and protons can resonate, like tuning forks, and should store information and energy in the process.
- "Simple" molecules like water, and "complex" molecules like DNA should be alive, vibrant, and collect histories as they live.
- Every cell on the earth, including every cell in your body, should store information concerning everything it comes into contact with.
- In the same way that your brain learns, your heart should learn, the tree should learn, the earth as a whole should learn, the sun should learn, the solar systems should learn, the galaxies should learn, and even the universe as a whole should learn.
- Everything that learns should be eternal, alive, and evolving; the history of everything should live on in the vacuum of space as info-energy systems.
- A creative consciousness must have existed at the beginning of either the big bang and/or the big bloom and continues to evolve, i.e. a God process exists and cannot die.

On first hearing, some of this may sound fantastic.

However, we should gently remind ourselves that the same was once said for the idea that the earth was round, that the earth revolved around the sun, that germs could cause disease, and that machines could fly. The list of once fantastic if not outlandish ideas is quite large.

Today we know there is more than our uneducated common sense teaches us.

Science has taught us that the earth is not actually flat; it only appears that way until we look more closely. Science has taught us that the sun does not actually revolve around the earth ; it only appears that way until we look more closely. And science is now teaching us that energy and matter are not without life and intelligence; it only appears that way until we look more closely.

In each case, we have revised our stories accordingly.

Just as there are levels of systems, there are potentially levels of life, of becoming, blooming, waiting to be discovered by the next generation of explorers. We are now ready to look more closely at a circulating universe potentially teeming with integrative systemic memory. We'll look closely at things we've seen before and things we've never seen, and see them all with new eyes.

PART III

Examples of Universal Living Memory

Happiness is what we feel when our biochemicals—of emotion, the neuropeptides and their receptors, are open and flowing freely. It is a scientific fact that we can feel what others feel—emotional resonance. The oneness of all life is based on this simple reality. Our molecules of emotion are all vibrating together.

Candace Pert

Chapter 7

Does the Heart Remember?

The Amazing Stories of Transplant Patients and the Plausibility of Memory in Every Cell

*If you wish to upset the law that all crows are black
it is enough if you prove one single crow to be white.*

William James

*I can see you've had a change in mind,
but what you need is a change of heart.*

Carole King

In order to understand how heart cells can learn, we should remember how brain cells learn. Brains cells learn as complex networks of feedback loops.

However, the story science has created for explaining how brains
learn applies equally well to how hearts, lungs, kidneys, or even
bones, can learn. Feedback loops do not care what form they take.
When they exist, they do what they do, regardless of their shape or
size. They create integrative systemic memories as time unfolds;
they create universal living memories. Period. At least, this is what
logic dictates. Feedback networks learn.

The first time I began to believe that the logic of systemic
memory might have meaning in the real world was the day William
Novak called Linda and me and told us about the book he was

helping Claire Sylvia write, called A *Change of Heart*. Frankly, I couldn't believe what he was telling us on the telephone. If Bill was right about Claire, then Claire's personality changes that followed her successful heart and lung operation could be taken as evidence in support of universal living memory.

Could Claire's experience be real?

For example, Claire recounted that six weeks after her transplant, when she was allowed to drive again, she drove straight to the nearest Kentucky Fried Chicken, a place she'd never been before, and this former dancer and fit, thin person ordered fried chicken nuggets. She later learned that the 18-year-old person whose heart and lungs now lived on inside her had had a fondness for them. Moreover, at the time of the young man's death in a motorcycle accident, uneaten chicken nuggets were found stuffed inside the pocket of his leather motorcycle jacket.

Claims such as these are typically and understandably treated as nonsense—that is, they don't make any sense—from a traditional reductionistic (Stage M) perspective.

They're explained as coincidences or misperceptions, side-effects of the immunosuppressant drugs, or the expression of preexisting psychopathology interacting with the stress of surgery. However, when systems are viewed not only as relatively static material systems (Stage I), but as dynamic, living (Stage L) and evolving (Stage E) informational energy systems as well, claims such as these, from select transplant patients, begin to make sense. After learning of Claire's experience, we were reminded of William James' famous phrase that introduced this chapter. To disprove the law that all crows are black, one need only discover one white crow, one exception to the rule. When Linda and I published our dynamical energy systems paper in 1997, in *Alternative Therapies in Health and Medicine* (in which we included the logic of systemic memory), we wrote: "It is possible that Claire Sylvia may be the 'white crow' of cellular memory."

Linda and I ultimately spoke with Claire and had the privilege of hearing her story firsthand. Claire's story is remarkable, and we'll share more of it with you shortly. We will also share with you stories of other transplant recipients described in Paul Pearsall's book, *The Heart's Code*. However, I must confess I have mixed emotions about these stories.

On the one hand, I know they are scientifically plausible. Modern science provides the logic and theory to predict that this kind of cellular memory should happen, at least in those transplant recipients who are open to receiving the personal information and energy that's predicted to be living inside their new organs. Moreover, Linda and I have studied the actual transcripts of ten of the heart transplant patients Paul Pearsall spoke with, as well as transcripts from family and friends of these recipients as well as family and friends of their respective donors. We are convinced that these reports are genuine and have helped Pearsall publish the verbatim reports in the scientific literature.

On the other hand, I still find these stories so remarkable that I say, "What? Can they really be true?" The skeptic in me pulls out every possible hypothesis that I can envision, and lays them out, one by one, on the conceptual table.

Of course, this is precisely what a scientist should do. Scientists have a professional responsibility to be open to all possible hypotheses, and to consider their merits in terms of both logic and data. But my reluctance to believe that these stories reflect a universal living memory process is more than scientific. There is, to put it bluntly, fear.

If these reports are true, then the implications are nothing short of staggering—medically, psychologically, spiritually, and ethically. We will address some of these concerns after we share the stories. As strange as the following stories may seem to you, they're actually but a prelude to the wonders of systemic memory and the universal living memory hypothesis.

"Amazing Transplant Stories"

Those were the cover words to the April 1998 issue of *Natural Health* magazine that ran a feature article on *The Heart's Code* entitled "The Heart Remembers," reprinted from Pearsall's book. What stories did editors consider to be so amazing?

Consider Glenda who lost her husband David in a car crash. Glenda is a practicing family physician. Three years after the accident, Pearsall arranged a meeting between Glenda and the young man who had received one of the most precious gifts one person can give to another—one's heart. In the case of heart transplants, we're not simply speaking about the gift of one's emotional heart or one's spiritual heart, we are speaking literally about the gift of one's physical heart.

Apparently the young man and his mother were almost a half-hour late for their meeting in the hospital chapel. Pearsall wrote, "I was ready to suggest to Glenda that we leave. The issue of recipients meeting the donor families is a very sensitive one, and I understood why the man may have changed his mind." However, as Pearsall took Glenda's hand, she said quietly, "No, we have to wait. He's here in the hospital. I felt him arrive about thirty minutes ago. I felt my husband's presence. Please wait with me."

Yes, this was an M.D. speaking. Pearsall wrote, "She [Glenda] is well versed in bioscience, and, as I do, admires the rigor and healthy skepticism of modern science."

Glenda went on to say, "David's heart is here. I can't believe I'm saying that to you, but I feel it. His recipient is here in this hospital."

At that moment, the door opened, and the young man and his mother walked hurriedly down the center aisle of the chapel.

"Sorry we're late," said the young man, with a heavy Spanish accent. "We got here a half hour ago, but we couldn't find the chapel." Hmm . . .

Could Glenda have really recognized David's heart information and energy as his heart entered the hospital in the body of the young man she was about to meet?

According to the systemic memory process, this is both plausible and probable.

Remember, information and energy continuously span out into space, and like lightning, the info-energy that actually precedes us is traveling close to the speed of light. This means that the information and energy arrives much sooner than the physical system does.

Our electromagnetic signals always precede us. Some physicists go so far as to propose that personal information actually "travels" instantaneously (the technical term is nonlocality), the electromagnetic waves "merely" travel at the speed of light, while the body, obviously, lags way behind at a snail's pace.

Pearsall continued, "After introductions and awkward attempts at humor about a heart-to-heart meeting between the young wife and her husband's heart, the usually shy Glenda blurted out, 'This embarrasses me as much as it must embarrass you, but can I put my hand on your chest and feel his—I mean your heart?'

"The young man looked at me, and then his mother, put his hand to his chest and finally nodded his head. As Glenda reached forward, he unbuttoned his shirt, took her hand, and gently placed it against his naked chest. What happened next transcends our current view of the brain, body, heart and mind.

"Glenda's hand began to tremble, and tears rolled down her cheeks. She closed her eyes and whispered, 'I love you, David. Everything is copacetic.' She removed her hand, hugged the young man to her chest, and all of us wiped tears from our eyes. Glenda and the young man sat down and, silhouetted against the stained glass window of the chapel, held hands in silence.

"Speaking in her heavy Spanish accent, the young man's mother told me, 'My son uses that word copacetic all the time now. He never used it before he got his new heart, but after his surgery, it was the first thing he said to me when he could talk. I don't know what it means. He said everything is copacetic. It is not a word I know in Spanish.'

"Glenda overheard us, her eyes widened, she turned toward us, and said, 'That word was our signal that everything is okay. Every time we argued and made up, we would both say that everything is copacetic.'"

This seems unbelievable, but fits the logic of the systemic memory process if we are open to the logic of positive feedback loops and circular causality. This story touched Linda and I deeply, but there's more. Pearsall writes:

"Our discussion about a magic word that seemed to reveal a code of the heart within him stimulated the young man to share story after story of changes he experienced following his transplant. Described by his mother as a former vegetarian and very health-conscious, he said he now craves meat and fatty food. A former lover of heavy metal music, he said he now loves '50s rock and roll. He reported recurrent dreams of bright lights coming straight for him. Glenda responded almost matter-of-factly that her husband loved meat, had played in a Motown rock and roll band while in medical school, and that she too dreams of the lights of that fateful night."

A Sherlock Holmes Heart

Glenda's is not an isolated story. Again quoting Pearsall:

"One of the many cases that seems to reinforce this principle that the heart's memory and intelligence lie outside that brain's control was revealed to me recently when I spoke to an international group of psychologists, psychiatrists, and social workers meeting in Houston, Texas. I spoke to them concerning my ideas about the central role of the heart in our psychological and spiritual life and, following my presentation, a psychiatrist came to the microphone during the question and answer session to ask me about one of her clients, whose experience seemed to substantiate my ideas about cellular memories and a thinking heart. The case disturbed her so much that she struggled to speak through the tears.

"Sobbing to the point that the audience and I had difficulty understanding her, she said, 'I have a patient, an eight-year-old girl who received the heart of a murdered ten-year-old girl. Her mother brought her to me when she started screaming at night about her dreams of the man who had murdered her donor. She said her daughter knew who it was. After several sessions, I could not deny the reality of what this child was telling me. Her mother and I finally decided to call the police, and using the description from the little girl, they found the murderer. He was easily convicted with evidence my patient provided. The time, weapon, place, clothes he wore, what the little girl he killed had said to him . . . everything the little heart transplant recipient had reported was completely accurate.'

"As the therapist returned to her seat, the audience of scientifically trained and clinically experienced professionals sat in silence. I could hear quiet sobbing and see tears in the eyes of the doctors in the front row. Unlike many presentations at scientific forums, this time there was no expression of doubt or skepticism. The very real possibility of a heart that remembers seemed to touch all of these scientists in their own hearts."

Can you believe this?

Can a mechanical pump, even if it has a nervous system of sorts, store so much information that it can remember the description of a murderer and be a Sherlock Holmes of sorts?

Yes, the systemic memory process requires that we entertain this claim seriously, and that we not "rush to judgment" and dismiss such reports as statistical coincidence or faulty perception. Something very real seems to be going on here.

Is There More to the Story Than This?

The problem with these cases, as dramatic as they are, is that they don't express the whole story, the whole truth. The truth is, there are weird aspects to these stories, often not repeated because of fear of ridicule, that make the implications seem even more difficult to accept. We realized this challenge right at the outset, when we heard Claire's transplant story.

Here's what happened to Claire. Briefly, she received one of the most difficult of transplant operations, a combined heart and lung transplant for a congenital condition, not a behavioral condition. Claire was not a smoker, she was not a drinker. She was super health conscious, in touch with her emotions and her body in a manner befitting a creative choreographer and dancer.

Since Claire's was the first heart-lung transplant in New England, the press was eager to speak with her. When she was able, she was posed a question by a reporter that essentially asked, "Now that you have a new heart and lungs, and a new lease on life, what do you want to do?" What came to her, and what she blurted out to her great embarrassment, was "I want to have a beer!"

Now this is not the kind of deep emotional and spiritual response that the press was expecting. Her subsequent visit to Kentucky Fried Chicken was just one of many changes that led her to wonder whether she was somehow in contact with the memories, the spirit and soul, of the person's heart and lungs now living inside her.

However, what follows are two examples that reflect the really weird part of her story.

83

Like many transplant recipients open to this kind of phenomena, Claire began to have a recurrent dream. Her dream involved a man whose name was Tim. He told Claire that he loved her. In her dream, Tim would come to her, and then he entered her through her lungs. Of course, this might be "just" memory from her new heart and lungs. But could it be more?

Could Tim's spirit and soul be connected to Claire *through* his heart and lungs?

Claire desperately wanted to meet someone who knew the person in her dream who called himself Tim, to see if he was really living inside her. The question was, how could she locate Tim? Would the medical staff at Yale give her the name of Tim's parents?

Of course not. Information about the identity of the donors and their families is usually kept strictly confidential. Then how did Claire ultimately get to Tim's parents?

The part of the story that most scientists avoid is that Claire met a person at a party who was purportedly "psychic." In a dream, he saw in a newspaper what appeared to be the obituary of Tim. After the psychic shared his dream with Claire, she went to a local library, sought the newspaper, and discovered Tim's obituary, just as the psychic had described it. This is how she ultimately came to meet Tim's parents, and the entire story came to light.

Did Tim actually come to the psychic? Did Tim come because Claire and her friend shared physical energy, so that the energy and information now in Claire's cells entered (or at least could resonate with) the cells of her psychic friend? Does Tim live as a systemic memory (a soul and spirit) *independent* of his heart and lungs, and does he resonate with his own heart and lungs so as to communicate better with Claire?

Do we really have to address questions such as these as we address the logic of the systemic memory process and the existence of universal living memory?

The answer is simple and straightforward. If we wish to be honest and honor the theory with integrity, then we must entertain such questions.

As Paul Pearsall said to Linda and me one year after he published *The Heart's Code*, he seriously entertains the possibility that some transplant patients may have a conscious wish to communicate with the donor's spirit and soul, and that this may facilitate accurate reception. The communication may be a three-way process—between the recipient, the donor's heart, and the info-energy system reflecting the living memory of the donor's spirit and soul—i.e. living energy system.

As the story of universal living memory continues to unfold, it is prudent that we

- remember Glenda and her copacetic relationship with David,
- stand in awe of the possibility that the little girl whose transplanted "Sherlock Holmes" heart may have helped find her murderer,
- wonder about the uneaten chicken nuggets found in Tim's motorcycle jacket and his spirit—his living energy system—that may have brought Claire and his physical heart back to his parents.

If stories like the above turn out to be true, the heart of a system, and the heart of health, may be universal living memory.

Could it be that the pulsing vibrations that reverberate and remember throughout the evolving universe reflect the essence of the heart of the cosmos, the gift of loving energy to us all? Is the heart of the universe universal living memory?

Our logical brains have been trained to say, "It can't be so."

Our hearts simply say, "I hope so."

Chapter 8

Does Water Remember?

The Plausibility of Homeopathy and Other Anomalies in Physics, Chemistry, and Medicine

In general we look for a new law by the following process: First, we guess it. Then we compute the consequences of the guess to see what would be implied if this law that we guessed is right. Then we compare the result of the computation to nature, with experiment or experience, compare it directly with the observation, to see if it works. If it disagrees with experiment it is wrong. In that simple statement is the key to science.

Richard Feynman

This is the kind of phenomena I wouldn't believe, even if it were true.

Anonymous, spoken to
Margaret Mead

Dr. Iris Bell sat in my university office for our weekly research meeting and said: "You know, some of the clinical observations in homeopathy are really weird!"

Coming from Iris, this statement is telling. Homeopathy is a con-troversial approach to medicine that hypothesizes, among other things, that water can store energy and information (that water can presumably have memory). Homeopaths believe that in high dilu-tion solutions, even solutions so dilute that virtually no physical molecules of the material dissolved in the water can be measured, the information and energy of the dissolved materials still remains in active form, and can be used to help cure disease.

Is homeopathy merely a medical "misadventure," or is it a medical manifestation of the systemic memory process?

A little history. Just at the time I was receiving my Ph.D. at Harvard in 1971, I met a pixie of a woman (she's maybe 4'11"), an undergraduate biology major at Harvard, and we became, and remain, friends and mutual teachers. Iris Bell decided she wanted to do her honors thesis with me on biofeedback and the voluntary control of heart rate. She conducted a first rate experiment, and her first scientific publication (Bell and Schwartz) was accepted for publication in the journal *Psychophysiology* before she left for graduate school at Stanford University. Like Linda, Iris has a deep feeling for systems and feedback, relationship and interaction. In addition to her profound capacity for reasoning, she has the gift of profound intuition.

Iris is not only brilliant, she has earned exceptional credentials as well. She received a Ph.D. in neuroscience at Stanford and then went on to receive an M.D. from the Stanford University Medical School. In addition to completing a residency in psychiatry at the University of California Medical School in San Francisco, with a focus on genetics and psychopharmacology, she received clinical certification in biofeedback and began training in homeopathy. After returning to Harvard as an assistant professor of psychiatry at MacLean Hospital, she came to the University of Arizona where she is currently an associate professor of psychiatry, psychology, and family and community medicine.

Since arriving at the University of Arizona in 1992, Iris and I have coauthored more than thirty papers in scientific journals. In addition, Iris conducts systematic research on one of the most controversial areas of modern medicine—homeopathy. In her spare time Iris went back to school, and recently added homeopathy to her list of medical licenses.

Why would someone as smart as Iris, who deals with psychiatry every day spend her time and energy pursuing the controversial area of homeopathy? Is she crazy, or does she know something you and I need to learn and understand?

Before meeting Iris, what I knew about homeopathy was what I read in popular magazines. Though I realized in the early 1980s that the systemic memory process predicted phenomena like homeopathy, I never expected to take homeopathy seriously, and ultimately to become personally involved in homeopathic research. The truth is, some of the claims and current research findings in homeopathy are weird.

The word "weird" can be seen in three ways:

- The everyday meaning of the word, which means "strange."
- The older meaning of the word, which means "spirit."
- The oldest meaning of the word, which means "fate."

When I explained this to Iris she said, "Hmmm . . . homeopathy truly deserves all three meanings of the word weird":

- Homeopathy is "strange."
- Homeopathy does address the idea of "spirit" (invisible information and energy).
- Homeopathy incorporates the deep meaning of the word "fate" (that specific personalities store an accumulated history of previous diseases that may even transcend lifetimes, and that true cure ultimately involves the treatment of the entire history).

Universal living memory addresses all three levels of weird not only in homeopathy but in everything else. In this chapter, we will examine homeopathy and the possible evidence of the systemic memory process in physical objects in physics, chemistry, and biology. We will look more closely at controversial claims such as memory in "electrons" as conveyed in crystal growth in physical chemistry, and even the possibility of universal living memory in DNA and RNA.

However, before examining the controversial claims and observations, let's begin more simply, and look at two tuning forks. Let's examine how resonance works in physical objects from a dynamical energy systems (DES) perspective.

Sympathetic Vibrations Between and Within Tuning Forks A and B

Most people have witnessed or played with tuning forks. When we have two tuning forks that are similar in shape, size, and constitution (we will call them A and B), and we strike one of them (A), the other one (B) will begin to vibrate as well. The technical term physics uses is "resonance," which means "re-sound."

When I was taught how resonance works, the explanation used was reductionistic. The causal mechanism was described as a one-way street from A to B—not a two-way street of information and energy flow between A and B. The "re" sound only traveled from A to B, not back from B to A again, and certainly not over and over again.

The non-systemic (reductionistic) story is that when we strike tuning fork A and it begins to vibrate, the air begins to vibrate, and this vibrational wave travels to tuning fork B. Since tuning fork B is like tuning fork A (same size, shape, and constitution), it responds to the vibrating energy coming from tuning fork A and begins to vibrate in synchrony with it.

Of course, what my elementary physics class failed to tell us was that after tuning fork B began to vibrate and generate sound, those sound vibrations would begin to travel back to tuning fork A. The continuing sound coming from tuning fork A would bump into the new sound coming back from tuning fork B. Moreover, the sound from B would ultimately and very quickly reach A, and A would now have the possibility of resonating with B!

If tuning forks A and B became a two-tuning fork system, then tuning fork B would affect tuning fork A like tuning fork A affected tuning fork B. This is easy to verify scientifically. All we need to do is measure the vibrations of tuning fork A and simultaneously measure the vibrations of tuning fork B.

As our control condition, we would first strike tuning fork A in the absence of tuning fork B. We would measure the pattern of vibration arising from A as it changes over time.

Then, for our experimental condition, we would bring tuning fork B into the room, strike tuning fork A, and measure the patterns of vibration arising from A as it changes over time again. This time however, due to the presence of B, the patterns arising from A should appear to be more complex. In the language of chaos and complexity theory, we should observe increased "dimensional complexity" in the pattern of waves arising from A's interaction with B.

This point is simple enough. Now, recall the logic of the systemic memory process in chapter 6, and remember that when A and B interact, they create ($a_{t+}b_{t++}a_{t+++}$. . .), that is, integrative interactions that preserve the history of the unfolding interactions of A and B as they accrue over time. This implies that tuning forks A and B become an A-B system, they accrue integrative systemic memories. Again, this is easy to verify in principle, using modern recording, computer, and statistical analysis techniques.

We can extend the logic from what is happening *between* tuning forks A and B to what is happening *within* tuning forks A and B.

Tuning fork A is composed of billions of molecules, and they are spontaneously vibrating even when the tuning fork is just "sitting" there (before we strike it). We don't hear the sound it continuously generates because the intensity is below what our consciousness normally detects. However, physical measuring instruments do confirm that tuning fork A is continuously and spontaneously resonating as a complex tuning fork network system. Tuning fork A is really a "network of A's" that can be thought of as a complex network of resonating A-A systems. The molecules in tuning fork A are continually dancing with each other, and in the process they are accruing systemic memories.

Now imagine that we repeatedly perform our experiment with tuning forks A and B; we strike A again and again and again. What would the logic of the systemic memory process predict? The prediction we are forced to make is that the "A-A network" system that comprised tuning fork A should store the evolving systemic memories that reflect not only the history of striking A, but the information coming from B as well. Hence, tuning fork A should be changing and evolving its integrative systemic history through its continued relationship with B.

If tuning forks A and B are then separated, should tuning fork A still remember that it spent significant time in the immediate past resonating with tuning fork B? If the logic of the systemic memory process is correct, the answer should be "yes."

How could we tell scientifically whether tuning fork A contained memories of its relationship with B? One approach would be to measure carefully the spontaneous dimensional complexity of tuning fork A before and after its history with tuning fork B.

A second approach, which would be more powerful and definitive, would be to reconnect tuning forks A and B, and see if when tuning fork A is struck, does it "recognize" the presence of tuning fork B by responding differently than it did before it had a resonant history with B?

Does tuning fork A now "know" tuning fork B? Has tuning fork A now developed a "noetic" (meaning knowledge) sense for tuning fork B? Has tuning fork A become a "noetic antenna" for the presence of tuning fork B? These questions all follow from the logic of the systemic memory process, and they are all testable.

Let's be clear here. We used the word "recognize" purposefully and carefully. The fact is, it is one thing to develop a theory to explain how information is stored dynamically in a system (the logic of the systemic memory process), but it is another to explain how the information is retrieved once it is stored. Just because the information has been stored does not mean that it can be retrieved.

The Mystery of Memory—Storage, Recognition, and Retrieval

Here's a way to develop a deep feeling for the distinction between the storage of information, the recognition of information, and the retrieval of information.

When I was a professor at Yale, I memorized my office number, and stored it in my mind. Now, if you ask me today "do I remember my Yale phone number," my answer is simple and to the point. No. I cannot "retrieve" it. Has the memory for the Yale phone number disappeared? Has it been permanently erased? According to universal living memory, probably not. A more likely explanation is that it's still somewhere in memory, but I don't know how to retrieve it.

If someone placed five phone numbers in front of me, and one of them was my Yale phone number, I suspect that I could recognize it and pick it out of the phone number line-up. The Yale phone number memory is still in my brain, waiting to be recognized and potentially retrieved. Simply put, to "forget" does not mean to "erase." As you know, once you learn how to ride a bicycle it is easy to learn how to ride it again, even if you haven't for many years.

We need to remember the fundamental distinction between storage, recognition, and retrieval, as we look incredulously at tuning forks and water, complex crystals, and DNA, and feel "these

91

things can't have memories! They don't look like they learn or re-member to me." Well, maybe we haven't looked closely enough yet, or scientifically enough yet, and maybe we haven't tested their memory properly.

It is curious (and humorous) that I can't remember my phone number at the university where I stumbled upon the logic of the sys-temic memory process. However, maybe my missing number can help remind all of us to be open to the possibility that in the same way that the Yale phone number is probably still a part of my dynam-ically resonating systemic memory, tuning fork B is probably part of tuning fork A's dynamically resonating systemic memory. Both memories are waiting to be recognized, and ultimately retrieved.

The "Weirdness" of Homeopathy—Evidence for Universal Living Memory in Water?

Homeopathy was discovered and developed over two centuries ago by a German physician, Samuel Hahnemann. One century ago, homeopathy was practiced widely in the United States, but it was squashed by the evolution of "allopathic" medicine as modeled by the American Medical Association. The AMA attempted to label the practitioners of homeopathy as unscientific quacks. However, homeopathy refused to die, and is experiencing a resurgence today in the United States and around the world. It was and still is widely practiced in Europe.

Homeopathy evolved because of clinical science and the power of systematic observation. The problem is, the observations so ob-tained seem like nonsense—that is, they don't make any sense—in the context of reductionistic science and classical physics.

However, the observations do make sense—they are even pre-dicted—in the context of systems science and quantum physics, especially when the science is viewed dynamically and inte-gratively.

Take a molecule such as salt, and dissolve it in water, then "succuss it" (meaning you shake it), many times (eighty times is a common number used in homeopathy). Then dilute the solution tenfold. This means you take out one tablespoon of the liquid and add it to ten tablespoons of plain water, making the solution one tenth as concentrated in terms of the salt material. Then succuss (vigorously shake) it many times, then dilute the solution again tenfold; do this over and over and over. The material substance becomes more scarce in the water, and ultimately it is so scarce that it cannot be measured by modern physical instruments.

Homeopaths have observed that if this ridiculously dilute succussed solution is given to the right patient, with the matching health problem, this patient may experience remarkable clinical relief. In classical homeopathy, it is claimed that the process of matching the right remedy with the right personality is key. The language homeopaths use is that the remedy must "resonate" with the personality of the patient in order for optimal health to be achieved.

The homeopath must discover which remedies are associated with which personalities. By "personality," homeopaths mean the biopsychosocial-spiritual personality; their assessment includes a physical history of the patient's past illnesses, psychological and emotional preferences, dreams, spiritual values. The procedure for matching remedies with personalities is comprehensive and integrative, based upon a systematic discovery procedure they call "provings."

Provings are conducted in normal, healthy individuals. Provings were originally conducted by practicing homeopaths; today they are conducted primarily by researchers working for remedy manufacturers. Substances under consideration as potential remedies are given to presumably "healthy" individuals, and the homeopathic researchers look for the development of symptoms in specific personalities. The goal, of course, is not to make healthy people ill, but rather to discover the match between specific remedies and specific personality types.

Homeopaths posit "the law of similars." The thesis is that specific remedies that generate specific symptoms in healthy persons with specific personalities should lead to the reduction of similar symptoms in diseased persons with similar personalities. Hence the goal in homeopathic treatment is to administer the matching remedy to the patient who is currently ill. The prediction is that somehow the remedy resonates with the personality and the disease, initiating a memory recognition and retrieval process of sorts that activates the healing mechanism, and ultimately brings the patient back to health. Along the way, as the memories are retrieved, the patient reexperiences earlier symptoms reflective of earlier diseases as the healing history unfolds.

From a simple materialistic, non-systemic perspective, this sounds weird. How can "nothing" (remember, the physical material dissolved in the water is virtually gone) cause subtle physical symptoms in specific healthy individuals? How can "nothing" when given to specific patients, lead them not only to improve their health, but reexperience their history of illnesses in some complex, inexplicable order? How can "nothing" resonate with the material substances that comprise physical beings? It doesn't make any sense. From a material, non-systemic perspective, it is nonsense. However, from a dynamical energy systems (DES), systemic memory perspective, it makes substantial sense.

When we dissolve material substances in water, what is happening in the water?

Remember that quantum physics tells us that everything is ultimately information and energy. The information and energy of the salt, for example, enters the dynamic network of water molecules, and they engage in a continuous dynamic resonance, thus creating systemic memories in the water system as a whole.

Furthermore, when we succuss the water, the continued mixing further accentuates the dynamic resonant interactions taking place within the water. With each successive dilution and series of successions, as the material concentration decreases the resonant information and energy increases. Hence, from an info-energetic perspective, the "weaker" solutions materialistically are actually more "potent" info-energetically.

What kind of a person is likely to resonate with salt? A person who has some kind of "salt history." The origin of this history may involve many possible mechanisms. Just because we do not know the origin of the history does not mean that we cannot specify the empirical relationship.

If unique systemic memories exist in solutions and people, how does the remedy correct the health history of the patient? The solution may have something to do with the "recognition" and the retrieval of systemic memories. If the logic of the systemic memory process is correct, the history of our illness is accumulated in our bodies as living systemic memories.

Is the pattern of this so complex, and so random, that no specific order can be found? Or is there a "table of diseases" like the periodic "table of elements," waiting to be discovered in the future?

Homeopaths are deeply systemic in their thinking, so they are comfortable in searching for patterns, even if they cannot describe their origin. However, if there is a yet to be discovered order, the mathematical formula that explains this order may be simpler than we think. The relationship of remedies to disease history may be like $E=mc^2$ is to atomic explosions. The formula that explains it all may ultimately be simple.

Of course, homeopathy, carried to its logical extreme, suggests that the disease history may be carried in the genes from generation to generation, since genes can carry information and energy. In this sense, the deep implications of homeopathy bring us to "spirits" (info-energy systems) and "fate" (the accumulation of history that plays a role in our destiny). In this sense, homeopathy in particular, and the systemic memory process in general, may always remain weird as in the deep and correct meaning of the word.

However, homeopathy in particular, and the systemic memory process in general, need not necessarily remain "strange." On the contrary, the idea of memory in water, unique resonances with personalities, the "recognition" of living systemic memories and the recapitulation and resolution of health histories, are no longer "strange"—they logically and empirically, make "sense."

To have feedback with resonance is to remember, over and over and over.

Do Electrons Carry Information, and Can This Information Affect Matter?

In a 1997 article, "Testing the Survival of Consciousness Hypothesis: The Goal of the Codes," we mentioned very briefly that the systemic memory process could provide a plausible explanation for survival of consciousness after bodily death. One of the people who read this article was Donald Eldridge from Australia.

Eldridge sent us a letter and a copy of a scientific article by Dr. Bevan Reid who in 1987 published an article in the *Journal of Biological Physics* claiming to have found evidence for "the ability of an electric current to carry information for crystal growth patterns." If Reid's experiments were valid, his work provided a paradigm for applying the logic of universal living memory to physical chemical systems.

If we take salt and dissolve it in water, and then take a drop of the solution and place it on a slide, as the water evaporates, it will leave telltale salt crystals of generally replicable shapes and sizes.

If we now add albumin to the salt solution, and then take a drop of the solution and place it on the slide, the water evaporates as it will leave telltale salt crystals, but their shapes will be more complex, and they will be surrounded by intricate fernlike crystal patterns. The difference in the crystal patterns between what the pure salt solution leaves and what the albumin-salt solution leaves is visible to the naked eye and is dramatically different when viewed under a microscope.

Now, here is what Reid did.

He took one beaker containing the albumin-salt solution and another beaker containing a pure salt solution, and placed them a few inches apart. He then took a simple 1.5 volt battery, and connected it to gold wires, creating an electronic circuit between the two beakers—one end of the battery was connected to the albumin-salt beaker with a gold wire serving as an electrode, and the other end of the battery was connected to the pure salt beaker with a gold wire serving as an electrode. To complete the circuit, a gold wire was placed from the albumin-salt beaker into the pure salt beaker.

Here's what he predicted. If electrons carried information, then as the electrons passed from the albumin-salt beaker into the pure salt beaker, the information of the albumin-salt beaker would travel through the pure salt solution, and in the process resonate the pure salt solution with the albumin-salt information. Since this was a continuous circuit, the current would circulate over and over, creating a dynamic systemic memory in the process.

If the crystal growth is an expression in part of information in solution, then the pure salt crystal bathed in the information of the albumin-salt should begin to look like the material of albumin salt, even though there was no material albumin in the pure salt solution. When Reid did this experiment, and the pure salt solution drop was evaporated on the slide, what he reported observing was an albumin-salt crystal growth in the absence of any material albumin!

Did these electrons carry the "spirit and soul" of the albumin-salt solution and pass it into the pure salt solution? Did the "spirit" of the albumin "materialize" in the pure salt solution? Is this modern alchemy, published in the *Journal of Biological Physics*?

If Reid's paradigm is true, then as the circuit time continues, as the battery wears down, it should store information about the albumin-salt solution. If this battery was then connected between two beakers that both contained pure salt solution, would this battery impart its albumin-salt memory, and would albumin-salt crystal patterns be observed?

Reid mentioned that there were many sources of contamination in these studies, one of which was that he discovered that he had to remember to use fresh batteries, because previously used batteries confounded the findings by creating albumin-salt crystals in pure salt solutions! If Reid's "confounding" factor is correct, another prediction of the systemic memory process may be demonstrable. Our recent research on the Reid paradigm is included here in appendix B.

Throughout the ages, stories have been told about the mystery and power of crystals. There are those who believed that crystals could be used to summon the gods, heal the sick, and help predict the future.

One of the most miraculous discoveries made in twentieth-century science is the pattern of background light that pervades the universe and presumably reflects the "first light" created at the beginning of the big bang. This was made possible by a crystal. Apparently, one of the major infrared satellite telescopes uses the diamond crystal to resonate with the light and amplify it to the point where it can be detected by sensitive electronic sensors.

Are crystals merely static, dead configurations of molecules, or do they, as quantum physics tells us, vibrate and resonate with the info-energy around them?

If we envision them to be dynamical systems, then the possibility arises that they accumulate systemic memories just as all dynamical systems do. If this reminds you of stories of "crystal" healing and psychics reading personal information from jewelry, you may wish to reconsider such claims in light of the systemic memory process.

Crystals are wonderful resonators. They are remarkable receivers of information. The heart of radio receivers is the crystal. According to anthropologist Jeremy Narby, a Ph.D. from Stanford University and author of the 1998 book, *The Cosmic Serpent: DNA and the Origins of Knowledge*, DNA can be thought of as a crystal too. He cites molecular biologist Maxim Frank-Kamentskii who explains:

> The base pairs in it are arranged as in a crystal. This is, however, a linear, one dimensional crystal, with each base pair flanked by only two neighbors. The DNA crystal is aperiodic, since the sequence of base pairs is as irregular as the sequence of letters in a coherent printed text . . . Thus, it came as no surprise that the one-dimensional DNA crystal, a crystal of an entirely new type, had very much intrigued physicists.

Based on his work with the ancient Ashaninca culture in the Peruvian Amazon's Pichis Valley, Narby suggests that DNA may function as a receiver for a class of photons called biophotons. Since all electromagnetic signals, including bioelectromagnetic signals, can be viewed as being "photons"—visible and invisible—the hypothesis that DNA and other molecules may function as selective resonators for photonic information and energy is challenging.

Is DNA more than a code? Does it function as a selective antenna? Is a homeopathic remedy more than a code? Does it function as a selective antenna too?

Are such crystal antennas "dead" (Stage M), or are they potentially systemic, living and evolving too (Stages I, L and E)?

From Static Structures to Dynamic Resonators: A New Look at DNA as a "Dynamic Noetic Antenna"

DNA and RNA are profoundly complex orders of only four fundamental molecules, and nobody knows how they are ordered nor what maintains their order.

However, the data are absolutely clear: the order of the bases is critically important to our existence and survival as physical systems.

If nature wanted to design a molecule to create systemic resonance, and store systemic memories, DNA and its sister RNA are wonderful; two strands of undulating patterns of molecules, resonating information and energy within and between the system.

If you think the physical structure of DNA is complex, you can imagine how outrageously complex the patterns of dynamic interactions between the molecules must be.

Linda has hypothesized that DNA may be designed to read unique systemic memories from the "zero point vacuum" like an antenna. Zero here means the sum of the energy in the vacuum is zero, yet information and energy are continually bubbling up and through the vacuum. Contemporary physics posits that the vacuum appears to sit at a "zero point" because it is actually balancing or integrating a profoundly complex, dynamically waxing and waning pattern of energetic interactions that on the average sums or cancels to "zero" but is actually potentially infinite in power and structure. If the logic of A-B interactions and integrations modeled in tuning forks is correct, then the individual genetic codes that define each of us may selectively resonate with those specific systemic memories that fill the sea of information in the vacuum.

We already know that the "vacuum" is filled with information and energy.

We live in a sea of radio waves that come from thousands of radio stations and TV stations and cellular phones. The sky is filled with millions and millions and millions of stars, each of their info-energy patterns mixing in areas smaller than the head of a pin.

How is this information ever read selectively?

Radios and TVs use specific antennas, crystals, and tuners to "tune in" to the desired patterns of frequencies. What came to me was an acronym. DNA might be the ultimate "Dynamic Noetic Antenna." Dynamic (D) meaning vibrant, evolving, systemic; Noetic (N) meaning knowledge, pattern, recognition; and Antenna (A) meaning antenna, receiver, tuner.

Maybe DNA is nature's version of a profoundly complex radio-like circuit that receives information rather than creating it. Of course, it will create information too, but it may be designed to selectively register and read electromagnetic patterns in the body and beyond. RNA could be similarly thought of as a "Resonating Noetic Antenna."

If DNA and her sister RNA can function as directional, pattern recognizing antennas, then DNA and RNA become exquisite dynamical energy systems (DES) beyond our current imagination. If Frank-Kamentskii's, Narby's, and Russek's hypotheses turn out to be correct, they will revolutionize molecular biology.

Is DNA designed to recognize our ancestors? Wouldn't it be amazing if the foundation of the biology of the cell, DNA and RNA, was designed to recognize the living information and energy of our parents and children? Logic suggests that the hypothesis is plausible, empirically testable, and refutable. We challenge the molecular biologists among you to create experiments to confirm or deny these possibilities.

If the systemic memory hypothesis is correct, homeopathy, DNA, and crystals in general may be discovered to operate by a universal "tuning" mechanism that selectively receives evolving knowledge remembered in the cosmos.

Chapter 9

Does the Soul Remember?

The Plausibility of Out-of-Body Consciousness
and Survival of Consciousness After Death

There are only two ways to live your life:
One is as though nothing is a miracle.
The other is as if everything is.
I believe in the latter.

Albert Einstein

The only solid piece of scientific proof about which I feel totally
confident is that we are profoundly ignorant about nature . . .

Dr. Lewis Thomas

There are two fundamental non-material concepts used through-out the sciences—information and energy.

Information refers to pattern, form, structure. Energy refers to force and power, the capacity to do work and overcome resistance. Energy does the work of information.

Information has energy, and energy has information. Information without energy is "powerless"; energy without information is "purposeless." Together they are quite a team. Soul and spirit are also quite a team.

Could it be that soul is to spirit as information is to energy?

This hypothesis enables us to envision a new scientific frame-work for specifying and therefore researching the ancient ideas of

101

soul and spirit using contemporary models and methods in physics, psychology, and statistics.

The following poem, inspired by Linda and put to paper by me, expresses this merging of intuition and reason, as Jonas Salk would say. Sometimes poetry expresses more completely what abstract equations merely describe. I dedicated this poem to Linda's father.

What, pray tell, are Spirit and Soul?
Are they one and the same?
Are Soul and Spirit a functional whole,
Derived from a common name?

Or is it the case that Soul and Spirit
Reflect two sides of a coin—
Where Soul reflects Information that fits,
And Spirit, Energy, that joins.

Is Soul the story, the plan of one's life,
The music we play, the score?
Is Spirit the passion, the fire of life,
Our motive to learn, to soar?

Soul represents the paths we take,
The visions that structure our flow.
Spirit feels very alive, awake,
The force that moves us to grow.

If Soul is plan and Spirit is flame,
Then matter is alive, you see.
Nature may play a majestic game,
Of Information and Energy.

I'd love to believe that wisdom and joy
Reflect God's plans and dreams,
That Soul and Spirit are more than toys,
And both—more than they seem.

Could it be that the Soul of God
Is the wisest of plans, so grand?
And the Spirit of God is the lightning rod
That inspires God's loving hand?

Could Soul be wisdom and Spirit be love?
Together, a divine partnership?
Purpose and passion, a duet from above,
The ultimate relationship?

The relationship of Spirit to Soul,
So simple, profound this team.
Through Spirit and Soul, our ultimate goal,
To understand this theme.

Soul as wisdom, Spirit as love—
Information, Energy;
Enlightened compassion, the flight of the dove,
Someday, pray tell, we'll see.

It is our hypothesis that these words reflect more than just poetry; they are an artistic expression of a foundational theory.

If soul and spirit can be likened to information and energy, then it logically follows that we can apply this premise to the systemic memory process, and consider this question: If information and energy are stored in a system, and the info-energy (the integrative combination) is stored dynamically and eternally, does this imply that the soul and spirit continue to exist in physical objects and even in the absence of physical scaffolds?

The answer is most definitely yes.

The systemic memory process may be the soul and spirit in all systems, and hence be the universal living memory process.

Can Living Energy Systems Exist in the "Vacuum," and Is This What We Mean by the Possible Survival of Spirit and Soul after Physical Death?

What you are about to read is one of the most interesting and inspiring implications that stems from the logic of the systemic memory process. If the concept of energy can be combined with the concept of a system, then a set of novel and far-reaching implications suggest themselves.

In the process of physical systems creating integrative systemic memories, they create virtual systems of dynamic memories—living energy systems—in the vacuum of space within the physical systems. These dynamical info-energy systems will not only have a "life of their own," but like all photons they will continue in the vacuum of space forever, even when the physical structure deconstructs.

We illustrate this essential insight in two figures below. The first figure shows the formation of a $V_{A\,to\,B} - V_{B\,to\,A}$ dynamical info-energy system in the vacuum between the physical components A and B. Note how the complex info-energy circulation within the vacuum mirrors the complex systemic memory process between A and B. It can be likened to an evolving systemic memory cyclone or vortex within the vacuum between A and B.

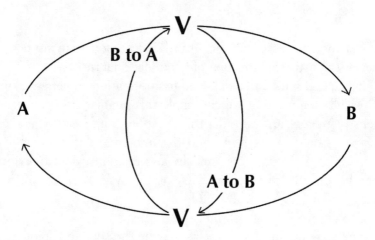

The second figure shows the continued existence of the $V_{A\,to\,B} - V_{B\,to\,A}$ dynamical info-energy system after the physical components

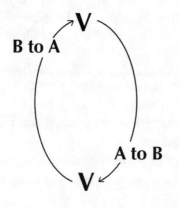

A and B have been removed. Note how the info-energy circulation within the vacuum continues to mirror the complex systemic memory process that existed between A and B. The info-energy system that continues within the vacuum is theoretically as alive and evolving as the original A–B system.

A and B interact and share information and energy. This sharing of complex information and energy occurs, by definition, within the "empty space" that separates all "material" manifestations of A and B. The "vacuum" (which we show as V for short) that connects the "matter" of A and B is the "empty space" between. Hence the material of A and B must be connected non-materially. This is elementary quantum physics, and taken by physicists to be a given.

In the same way that many contemporary scientists do not yet employ systemic thinking when they think about material objects, they similarly do not employ systemic thinking when they think about "non-material" objects.

However, if they did, they would realize that the same logic that we use to explain the existence of material systems requires that we posit the existence of non-material info-energy systems within the material systems. Hence the idea of living energy systems within material systems.

The reasoning is simple. Since the vacuum is ultimately a single integrative vacuum—meaning, the "space" allows information and energy to extend and mix in all directions—the information and energy traveling from A to B will interact in the vacuum with the information and energy traveling from B to A.

The fact is, at a fundamental level, there is no physical division between the two-way street of circular causality between A and B. The V on the side going from A to B is connected to the V on the side going from B to A. Hence, the A to B flow can interact with the B to A flow in a continuous, ongoing way. The circulation of energy and information within the vacuum between A and B creates a pure info-energy within V that mirrors the systemic memory process between A and B.

You can imagine it this way. The repeating circulation of information and energy traveling from A to B and B to A creates a living vortex (a dynamically swirling wheel of information and energy) that contains the emerging combination of info-energy comprising the evolving relationship between A and B. The material A–B system contains an info-energy A–B system within it that extends into "space" like the stars in the sky.

This realization not only provides an explanation for the origin of emergent/novel properties observed in systems, but provides an explanation for the creation of pure dynamical energy systems (pure DES's) within the non-material space that comprises everything.

This means that the essence, the profound complexity that defines all complex systems—the soul and spirit of each system, its dynamically organized information and energy—exists as an emergent dynamical energy system (a V-V system) that contains the identity, the personality and history of each complex system.

Note that the concept of a system includes the concept of information. A system, by definition, reflects an organization of components, and hence expresses information (form). When we understand that systems are not truly static, but are dynamic to various degrees at all times, then it follows that the information comprising the system is dynamic too. According to living systems theory (Stage L), if the "system" is living, then by definition, the "information" is living too.

Recall that energy is power and information is system—when we view them both as dynamic and interactive processes, we logically come to a new, living vision of energy and information, spirit and soul—the living energy universe.

If all physical systems create non-material info-energy systems (living energy systems) that non-physically embody their emergent wholeness in the "vacuum," then the capacity for people to see without their eyes and hear without their ears is no longer nonsensical. It is required! Our eyes and ears and brains and hearts, in fact, our "everything," exist as living energy systems in the "vacuum." And once our "everything" exists as a living energy system in the vacuum, it will continue and evolve forever. The logic is unavoidable.

Hence, everything that exists may actually have a spirit and a soul, a living history of non-material information and energy. This revision of our idea of spirit and soul makes it possible to reconsider the weird reports of people who claim to have died, left their bodies, and witnessed what happened as they were physically saved so that they could be brought back to physical life. And this revision of our idea of spirit and soul makes it possible to reconsider the weird reports of people who claim to receive messages from deceased people who wish to remain connected with their loved ones.

Hence, living energy systems = universal living memories = life eternal. That's the conclusion.

Now, what about data? Do observations support the inference? As Linda and I have learned, the answer appears to be yes.

Seeing Without our Eyes and Hearing Without Our Ears— Verifiable Out-of-Body Experiences during Anesthesia and "Death"

Most of us, most of the time, experience our consciousness inside our bodies.

When we wake up in the morning, for example, we do not worry that we will discover that our consciousness is hovering around the ceiling somewhere, looking down on our bodies, trying to figure out how to get back in. It seems obvious that our conscious experience is dependent upon our senses. If you close your eyes, you can't see. Cover your ears and you can't hear. These experiences are "no-brainers"—they are so obvious, so true, so replicable, that we understandably assume that they are true.

However, we make a big mistake when we assume that our "stories" about replicable experiences are true. We should learn to separate the "fact" of replicable observation from the "inference" of our stories about the observations. We should never "assume" something—because when we assume something we stop thinking about it.

When I wake up in the morning, there is no question that I see the sun rising in the east. It's a no-brainer that I see the sun as if it's revolving around the earth. It is so obvious, so true, so replicable. However, I no longer assume this to be true just because it looks that way.

I drive to the university, and every time I make the drive, I confirm that the earth appears flat. It's so obviously true, so absolutely replicable and verifiable to the naked eye, but I no longer assume this to be true either.

Science has taught me, and everyone else, that just because it looks a certain way, and can be replicated with the naked eye to look a certain way, does not make it a certain way. Even if it looks to the naked eye or to other instruments that can record what the eye sees that it is 100 percent replicable, this does not mean that the story we derive from the experience is true. The inference is not the observation. However, the inference that our eyes are necessary to see is hard to give up, and there may be some truth to the story.

If you understood the logic of the creation of living energy systems within living material systems, you will understand that physical eyes theoretically create non-material info-energy system eyes that can also "see." Theoretically our info-energy system eyes can process photons and convert them into info-energy neural impulses that travel to our info-energy system brain.

I didn't have this potential scientific story when I was a jazz guitarist at age seventeen and I had an out-of-body experience while playing a jazz solo. I simply had a weird experience that was totally unexpected, and I dismissed it as a trick of the mind. I was about to play a solo in a jazz combo and the song was Gershwin's haunting "Summer Time." I had played "Summer Time" probably hundreds of times, and my guitar playing was beginning to become almost effortless.

As best I can explain it, I went into a "flow" state, I was in the "zone." These are words that are sometimes used by artists and athletes to describe a particular "altered" state of consciousness involving time and space. Time suddenly slowed down, I was way out of my body, and I witnessed myself playing the solo with the combo from a distance above and behind the band. When the solo finished, I "came to," and felt dizzy. The audience was clapping wildly, and the combo looked amazed. After we finished the piece, the band told me that my solo had been the best they had ever heard me play.

However, for the life of me, I couldn't remember a single note! The shock for me was not the momentary out-of-body experience, which I simply assumed was a momentary mistake of the mind; it was my inability to remember what I had played, and that I had missed my own solo, that bothered me.

I never had another musical out-of-body experience, and did not think about that one weird experience much, until Linda and I met Joe McMoneagle in the summer of 1997. Being a skeptical scientist,

I had treated my out-of-body experience as a foolish trick of my mind and nothing more. But McMoneagle and his out-of-body experiences shook me to my core. You can read about McMoneagle and his amazing life in his book *Mind Trek*.

McMoneagle was a military person who had an accident and almost died. After he recovered, he discovered he had some uncanny, seemingly "paranormal" abilities that interested military intelligence and the CIA. The CIA conducted secret research on the possibility of what is called "remote viewing." This is a controversial claim in parapsychology that people visit distant places "in their minds" and report seeing things that can be later verified as true or false. McMoneagle was one of their prize "remote viewers."

However, it was what happened to him when he almost died a second time that shook me to my core. McMoneagle is a scientist in his mind and heart. He's very skeptical, and wants proof. This is why he was so happy to be researched systematically by a team of distinguished scientists at Stanford Research Institute. When he subsequently had his out-of-body experiences, he wanted proof too, and obtained written verification from his physicians.

After I learned of McMoneagle's amazing story, I met two more people quite unexpectedly who had equally amazing stories that they too had verified. One credible person called me after reading a feature article about the systemic memory hypothesis titled "Science at the Edge" in the fall 1997 issue of the *Arizona Alumni Magazine*. The person is an astrophysicist, the president of a telescope company, a hard-nosed engineer type.

The second, a less credible person, I met in the spring of 1998 in a federal prison in Tucson, where I was speaking on behalf of the Tucson Humanism Society. I told the group of prisoners about the systemic memory process, and a prisoner insisted on telling me his story. I asked him to put it in writing, and asked permission to call his physician to confirm his detailed story.

Here is a prototypic story that captures the key features of the three men's stories Linda and I have personally heard. This prototype also fits other stories that have been reported in the literature as well as other persons we have met since writing the prototype.

Imagine that you are having heart surgery, you are unconscious and your heart goes into ventricular fibrillation. This means that your heart cells are beating out of synchronization, so your heart is no longer able to circulate blood to your brain and the rest of your body. For most people, just a few minutes without blood results in serious and potentially permanent brain injury, and in a few more minutes, physical death may result.

Up to this point, you were unconscious. But around the time that your heart starts failing, you discover that you are awake, you are outside your body, and you are hovering over your body and the surgical team. You see the surgical tools, the defibrillator, the doctors and nurses. You witness, step-by-step, what they are trying to do, and who is doing what. You hear what they are saying, and you witness their alarm.

You are quite amused by all this. You know this is your body, you know that you may be dying, you may even see that your heart has stopped beating, and you hear that the team is worried that they will lose you.

You also realize that you are having an experience that you never, in your entire life, expected to have. You have never met anyone who has had such an experience. You were given no warning that you would have such an experience. You know that anesthetized people cannot be conscious. You also know that you cannot see without your eyes or hear without your ears.

But you are awake. You are conscious. You are seeing and hearing.

Whether you are Joe, the military man, or Jim, the astrophysicist, or Jack, the garage mechanic, your profession and education and religion doesn't seem to matter. You are witnessing the possibility that you are going to die. And you know there is no way that this can be happening.

You say, "I must remember this. If I survive I must find out if my experience really happened. I am going to put all this in my memory, to the best of my ability, and if I end up back in my body, I am going to write it down or tell somebody immediately!"

Note what you are *not* experiencing.

You are not witnessing bright lights, you are not having a life review, you are not meeting relatives or strangers who are waiting to accept you into the afterlife. None of the now classic reports of near-death experiences are happening to you. You are simply witnessing your surgery, and your possible death, and taking detailed mental notes of the proceedings.

Then, at some point, you lose consciousness, and when you awaken you are dazed and in pain. Up there, while the surgery was going on, you felt fine. There was no pain, not even fear, mostly interest and amazement.

If you are Joe, you scream for a nurse to give you a piece of paper and a pencil immediately to draw a picture and write down some words.

If you are Jim, you wake up and see an old woman, a volunteer, sitting beside you. You don't want to scare her, so you ask her if you can quickly share a dream you just had. As she hears the dream, she is amazed, and runs out to call in the staff to listen to what this patient is telling her.

If you are Jack, you wake up, and beg for the nurse to get your doctor right away because something has happened and you must tell him now!

Your story gets recorded, at least the parts you remember. To your astonishment and the medical staff's disbelief, what you witnessed is confirmed by their memory of what happened. You get your verification and their consternation.

Now, how do you explain to yourself what just happened to you?

You might have overheard someone redescribing the surgery after it was all over, while you were coming out of the anesthesia. But the nurses tell you that that was not possible since no one else was hanging around. You consider any and every possibility of which you can conceive. The big possibility of course is that you really did see without your eyes and hear without your ears, even though your brain was clearly anesthetized, and even though you may have been, technically speaking, dead while all this occurred.

Can your consciousness really exist outside your body? You know that some people believe that such things are possible, but you never experienced this before, especially during surgery, and especially when your observations were verified. As you read this book, you should be coming to realize that some scientists no longer assume that such things are impossible.

When we combine the concepts of system and energy, we derive the logic of the systemic memory process, and when we extend this logic to energy systems within material systems, the plausibility of seeing with energy system eyes and hearing with energy system ears becomes entirely plausible. Of course, we have to then hypothesize that consciousness is more than just a material system property of neurons, but may be an energy system property as well.

The point to remember here is that the logic of the systemic memory process ultimately takes us to a place where we begin to see that Joe and Jim and Jack may be telling us something important about how consciousness works. They may be "white crows" of living energy systems.

If consciousness is somehow involved with living energy systems, and living energy systems are normally constrained within living material systems, then our consciousness will typically be constrained inside our material systems. However, under special circumstances during sleep, with drugs, with special training of the mind, and ultimately with physical death, our living energy systems may escape the "gravity" of the material systems, and our consciousness may soar.

You may be wondering what is the "gravity" that keeps living energy systems within living material systems? The answer is, of course, no one knows.

Linda and I have proposed that, to honor the history and vision of systems theory that leads to the formulation of this general hypothesis, we use the playful word "systemity" to denote the "gravity" of material systems that keeps energy systems (i.e. systemic memories) within them. This "force" may involve flows (circulations) of energy and information within material systems and may comprise the so-called "weak" and "strong" forces in quantum physics that are used to explain how atoms are held together.

We use the term systemity because it reminds us to keep our minds open to the question of how integrative systemic memories remain in physical systems. We know that some of the information and energy leave systems through the vacuum and extend into space; however, for obvious reasons a system could not survive if it lost all of its info-energy and could not retain its core.

As James Miller of *Living Systems* reminds us, all systems have boundaries. It is the boundary that enables the system to maintain its integrity by semi-separating its insides from the outside environment.

If you accept the possibility that Joe and Jim and Jack may have had genuine experiences, that consciousness can exist outside the physical body and can continue to process information in a sense we can recognize, and that the systemic memory process provides a curiously plausible set of predictions about why such things should happen, you are ready to approach what we consider the ultimate question: the possibility and plausibility of survival of consciousness after physical death.

A Modest Experiment on the Mother of All Questions

When my academic colleagues hear me talk about survival of consciousness research, some of them roll their eyes, look away, or sneer. One of the fastest ways to lose credibility and destroy one's academic career is to talk about the possibility of survival of consciousness after death as being scientifically plausible and deserving of serious scientific investigation.

Fortunately, my colleagues at the University of Arizona are more open than most academics, and Linda and I have been tolerated by many and even encouraged by a few. We have formally established the Susy Smith Project in the Human Energy Systems Laboratory at the University of Arizona to pursue serious scientific research on this question with a local and international advisory board of scientists.

Susy Smith has devoted the last 45 years of her life to researching survival of consciousness after death. Susy was trained and worked as a journalist. She was a student at the University of Arizona and the University of Texas, and worked on the staff of newspapers in Florida and Utah. Married for a brief time as a Texas undergraduate, and stricken with an illness that made walking difficult, she lived alone with her miniature dachshund, Junior.

An agnostic and skeptic, Susy gave little thought to the question of survival of consciousness until after her mother died when Susy was in her early forties. Fortuitously, a friend loaned Susy a book by Steward Edward White called *The Unobstructed Universe*. Presumably communicated by White's deceased wife to one of her friends, this book provided a remarkably complex physics explanation for

113

how the afterlife worked. The book impressed Susy, and one day, while taking a walk with Junior she realized that if her mother were still alive she would want to resume contact. As Susy tells the story, around this time she experienced the "presence" of her mother—and it seemed genuine.

Initially Susy was skeptical. She knew tricks of the mind. She reasoned, "If this is my mother, there must be some way to prove it." With her small inheritance, she took a year off, initially went to the Parapsychology Laboratory at Duke University, and then on to the Parapsychology Foundation in New York. In time she became an expert on survival of consciousness.

Her first two books were academic classics. She edited the collected works of W.H. Myers, one of England's great early researchers in this area at the turn of the last century (the foreword was written by Aldous Huxley), and she wrote a book called *The Mediumship of Mrs. Leonard*, a biography of the best studied, and most convincing case of survival of consciousness in the scientific literature.

However, Susy couldn't live on her academic books, so she began writing books for the general public and ultimately published twenty-seven of them. They included her autobiography entitled *The Confessions of a Psychic* and a mind-stretching book titled *The Book of James*, purportedly written in collaboration with none other than Dr. William James of Harvard University.

Through our work with Susy Smith we learned that there was a substantial history of work, from Myers and James in the last century, to credible mediums like Mrs. Leonard and Mrs. Piper, in addition to lay persons interested in this work, that all point to the plausibility of survival of consciousness after death as a legitimate scientific field of inquiry, albeit controversial inquiry.

In the course of our research, Linda and I have witnessed legitimate mediums first hand. For example, Laurie Campbell, the chairperson of the Mediumship Research Committee of the Susy Smith Project in the Human Energy Systems Laboratory, told us about an instance where she made contact with a deceased husband, and learned from him that he secretly purchased a Japanese scarf for his wife, which was wrapped in a box that was still in the house. He had not been able to give it to her before he died. With the aid of her family, the wife searched the house and discovered to her amazement the box containing the beautiful Japanese scarf.

Had Laurie read the wife's mind? Clearly not, the wife did not know of the gift.

Did Laurie read the deceased husband's mind? Possibly. That is one way to frame the survival of consciousness hypothesis.

The logic goes as follows:

- if our consciousness somehow involves our essence, our information and energy, our soul and spirit, and
- if dynamical/living energy systems form within material systems as a natural aspect of being systems, and
- if the emergent, holistic nature of these dynamical/living systems have integrity and can exist in the "vacuum" after the body deconstructs,
- then survival of consciousness is both plausible and even probable.

Of course, there are a lot of "ifs" here. But that is what logic and mathematics are all about; sequences of logical inferences, one following the next, that take one on a journey—a "formula" that informs the flow.

Einstein loved thought experiments. Thought experiments are a prerequisite to actual experiments. Linda and I, with many colleagues, have enjoyed the process of performing thought experiments as well as empirical experiments on the possibility of survival of consciousness after death. Our first empirical experiment was an exploratory study to determine whether it was possible to design and conduct systemic research related to survival of consciousness. The experiment was conceptually challenging and the interpretation complex. The implications were controversial.

We presented the paper at the 1998 meetings of the Society for Scientific Exploration, an organization devoted to the critical examination of topics at the frontier of science. The response from this open-minded group of scientists was generally positive and appropriately cautious. Most took a "let's wait and see" attitude. Some found the implications preposterous.

One reviewer of the draft of the scientific paper, who believed that the findings only proved the existence of paranormal memory retrieval among the living and did not speak at all to the question of survival of consciousness, ended the review stating, "Do not publish, and do not even consider in revised form." Needless to say, the paper was rejected from that journal and published in another peer-reviewed scientific journal open to exploring alternative hypotheses.

We'll let you decide for yourself. The technical title of the paper was "Medium to departed to medium communication of pictorial information: Evidence for super psi and survival of consciousness?" However, as Linda puts it, the experiment is "from here to there and back again."

Here is how the experiment worked:

Step One: Medium One (who was Susy Smith), in the privacy of her home in Tucson, invited four deceased people she believed she could communicate with to serve as collaborators in the research.

The four people were Betty Smith, Susy's mother, deceased for forty-five years but with whom Susy believes she has been in more or less continual contact; Dr. William James, the great physician/psychologist, with whom Susy believes she has been in communication for close to forty years; Dr. Henry Russek, Linda's father, whom Susy believes she has been in contact with for two years; and Howard Schwartz, my father, whom Susy believes she has been in contact with for one year.

Step Two: Susy invited each of the deceased to pick something they would like Susy to draw for them (Susy is a decent painter). She drew each picture to the best of her ability. These were the experimental drawings.

Step Three: Susy selected an image of her own and drew a picture. This was the control picture (to test for possible telepathy, remote viewing, etc., on the part of Medium Two).

Step Four: Medium Two (Laurie Campbell), who had never met Medium One (Susy Smith), and had not even spoken to her on the phone, attempted in two, two-hour video recorded sessions at a later time, to contact each of the deceased purported collaborators, and receive information about each of their experimental drawings.

Step Five: Medium Two also attempted to receive information about Medium One's control picture.

Step Six: Medium One and Medium Two met (in the presence of video cameras) and Medium One showed Medium Two the actual drawings. Medium Two then attempted to first use her "reasoning" to guess which picture was drawn by which individual (Betty, William, Henry, Howard, Susy); and second to use the summary information that she received when she was attempting to communicate with the departed (Step Four), plus the information received in Step Five, to select which drawing was associated with which person. The three experimenters (Linda, Dr. Donald Watson, and myself) also and independently made both sets of decisions.

The results were most interesting. When Medium Two attempted to use reasoning alone to guess which drawing was associated with each person, her accuracy was at chance (she got one out of five correct). When we used our reasoning we did equally poorly (I got one out of five, Linda got zero out of five, and Don got two out of five; 20% accuracy on the average). However, when we used the summary color information derived from Steps Four and Five, each of us independently got five out of five correct (100%).

These were not the findings we anticipated.

If the survival of consciousness hypothesis were correct and psi (a term meaning the paranormal, particularly telepathy and action at a distance) was not involved, then Laurie would have been accurate in Step Four, but not in Step Five. If only psi was involved, Laurie could have gotten all five pictures correct. This is in fact what she did.

Of course, the systemic memory process predicts that a sensitive person should be able to retrieve information from both the physical living and the "dead," hence Laurie should be good with all of it. So how do we conclude that survival of consciousness may have been involved here?

Let's consider the control picture first.

Ideally, Susy would have made four control drawings, so there was an equal number of experimental and control pictures. The fact that Laurie "saw" (in her mind, Step Five) Susy's control picture as "purple and green, many circles and shapes, possibly a vase of flowers, a 'rainbow' of flowers," and Susy's drawing turned out to be a gorgeous, supercolor bouquet of flowers in a purple vase, was frankly eerier to Laurie.

More interesting was what Laurie experienced when she tried to connect with Susy. Laurie heard no dialogue. No communication was involved. She said she saw a living room with a couch, and a wall opposite it with paintings, and a chair to the left, and something that drew Susy's attention to the right.

When pressed to see Susy's picture, Laurie saw the purple and rainbow of color forms very clearly. The layout of the furniture turned out to precisely match the layout of Susy's apartment, a place she had never seen or heard about before. In remote viewing terms, Laurie scored a bull's-eye. Though she could have gotten Susy's layout telepathically from Linda's or my mind, she would have had to have gotten the actual drawing from Susy's mind.

The question is, can all of the data in this experiment be explained by remote viewing or telepathy with the living? We don't think so. The reason is that when Laurie was attempting to contact the departed hypothesized co-investigators, she was flooded with information, none of which was wanted! For example, we were frankly not interested, then, in hearing from Betty about how much she loved her daughter. And we did not ask for images about where Susy grew up as a child. However, Laurie reported seeing a farm-like house with a cow in the backyard, plus a flower and vegetable garden.

When the experiment was completed, and Laurie and Susy met and had the chance to talk, Susy told us that she did not live in a farmhouse, but there had been a cow in her backyard at one time, and her mother did have a flower and vegetable garden.

Who cared about a cow in the backyard? We, the "scientists" were interested in Betty's picture, not an old cow from Betty's and Susy's past. However, Laurie kept getting flooded with information and energy (facts and emotions) that distracted her from focusing on the drawing. It's hard to see an abstract picture when you are flooded with an image of a cow. All she could get was a vague "yellow and green" form, maybe a "flower, or a tree."

It turned out that there was only one picture that was yellow and green, and it was a sunflower, purportedly suggested to Susy by her mother Betty.

Similarly, we were not interested in

- William James' interest in dancing with Susy in the afterlife, or his continued commitment to the field of afterlife study, or
- Henry's profound feeling of love for his daughter, and his concern that his wife was still secretly crying in her bedroom in Boca Raton (information that was later confirmed, which none of us knew at the time), or
- My father's concern that we call my brother to find out about a major change in his life (my brother was making a significant personal decision at that time).

Something more seemed to be going on . . .

Are we convinced that these data prove the survival of consciousness hypothesis? Of course not. Are we convinced that our continuing research with Laurie Campbell in collaboration with superstar mediums George Anderson, John Edward, Rev. Anne Gehman and Suzane Northrop, as featured in the HBO special "Life Afterlife," will prove that consciousness survives bodily death? Maybe.

This kind of pioneering work provides the foundation for continuing investigations that, utilizing the model of the systemic memory process, can eventually prove or disprove the survival of consciousness hypothesis. The challenge is to stay open to the possibility, and design the kinds of studies that reveal the kind of extraordinary evidence necessary to support (or dismiss) this extraordinary hypothesis.

When the available data are looked at openly with scientific integrity, the following conclusion seems justified: though the data are clearly not definitive, they are curiously consistent with what Joel Martin and Patricia Romanowski describe in their book, *Love Beyond Life*. If universal living memory exists, as predicted by the systemic memory process, then not only should the spirits and souls of our departed loved ones remember, but they will be just as alive as we are.

Chapter 10

Does the Universe Remember?

A New Vision of Universal Memory, the Living Vacuum, and an Evolving God

There is no such thing as chance, and what we regard as blind circumstance actually stems from the deepest source of all.
Friedrich von Schiller

We are seeking for the simplest possible scheme of thought that will bind together the observed facts.
Albert Einstein

Einstein once said, "God does not play dice with the universe."

This belief does not, on the face of it, sound weird. However, when we address the logic of randomness from a systems perspective, and then apply this logic to the idea of the "vacuum," we come to a profound hypothesis that on the face of it will sound quite weird. In fact, this hypothesis is the most controversial implication of universal living memory and the systemic memory process.

Is it possible that everything that has ever happened in the universe is ultimately stored everywhere in the universe? Does the logic of the systemic memory process require that we envision such a possibility? Is this memory a living, evolving, and eternal memory? Is this universal living memory what we mean by the evolving mind of God?

120

Can we tap into this universal living memory, and retrieve information from any and every aspect of the past? And is this where fate resides as a living, evolving destiny?

Before we address the systemic logic of why order and memory exists everywhere in systems, and then, by definition the logic of why order and memory must exist in the vacuum as well, let's consider what ancient traditions have posited about the nature of mind and reality.

Ancient Ideas about Universal Memory and the Universal Mind

In Russel Targ's and Jane Katra's 1998 book *Miracles of the Mind*, about "non-local" consciousness and spiritual healing, they describe the ancient hypothesis called the *Akashic* records.

According to Targ and Katra:

> Two thousand years ago, Patanjali, the Hindu philosopher and Sanskrit writer of the *Yoga Sutras* (aphorisms or teachings), taught that we obtain psi data by accessing what has become known as the Akashic records, the aspect of nonlocal mind that contains all information past, present, and future. One accesses it, he said, by "becoming it," with a single-pointed focus of attention. His writings provide us with a mental tool kit to accomplish this. Patanjali tells us that in order to see the world in our mind, we must quiet our mental activity. We have learned to call these waves mental noise.

In 1997, at the same time he was studying physics at Yale University, Dr. Jeffrey Satinover published a controversial book titled *Cracking the Bible Code* that addresses the origin of order in the universe. Satinover is a practicing psychiatrist and former William James Lecturer in Psychology and Religion at Harvard, who holds a degree from MIT, the Harvard Graduate School of Education, and the University of Texas.

According to Satinover, things often "pop" into our minds, sometimes at the strangest times, and it happens to scientists and mystics alike. Satinover explains that Max Planck, the physicist who conceived the idea of quantas of energy "jumping" from place to place instantaneously "without passing between them," may have "received" this weird idea.

As Satinover said:

> Planck himself found his solution almost laughable, and states that he never could figure out exactly why he thought such a thing, since it made no sense whatsoever. His idea was both discontinuous with everything that preceded it, in physics and anywhere in science, and inconsistent with both common sense and everyday experience. He had not even the advantage of previous philosophical inquiries along the line of James. The idea simply appeared in his mind one night.

Whether Planck "received" it or not we may never know, but what is important is to raise the question: was the idea conceived by Planck's unconscious, received from a greater systemic memory, or some combination of the two?

Of course, Planck is not the main character in Satinover's book. Moses is.

According to Kabbalists and other mystical Jews, the original Torah was supposedly given to Moses, word for word, letter for letter, by God. Using the language of Patanjali, it appears that Moses may have tapped into the Akashic records (believed to be a universal repository of memory). Why was Moses able to do this? Was the Torah, which consists of five complete books, an expression of Moses' conscious and unconscious mind? Had Moses received the information from the universal memory, or was it some combination of the two?

Here is how Satinover saw it: "Was it because of his accomplishments and spiritual technique? According to the Torah, it was chiefly because 'he was the most humble of men.'" Because Moses was so humble, he did not filter or modify the information, and was therefore a pure channel for it. He was truly an open and humble scribe for the information "from above." Satinover takes the lesson of humility and extends it to science itself. As he put it, *Science is merely the mathematical formalization of humility.*" (our italics)

We can see that the idea of an ancient record, a code, accessible to humans anywhere if they are of the right frame of mind and heart, is an old and cherished idea. Hopefully, science is learning the lesson of humility, and with the systemic memory process driving it, may attempt to return to this ancient belief and see it with new eyes as a possibly living code.

Contemporary Ideas about Universal Memory and the Universal Mind

A few frontier scientists have addressed this idea in light of contemporary data and physics. Probably the best known is Rupert Sheldrake, a scientist with exceptional credentials. (Linda and I keep mentioning credentials because we appreciate that some of you may be more willing to listen when you realize that the kinds of scientists who address these questions are actually quite exceptional—they tend to be very smart, very well trained, and very devoted to their science.) Sheldrake did his Ph.D. in biochemistry at Cambridge University and studied at Harvard University. At one time he was a Research Fellow of the Royal Society.

In 1981, Sheldrake published the controversial book *A New Science of Life: The Hypothesis of Formative Causation*. The distinguished journal *Nature* called it "the best candidate for burning there has been for many years." Britain's distinguished *New Scientist* was less prejudicial. They stated, "It is quite clear that one is dealing here with an important scientific inquiry into the nature of biological and physical reality."

Sheldrake's thesis is that objects come into being (atoms, cells, organs) not only because of information inside them, such as the genetic code, but because of information and energy outside, called "fields" in physics.

The idea of morphic (form) fields that help form objects has existed in science for some time, though it is believed to have been put to rest with the advent of modern molecular biology. However, as Sheldrake reviews in *A New Science of Life* and his second book on the thesis, *The Presence of the Past: Morphic Resonance and the Habits of Nature*, many phenomena appear in physics, chemistry, and biology that are consistent with the idea that external fields play a role in helping to shape the creation of objects.

Now, the great leap that Sheldrake took was he proposed that this morphic field grew with experience; meaning, each time an object came into existence, it added its form information to the overall morphic field. Hence, the field was continuously evolving, accumulating information with each new thing. With continued replication, the birth of atoms, crystals, cells or organisms should be easier to occur over time.

Now, where was this information stored? What locale?

What Sheldrake proposed was that the information was stored everywhere, equally, and this storage transcended space and time. We do not know if this "beyond space and time idea" came to Sheldrake like the idea of quanta instantaneously jumping from here to there came to Planck. What we do know is Sheldrake's idea fit nicely with ancient beliefs of the evolution of some sort of universal memory that transcended space and time.

I learned about Sheldrake's 1981 book after reading an issue of the *Brain/Mind Bulletin* that featured his thesis. At this point, I had taught the human psychobiology and systems theory seminar and had conceived (received?) the systemic memory hypothesis. When I read about Sheldrake's thesis, I realized that the systemic memory process might help explain the origin of morphic fields.

Inspired, I made contact with Sheldrake, and he explained that he was testing his thesis in a most creative way. Sheldrake went on television in Britain and showed the TV audience an embedded figure that had never been seen by anyone except the artist who drew it. Embedded figures are forms hidden in a morass of lines. The task is to look at the seeming chaos until the figure ultimately pops out. Once you know what the figure is, the solution is easy.

Sheldrake predicted that if millions of people saw a new embedded figure, and if other people around the world were then shown the embedded figure, they would recognize it more quickly because millions of people had created a morphic field for the figure. New people could tap into this field through morphic resonance; this is like the tuning fork idea discussed in chapter 8.

Being a careful scientist, Sheldrake understood the need for controls. He originally had four embedded figures drawn, and randomly selected one of them to show on television in Britain. Then, in various places around the world, groups of people, none of whom had seen the television program, opened envelopes containing the four embedded figures. They attempted to find them.

Sheldrake predicted that on the average, the people would find the embedded figure more quickly (slightly yet statistically significantly) in the figure that happened to have been shown on the British TV, and that this effect would occur more or less equally around the globe.

What he found was that a slight and statistically significant effect was obtained, but the magnitude generally decreased the further away people were from Britain.

He subsequently conducted a similar type of experiment using German TV, and a similar pattern was replicated. There seemed to be some sort of a morphic resonance effect, but the effect seemed to decrease with distance. This is not what Sheldrake anticipated.

However, when I learned of these observations, I was both amused and alarmed.

This was what the systemic memory process would predict. The effect would begin locally and spread out as the systemic memories resonated and expanded into the great network of matter and "vacuum." I was further encouraged that the systemic memory process might be relevant to Sheldrake's hypothesis when I learned of physicist David Bohm's attempt to explain how morphic fields might develop in the vacuum.

In an interview between Sheldrake and Bohm published in 1982 in *ReVision*, Bohm speculated how it might work. The language is technical; the key concept to appreciate is Bohm's use of words with the prefix "re." Here is how we described it in our first scientific paper on the systemic memory hypothesis (included in Appendix A):

> The logic that leads to the conclusion that the vacuum may be the ultimate storage device for recurrent feedback energy systems interactions is implicated in Bohm's recurrent process explanation of Sheldrake's morphogenetic resonance hypothesis (Sheldrake and Bohm, 1982). After Bohm published his seminal book on wholeness and the implicate order (Bohm, 1980), Bohm went on to employ the circular concepts of "re-injection", "re-projection" and "recurrent actuality," to explain the origin of memory and wholeness in nature. Simply stated, Bohm hypothesized that implicate memories emerge through "repeated cycles of re-injections and re-projections." Repeated cycles of re-injections and

re-projections described at the quantum level can be viewed as being a special case of the process of recurrent feedback interactions that occur in all systems at all levels—the implicit logic is the same. According to Bohm, our everyday concept of "actuality" (what we term "reality") should be reconceptualized as being a dynamical process, a *"recurrent* actuality."

"Recurrent feedback interaction" is the technical term used to explain how circular causality, the inherent process involved in all systems, takes place. Bohm's terms re-injection, re-projection, and recurrent actuality are appropriate terms to describe the process of systemic memory and therefore universal living memory.

Over a hundred years ago, William James wrote that "When two elementary brain-processes have been active together or in immediate succession, one of them, on re-occurring, tends to propagate its excitement into the other." Rephrasing James, we could say "When two elementary processes, A and B, have been active together or in immediate succession, one of them, on re-occurring, tends to propagate its excitement into the other." Sounds just like systemic memory, doesn't it?

The re-occurring of propagating one's excitement into the other, as James put it, is the *re*-injection, *re*-projection, and the creation of *re*-current actuality, as Bohm extended it a hundred years later. The key, as you see, is "re." The rest is history, only now the history is living.

In 1981, the Tarrytown Group, a membership society affiliated with the Tarrytown Conference Center in Tarrytown, New York, offered a $10,000 prize for "any completed experiment that documents the validity, or the invalidity, of Rupert Sheldrake's theory." The contest closed December 31, 1985. Sheldrake asked me if I was interested in designing research to compete for the prize, and I said no. However, an experiment "popped" into my mind one night that would not leave me alone.

I had attended a research seminar given by Sheldrake in New York City, and shortly after the seminar an experiment hit me that integrated my evolving secret interest in the science and mysticism of Kaballah. Being a scientist, I wanted to figure out what was going on, but I was not about to become a mystic myself. However, I was curiously reminded of mystical Hebrew every day at Yale University, a university founded originally as a conservative school of divinity in response to Harvard's liberalism.

That's correct, I was reminded of mystical Hebrew at Yale University every day.

The reason was that I had five Yale chairs in my office, and each carried Yale's insignia for all to see. It turns out that Yale's seal contains four Hebrew letters, and I could not fathom why a Christian University would use Hebrew letters in its seal.

With some digging in the venerable Yale library, I learned a possibly apocryphal story that gave me the chills.

The first president of Yale University supposedly had a good friend who was a rabbi. One night, while the president was sleeping, a set of Hebrew letters came to him in a dream. Not knowing what they meant, he wrote them down, and showed them to his friend the rabbi. The rabbi was amazed because the letters had some mystical meaning in Kaballah, and they were related to Yale's Latin motto of *Lux et Veritas* (Light and Truth).

The experiment that came to me involved the Hebrew language. The Hebrew language has been spoken for thousands of years, and people still read the Torah just as it was read thousands of years ago. If ever there was a language that should have a living morphic field, it is Hebrew.

Here is the experiment that popped into my mind. What would happen if we selected three letter words from the Torah, and then created nonsense syllables from them. Since I don't read Hebrew, it's all nonsense to me. However, thanks to the efforts of Jake Burack, then a graduate student at Yale University who was raised as an orthodox Jew and whose father was a distinguished rabbi, we were able to go to the Torah and obtain 48 three-letter words.

Jake selected 24 verbs and 24 nouns. It turns out that some careful scholars of the Torah had taken the time (before computers) to count how often each and every word appeared in the Torah. This made it possible for us to select 24 high frequency words (12 verbs and 12 nouns) and 24 low frequency words (12 verbs, 12 nouns) as used in the Torah.

Of course, it was improbable that this frequency difference reflected the total history of the use of these words in all contexts (for example, general speech or newspapers), but at least it reflected the frequency used in a set of books that have been read for thousands of years.

Once we had the actual words, the next task was to create nonsense words. We could not simply leave this to chance, because a given set of three letters could create multiple meaningful words. The words "god" and "dog" have the same letters, and both have meanings. Since Jake knew Hebrew, he made sure that the 48 scramblings of the 48 words all resulted in 48 nonsense syllables. The 48 words and the 48 nonsense syllables were then arranged in a counterbalanced order such that each set of eight presentations contained one of each type of real and nonsense words (high and low frequency verbs and high and low frequency nouns), and the order of the eight types was different from set to set, for the entire 96 words.

Yale students who did not know Hebrew were invited to participate in a language experiment. The students were told that they would be shown 96 different Hebrew words, and that their task was simply to write down the first thought or image that came to mind when they saw each word. We explained that since they did not know Hebrew, they probably would get most if not all of the meanings wrong. We did not care. We were interested in their free associations, whatever came to mind.

After each free association, the students were asked to rate the confidence of their guess—that is, what was their hunch that a given free association might reflect the true meaning? Students used a simple four number scale, from complete guess to certainty, and they were encouraged to be creative and open to their intuitions. Students were not told that half the words were nonsense syllables.

This experiment was originally designed to be the pilot phase for a subsequent Hebrew learning study. We wanted to be sure that subjects did not know Hebrew, and we therefore wanted to select only those who got a score of zero on the meaning portion of the test.

It was our hypothesis that the brain can register and detect information that is even below our level of conscious awareness. Hence, we wondered, would the subjects unconsciously recognize if a word was meaningful or nonsense? Would the confidence of their guesses be slightly but statistically significantly higher for the real words than the nonsense words? And would the confidence of their guesses be slightly but statistically significantly higher for the high frequency words compared to the low frequency words?

The results were, in a word, unbelievable.

In fact, because we could not believe them, we repeated the experiment five times with five independent samples of students. I was reminded of the words spoken to the distinguished anthropologist, the late Margeret Mead, which are rephrased slightly here: "These are the kind of data I wouldn't believe, even if they were true."

The obvious prediction, that the subjects would get virtually all of the meanings of the words wrong, was found. These findings were easy to believe! However, the rating of confidence of their guesses showed a slight but statistically significant difference. Their intuition of confidence was higher when the words were real compared to nonsense, and their intuition of confidence was higher for the high frequency words compared to the low frequency words. These findings were nearly impossible to believe.

This "implicit perception" (implicit means subliminal or unconscious) effect only appeared when subjects were given the task of simply free associating, and they did not know that half of the words were nonsense. When we gave the same subjects the 96 words again, only this time told them that half of them were real and half of them were nonsense, and asked them to try and figure out which was which; as a group they could not do it! When they became more logical, more analytical, more "left-brained," they could not perceive the difference. However, when they functioned in a more open, holistic, more "right-brained" manner, subtle awareness of the original words was observed. This discovery, replicated five times, is important.

All too often paranormal-like phenomena that occur spontaneously, in dreams or moments of openness, when brought into the laboratory in tasks that require people become analytical, seem to disappear. Is the mode of subtle information processing different when we attempt to detect subtle information, possibly of systemic memory?

We told Sheldrake of our findings, and he asked us to write them up to be considered for the Tarrytown prize. My mother was dying at the time, and this research, though important, did not have my

129

highest priority. Sheldrake insisted, and said he would find out if the deadline could be extended. The deadline was extended for four months, and we prepared the findings for publication.

Curiously, during this four-month period, after we had come to our discovery, a professor and his students in Britain came to a similar idea using Farsi, the language of Iran, and they obtained positive results too. They submitted their paper for the prize as well. The prize was shared by our two laboratories. The Tarrytown Society increased the prize to $20,000 so that each laboratory received $10,000. *Time* magazine wrote an article about the prize and the award ceremony, and essentially said what *Nature* did: the theory is ridiculous, hence the research must either be flawed or have a simpler, non-controversial explanation.

The reaction of some of my colleagues was so negative and cruel that I decided that I would not attempt to publish the findings. Enough damage had been done.

I went back to being a "regular" Yale professor, publishing mainstream research on my National Science Foundation grant on the psychophysiology of personality and emotion. And I tried to put Sheldrake's morphic resonance out of my mind.

Years later, after I was invited to be a professor at the University of Arizona, I was approached by a peer-reviewed scientific journal for the International Society for the Study of Subtle Energies and Energy Medicine, which begged me to submit the findings.

I declined, saying the findings were too controversial. Moreover, I still found the findings hard to believe myself.

Then, a few years after I turned down the invitation to publish the Yale findings, a student at the University of Arizona who was a dual major in psychology and Judaic studies asked me if I had a project she could work on for an honors thesis that integrated her two interests. I pulled out the Yale manuscript, and suggested that she might find something of interest there. Her name was Penny Delman, and she taught Hebrew. Penny was very interested.

Penny and I designed a related experiment. We gave subjects a set of cards containing three letters, and simply asked them to rearrange the cards in a way that seemed pleasing to them and that might make up a Hebrew word. There were 20 sets of cards, 10 verbs (5 high frequency and 5 low frequency) and 10 nouns (5 high frequency and 5 low frequency). To my surprise, the data replicated and extended the Yale findings. The subjects' arrangement of the letters was slightly but statistically significantly greater than chance, especially for high frequency words, and the subjects had no idea what the words meant.

The Yale and Arizona studies were published in a book, in German, in 1997 titled, *Scientists Discuss Rupert Sheldrake*. I discussed Sheldrake's theory in the context of systemic memory, and illustrated how the two theories could be compared and contrasted in future research. The chapter ended with the following conclusion:

> *The logic of systemic memory, implicitly used by Bohm to explain morphic resonance, is potentially powerful because it bridges traditional systems theory and quantum systems theory (see also Laszlo, 1995). It is possible that the logic of systemic memory can help bring the concept of morphic resonance into mainstream science. However, until research funding is made available to test morphic resonance and systemic memory predictions, the predictions will remain as they are, thought provoking curiosities waiting for empirical investigation.*

What organization or person is going to fund serious research on universal memory and ancient languages, especially in today's scientific and financial climate? It will take a special calling of a dedicated person or group who understands and shares the vision, and is in a position to do something about it.

Laszlo and the Quantum Vacuum

A hero of mine is Erwin Laszlo, an integrative systems theorist who, like James Miller, thinks broadly and deeply. In two recent books, one technical, titled, *The Interconnected Universe: Conceptual Foundations of Transdisciplinary Unified Theory*; the other popular, titled, *The Whispering Pond: A Personal Guide to the Emerging Vision of Science*, Laszlo paints a sweeping vision of the future of science, focusing on the vacuum.

His inspiration comes not only from Bohm and Sheldrake, but from a team of contemporary physicists, Bernard Haisch, Alfonso Rueda, and Harold E. Puthoff. Their technical articles on "zero point energy" (the energy that appears zero but is actually infinite in the zero point vacuum) make one's head spin, but their less technical articles, especially "Beyond $E=mc^2$" in *Discover* magazine, express an exceptional and exciting new vision of "empty space" that runs contrary to common sense or the "void" as perceived by Buddhist mystics.

Like Sheldrake's idea of the morphic resonance process (extending the concept of tuning fork resonance to morphic fields), and our idea of the systemic memory process, the idea of "zero point energy" in the "quantum vacuum" is exceptionally simple at its core, and exceptionally complex in its details.

These physicists posit that the vacuum is far from empty. On the contrary, as I intuited from the high-rise in Vancouver, the vacuum is overflowing with information and energy. Haisch and his colleagues believe that the quantum vacuum is actually a quantum sea of possibility, a profound energy waiting to be discovered, studied, and tapped.

Our book cannot go into their theory in any depth. If you're interested and prepared to be inspired, read *The Whispering Pond*. It was in Karl Pribram's afterword to Laszlo's *The Interconnected Universe* that we learned of McCulloch's wonderful phrase—"Do not bite my finger, look where I am pointing."

So let's take James' and McCulloch's and Pribram's and Bohm's and Schwartz's and Russek's ideas of recurrent processes, and add them to the evolving model of the vacuum. As we do so, try not to bite.

Here's the core idea. All so-called material objects exist within a gigantic vacuum that is bubbling with information and energy. The vacuum is so complex, it is filled with so much information and energy, including the history of all the stars in the sky, and even the background radiation from the very beginning of the universe, that it is unimaginable.

My mind boggles at the thought of all this information and energy, and wonders constantly how one ever retrieves anything out of it, but the fact is we do.

Now, when we take the idea of energy, and combine it with the idea of system, particularly a dynamic energy system (what Linda and I call DES), we recognize that the vacuum may be teeming with these energy systems, and they are as alive and evolving as physical life itself. The visible world contains the invisible world, and the in-

132

visible world spreads out into "space" which is actually super-connected since it is all energy.

If the idea of living energy systems has plausibility, and living energy systems live in the vacuum, then everything that lives will be connected energetically to everything else that lives to various degrees. Living energy systems will have relative locality (beginning in a specific place and extending out into space in all directions) and ultimately non-locality (being "everywhere" as contemporary quantum physics proposes) as well. However, the logic will not be local *versus* non-local (the Stage M, reductionsitic vision), but local *and* non-local (the Stage I and beyond, systemic vision).

Sound travels in the air, but it travels faster and easier in water, and travels even faster and easier in solid objects that resonate with it. The more that things are interconnected and open, the more readily the information and energy are conducted. At close to zero degrees, weird things happen: compounds can become superconductors, encountering no resistance at all.

If the vacuum is a gigantic network of living energy systems as DES suggests, then "sound" (electromagnetic vibrations) may be especially rapidly and readily conducted everywhere to everything to various degrees. Though solid objects will selectively resonate with information and energy coming from their respective environments, since all systems are ultimately "open" to various degrees, they will ultimately receive the information and energy of "everything" to various degrees.

The argument should not be wave *versus* particle, or local *versus* non-local. It should be wave *and* particle, or local *and* non-local, at least when we are thinking systemically. The challenge in science is to learn how to wear different conceptual hats, to try them on for size, and to see how they give us different complementary visions of what ultimately may be "one" universe (what Linda and I call integrative-diversity in our scientific papers).

According to Laszlo, nearly every current anomaly seen throughout history and documented in contemporary science (such as out-of-body experiences or telepathy over long distances), becomes plausible when we entertain the idea that the vacuum is actually the place where all is connected, the space we all share. When we add the systemic memory process to Laszlo's logic, the vacuum of space itself becomes eternal, alive, and evolving. And our visions of the Grand Organizing Designer become even more exciting. The universe becomes an organizing and remembering universe, a living energy universe.

Does all this sound like magic?

Here's how Harold Puthoff ended his 1998 scientific article, "Can the Vacuum be Engineered for Space Flight Applications? Our View of Theory and Experiments," published in the *Journal of Scientific Exploration*:

> As we peer into the heavens from the depth of our gravity well, hoping for some "magic" solution that will launch our spacefarers first to the planets and then to the stars, we are reminded of Arthur C. Clarke's phrase that highly advanced technology is essentially indistinguishable from magic. Fortunately, such magic appears to be waiting in the wings of our deepening understanding of the quantum vacuum in which we live.

Why the Universe Cannot Be Random—
The God Hypothesis Explained

In Heinz Pagel's *The Cosmic Code*, he pointed out that when mathematicians look for randomness in nature, they never quite find it. If they look hard enough they will discover a hidden order, a formula that reveals a hidden form. Today we call this branch of systems science "chaos and complexity theory."

Around the same time that I stumbled upon the logic of the systemic memory process and the logic that ideas are alive, I came to an explanation about why it was impossible for pure randomness to occur in the universe if systems theory is true.

What I mean by this is that if everything in the universe is ultimately interconnected and functions as layers and layers of systems, then the very conditions that define how randomness can occur are not present, and therefore randomness is predicted not to be present. Stated another way, if we take seriously our understanding of randomness, then a system cannot be random.

Sometimes either/or thinking is necessary. When we understand systemic thinking, we see that even the dichotomy between order and disorder may be oversimplified. The argument may not be order versus disorder, but order and disorder. Statistics tell us that to obtain a random distribution, each event must be independent of every other event. This is the bedrock of the mathematics of statistics. The key here is independent. Each time you flip a coin, the flip must be independent of all previous flips.

There can be no learning. There can be no wear and tear on the coin. The random process requires complete and total independence and constancy from flip to flip. Now the question is, are systems ever completely independent? Do things in nature ever act in such a way that they are completely independent from each other, and independent over time? Can systems in nature be treated as if they are completely closed and not interacting with their environment?

Of course, we can make up such an abstract story, and even model it mathematically.

The question is, does nature fit this condition, this essential requirement of independence? What systems theory tells us is absolutely, positively, no.

When we put on our system's hat, we come to Laszlo's vision of *The Interconnected Universe*. In an interconnected universe, randomness is not possible.

No independence, no randomness. Simple. However, if things are independent, then you will observe randomness. In fact, if there is complete independence and no ordering process, the probability of getting a random distribution is actually 100 percent! If you doubt this, try the experiment yourself.

Have a computer randomly select ten numbers from 1 to 10 and calculate the mean of the ten numbers selected; repeat this procedure a thousand times, and plot the resulting distribution of the means. Then do it again, and again, and again, and again. What you'll see, over and over, is an upside down U-shaped function, which is called, curiously, a random "order." It is not called a random "disorder" because it really is an order.

The truth is, randomness does not occur by chance. Randomness can only occur when events are completely independent of each other, and that only happens in abstract systems. To the extent that randomness occurs, it gives everything that is possible a chance to occur. *Randomness does not occur by chance, it provides the chance for*

135

things to occur. To the extent that things are interdependent, the capacity for true randomness is constrained accordingly.

Now, think about the universe and what physics sometimes refers to as the quantum "sea," the vast ocean of dynamic activity that occurs in the space that is everywhere. Think about the swarms of stars and energy. Think about the profound complexity of the organization of DNA and even the simplest of the simplest of cells.

Now let's add the logic of the systemic memory process to all of this.

If everything is ultimately interacting to various degrees, sharing information and energy—sharing the same ultimate space, the same quantum vacuum, the same quantum sea—and this information and energy are evolving as a dynamic, creative memory, then not only is the memory potentially everywhere to various degrees, but it's evolving and living in the deepest meaning of the term.

When the poet Freidrick von Schiller said, "There is no such thing as chance, and what we regard as blind circumstance actually stems from the deepest source of all," he probably overstated part of the case and understated another. The overstatement is that "chance" exists to a degree. Things are not totally connected; flexibility clearly exists in nature.

The understatement concerns the "source of it all." The source of order may come from two deep sources:

- the origin of the order from which all emerges, and
- the evolving creation of systemic destiny as the history of the all is dynamically stored and remembered everywhere to various degrees.

One of science's greatest dreams is to discover certain principles that integrate, explain, and predict large numbers of seemingly disconnected phenomena. As Einstein put it, "We are seeking for the simplest possible scheme of thought that will bind together the observed facts." Could it be that the idea of system, combined with the idea of energy, that leads to the logic of the systemic memory process, provides a "possible scheme of thought that will bind together the observed facts"?

If memory is a core consequence of the feedback process ubiquitous in all dynamical systems, then the universal living memory hypothesis serves as a powerful scheme of thought that binds together—integrates—the observed facts, from the conventional to the controversial, and beyond. Everything that "is" remembers, from the small to the all.

PART IV

Implications of Universal Living Memory for Everything

It's tough to make predictions,
especially about the future.

Yogi Berra

Chapter 11

The Living Energy Universe

Implications for Twenty-First-Century Science,
Education, Business, Healthcare and Spirituality

We shall not cease from exploration
And the end of all our exploring
Will be to arrive where we started
And know the place for the first time
T.S. Eliot, "A Little Gidding"

Give us more to see.
Stephen Sondheim
Sunday in the Park with George

Imagine that it is sometime in the not so distant future, and that the scientific community has embraced the challenge of testing the many guises of the systemic memory hypothesis.

Imagine that scientists in numerous disciplines and professions—physics, chemistry, biology, psychology, sociology, medicine, geology, ecology, astrophysics—have not only examined the logic of the systemic memory process, but have conducted controlled experiments to determine whether the systemic memory mechanism is operative in their domains. Let's posit that after the dust has settled, the conclusion turns out to be—systemic memory, and hence universal living memory—is real. Let's imagine that the summary consensus of the scientists is that everything, yes everything, appears to be eternal, alive, and evolving.

How would this conclusion change our vision of science, business, education, healthcare, spirituality, life in general? How would our vision of the universe, and therefore everything around us, change? Would we smile? In this chapter we are not asking you to "believe" that this hypothesis is true. We are simply asking you to "entertain the possibility" that it might be true. The potential implications are extremely wide-ranging, and some will seem wild.

As a rule, scientists do not like premises that promote "wide and wild" speculations. This may be one reason why conservative scientists tend to favor reductionistic thinking (Stage M science) over systemic thinking (Stages I, L, and E science). However, since reductionistic science fails to address adequately

- the question of the evolution of order in nature and the universe,
- emergent properties and holism in nature and the universe, and
- phenomena that require an appreciation for unpredictability, complexity, and self-organization in nature and the universe.

It is prudent if not essential to entertain the implications of systemic thinking. To help you keep track of the many implications, we organize the implications into a series of broad questions.

What Are Some Implications for Physics?
Physics May Become a Behavioral Science

If the systemic memory process is true, physics will never be the same.

As Sheldrake expressed it in his morphogenic resonance hypothesis, the "laws" of nature may turn out to be "habits" of nature. What we have called independent laws, may actually be interdependent habits. The very "laws" themselves may be evolving. If the laws function systemically, then they may be alive and evolving themselves. If physical phenomena, even the "laws" themselves, have memory and learn over time, then physicists will ultimately have to become behavioral scientists, even psychologists! If physicists are to learn how to conduct research on learning, they will need to spend time with scientists who are experts in learning. Physicists will have to take courses in psychology as part of their scientific training.

Psychologists will have to expand their education too. Most psychologists believe that humans, primates, rats, sea slugs, fruit flies, and even paramecia can learn. However, psychologists typically do not believe that DNA, water molecules, and photons can learn. The former are alive, the latter are dead. Case closed.

However, like Miller and Sheldrake, we are suggesting that all science is ultimately "behavioral" science. If the systemic memory process is true, then all systems at all levels do more than simply "behave." They behave dynamically, evolve over time, and express the very essence of life. This principle applies even to the "laws" of science. It is all process. It is all an expression of universal living memory.

Of course, laws that have been around for a long time, that have accumulated billions of years of integrative systemic memories, should on the whole be very stable. However, just because the laws appear to be stable does not mean that they are therefore fixed, unchanging, dead. Theoretically, there can be degrees and levels of flexibility in physical phenomena just as there are degrees and levels of complexity in physical phenomena.

If nothing is independent of everything else, and the systemic memories for the whole of the universe are to various degrees spread out throughout the quantum vacuum, then everything that exists today can potentially be influenced by the history of the entire universe.

Hence, there may be "nothing new under the sun." The sun itself may be alive, expressing a living code in the visible and invisible flames that extend from its core and reach to the far corners of the universe. This code may have profound physical, chemical, and biological implications and commercial applications.

The systemic memory process potentially provides a new explanation for the controversial claims of so called "cold fusion." Courageous physicists, chemists, and engineers are continuing to conduct serious research in this area. Contemporary research suggests that under special circumstances, energy can accumulate in physical systems. Under the right conditions, the energy may accumulate and create a "cold" fusion of useful energy. The systemic memory process also helps explain sonar luminescence—the conversion of low intensity sound in water to high intensity heat and light.

The systemic memory process helps explain the observation of time irreversibility. If all things accumulate history over time, then it is impossible to repeat the same thing over time absolutely exactly. Perfect replication is not possible because material itself wears its history—the revised vision is that things do not so much wear "out" as wear "on" over time. In a deep physical sense, it may be impossible to go backwards, to go "home"—because the present contains the past in an evolved form, for all time. The idea that one can travel "back" in time may need to be revised accordingly.

It is even conceivable, as Linda suggests, that time and space themselves may be dynamically circular, and therefore be alive and evolving. If everything is eternal, alive, and evolving, this thesis may apply to the fundamentals of time and space themselves. If this vision causes your mind to "spin," the effect may be more than poetic—it may actually be instructive of the spinning nature of the universe and everything within it. Though the systemic concept of circulating time and space complicates the mathematics of physics even further, the end result may be increased understanding and appreciation of the universe in which we live.

Photons, and phonons, and all other wild and weird phenomena in quantum physics, may accumulate histories as well. Systems are likely "entangled" (quantum physics' term for intimately connected) not only in a "classical" sense (electromagnetically and locally), but in a "quantum" sense (probabilistically called Bell's theorem of nonlocality) as well. If William Tiller's hypothesis, as described in his book *Science and Human Transformation: Subtle Energies, Intentionality, and Consciousness*, is correct, the systemic memory process will extend all the way to quantum entanglement and even to the fundamental "loops" of physics (loops are circles, like feedback loops; modern physics miniaturizes them to imaginary "strings").

If the evolving "theory of everything"—so-called "superstring theory"—is correct, then everything is ultimately made of tiny little "loops" (strings) that vibrate in a myriad of ways. Recall that the heart of the systemic memory process is the circle, the loop. Systems reflect circulations of information, energy, and matter. Memory is circulation, from the micro to the macro. And memory plus recurrent circulation yields evolution ($E = mc^R$). For all its evolving complexity, the universe may be elegant in its core simplicity, as Brian Greene tells us in *The Elegant Universe*. With the superstring may come supermemory as a foundational concept in physics.

Note that the concepts of "self-perception," "self-consciousness," and "self-awareness" involve systems processing information and energy about themselves in a dynamically circular fashion. This is, of course, what is meant by circular feedback in systems. The systemic memory process implies that self-awareness exists not only in human systems, but it exists at every level, from the micro of quantum physics to the macro of astrophysics.

Contemporary scientists interested in consciousness and the quantum mind, such as Dr. Stuart Hameroff, an anesthesiologist at the University of Arizona, and Roger Penrose, a physicist at Cambridge University, imply that the systemic memory process extends to the quantum level and even the nonlocal. Hameroff and Penrose focus on the "microtubules" in neurons, but the same logic applies to all levels where feedback loops operate. Self-consciousness and self-organization may be two sides of the same coin, an expression of self-revision, integrated by the concept of the systemic memory process.

Simply stated, even electrons, photons, and superstrings may have "self-consciousness," "self-organization," and "self-revision" in their own way and form.

What are Some Implications for Chemistry and Biochemistry? The "Soul of the Rose" and Aromatherapy

Clearly, if the systemic memory process is true, then molecules will store integrative systemic memories. Depending on the flexibility and complexity of particular molecules, the nature of their memories will vary. The study of learning in molecules should be fascinating.

145

As Linda suggested, DNA and RNA may function as dynamic noetic antennas and resonating noetic antennas, selectively tuning into the mix of memories contained in the vacuum, between every subatomic particle that ultimately comprises what science labels as molecules.

As we discussed in chapter 8, crystals may be especially good at storing systemic memories. Water may be among the very best crystallizing molecular systems. Homeopathy may work because of memory in water. Even the idea of "holy" water takes on a new plausibility.

If the systemic memory process is correct, then alcohol compounds contained in roses and other flowers should have a different systemic history than the same alcohol compounds created artificially in the laboratory.

The alcohols that have "lived in the rose" will contain information about "roseness," including the environment in which the rose was born and grew up. If the soul of the rose is contained within the alcohols, then the effects of rose memory alcohols should be different from laboratory memory alcohols. Even though the rose and the laboratory alcohols will have the same physical structure, they will not contain the same information and energy. The info-energy systems that live on in the rose memory alcohols will be "rose" info-energy systems, whereas info-energy systems that live on in the laboratory memory alcohols will be "laboratory" info-energy systems.

This implication may help explain why aromatherapy and other natural remedies such as herbs work. When the distiller extracts the "essential" oils from a plant, he or she may be extracting the "essential systemic memories" that reflect the wholeness of the plants themselves in addition to the unique combination of physical components that comprise the individual plants. If chemicals have memory, as systemic memory predicts, then chemists will need to study psychology too, and vice versa. That's because if molecules can learn, then chemists will have to study molecular learning just as psychologists study intellectual learning.

What are Some Implications for Biology, Evolution, and Medicine? (Cellular memories, diseases of systemic memory, eating of abused animals, living drugs, aging, remembered breathing . . .)

The logic of the systemic memory process leads inexorably to the conclusion that all cells have memories and learn, from individual single-celled organisms to each of the sixty-plus trillion cells that comprise our bodies. Miller explicitly stated this conclusion in *Living Systems*. Using the logic of the systemic memory process we extended his conclusion downward to apply to every component contained within cells, and upward to apply to living systems at the global level.

In the same way that our body records physical scars, the prediction is that the body records informational and energy scars as well. Theoretically, the systemic memory scars remain with us forever, to various degrees.

Biological science tells us that every seven years or so, every molecule in each of the sixty-plus trillion cells within our bodies is replaced. Why would the body do this? Molecules are molecules, aren't they? They don't age (the old "dead" science story). Or do they (the new "living" energy systems science story)?

The systemic memory process suggests that the myriad molecules that comprise our cells are alive. They store information and energy about our history, including our pains and sorrows, to various degrees. What ongoing molecular replacement may achieve is to give us a new physical scaffold to support our evolving internal living info-energy systems.

Hence, the way we eliminate some of our "physical" storage of our systemic histories is to release our "old" molecules back to the earth and replace them with "new" molecules. However, since these molecules are not really "new," we actually continue to mix our memories with those around us. We become ever more a *Society of Mind*, the title of Marvin Minsky's book, or a collection of "souls" of systemic memories.

As our cells accumulate more and more systemic memories, they may reach a point where their physical systems can no longer sustain their structure. If too many memory scars are accumulated, and the

147

physical scaffolding is not replaced, the system may collapse under its own systemic memory weight.

The kind of air, water, and food we ingest should influence the environmental systemic memories we mix with our own. Individually and collectively we may be suffering from more than physical environmental pollution; we may be suffering from systemic memory pollution as well.

One of the most controversial biophysical and political implications of this thesis concerns how we raise and ingest meat. Animals are too often raised under stressful and abusive circumstances, and we ingest their cells into our bodies. Their molecules replace some of our molecules. Hence, we live with the info-energy of their pain and suffering. If future research documents that this hypothesis is valid, one can imagine what some of the profound implications will be, for our eating habits, the way we raise and care for animals, the way the food industry is allowed to function and is regulated.

Many, if not all, diseases may ultimately be related to the systemic memory process. Conversely, many if not all treatements may ultimately benefit by understanding the systemic memory process. Diseases like Alzheimer's may be re-envisioned as alterations in the storage and retrieval of systemic memories. Maybe patients with Alzheimer's have not "lost" their memory, but their ability to use their compromised biochemical machinery to express their memory.

The transplant paradigm will need to be reconsidered, and we may be able to improve the likelihood that the transplant is accepted with little rejection by teaching people how to connect with, invite, and honor the new memories that will be sharing their physical body. New energy medicine paradigms could provide complex dynamic information that expresses the essential memories that sustain life in selective types of cells. The possibilities for medicine and health are vast.

Most of the time we do not have to remember to breathe. Our respiratory systems remember to breathe for us. The complex circular feedback loops comprising the "autonomic nervous system" theoretically engage in a continuous systemic memory process of "remembering" for us. Thirty years of research in biofeedback tells us that humans and animals can learn to gain conscious control over organs regulated by the autonomic nervous system. We can add new memories, and new levels of self-regulation, to the system that is designed to remember for us.

As Linda sees it, the evolving universe is a "remembering universe." In a deep sense, the stars may "remember" to "beat" as galactic systems in the same way that heart cells remember to beat in the cardiac system. The process may be generic, universal, and meaningful. The implications of the systemic memory process for re-envisioning evolution are also vast.

If the systemic memory process is true, then evolution cannot simply be an expression of random mutation, what Richard Dawkins dubbed the "blind watchmaker." Not only may there be a grand "plan of plans," or a grand "implicate" order as Bohm put it, but there should be an evolving, manifesting plan that accrues over time through the storage of systemic memory. The words "universal living memory" convey this idea more vibrantly. Flexibility may be built into the plan, allowing for relative freedom and opportunity, but if the system is indeed a system, its existence and evolution can not be explained by pure chance alone.

It is worth remembering that Darwin did not have access to Miller's *Living System* book. Darwin did not know about the implications of systems thinking—general, living, and evolving systems theory—for the logic of randomness. One wonders, if Darwin had known then what contemporary systems science knows now, would he have written a different *Origin of Species?* We suspect so. And if Darwin had written a different *Origin of Species,* would other "Darwinians"—including certain chaos and complexity theorists—have expressed this revised vision in their writings? We would hope so.

Everything, including science itself, is potentially an expression of an evolving process (Stage E). If the systemic memory process is correct, it is possible that what we call "evolution" may itself be "evolving." A conceptually challenging premise to ponder.

What are Some Implications for Psychology?
(Memory everywhere, learning everywhere, consciousness everywhere, mind-material interaction everywhere . . .)

If learning and memory are the rule, not the exception, in nature, then the discipline of psychology, like the discipline of mathematics, will ultimately become a generic discipline, universally applied to quantum physics (the micro) and astrophysics (the macro), and every discipline in between.

The study of learning and memory will continue to play a central role in psychology. However, psychologists will need to understand how the learning takes place systemically in all systems at all levels. If the systemic memory process is true, then memory is not limited to the brain. Every cell, and every molecule within every cell, will accumulate a unique story. Every story will include the story of the whole as it is perceived through its unique relationship with the whole. The phenomenon of memory will become ever more interesting and even more complex than currently envisioned.

Psychologists will want to build better bridges with physicists and chemists to address the deep question about how systemic memory is retrieved, especially through conscious intention.

Can we develop better procedures for helping people retrieve memories, first of their own individual pasts, and then of their greater past? Yes, psychologists will have to re-entertain the idea that "spirits" and "souls" exist as info-energy systems that play a role in what all of us do. Moreover, we will have to become more humble about claiming that "our" thoughts come exclusively from "us."

The truth is, when a thought "pops" into our head, we don't really know where it comes from:

- Did we "create" it?
- Did it come from "our" unconscious?
- Was it a "random" event?
- Did we receive it from someone else?
- Did it come from the "present" or the "past" (and if the "past" is actually present, as Sheldrake reminds us and the systemic memory process requires, then is it all "present")?
- Did we receive it from a higher "soul," an "angel"?
- Did we even get it from the Grand Organizing Designer of the universe him/herself? Did we get it from the universal living memory?

The truth is, science doesn't know. If memory can be everywhere, including in info-energy systems living in the vacuum, then where is consciousness per se located? Is consciousness primarily a construction of the brain, or is the brain just one magnificent tool for experiencing consciousness?

As we mentioned in the section on physics, if the systemic memory process is true, then everything theoretically has some level of consciousness, from the superstrings of microloops to the superclusters of billions of galaxies. Self-consciousness arises from the fact that everything ultimately "sees" itself because it receives information and energy about itself from the "past" through the "eyes" of others. In the simplest abstract terms, A sees itself through B in a continuously, dynamically, recursively unfolding way. The systemic memory process extends the contemporary philosopher David Charmer's "dual aspect" theory, that says every "thing" that is informational has both a "physical" and a "conscious" component.

In a deep sense, we are our living memories. This is a key take-home message: We are what we remember—we are our living memories.

To the extent that our memories are eternal and living, as systemic memory suggests, then our histories can continue to grow and evolve forever; ours and the history of everything else. Stephen Hawkin's *A Brief History of Time* becomes a *A Brief History* of Memory. From a systemic perspective, time = memory.

If consciousness is everywhere, and everything is connected directly through the vacuum, then everything is intimately connected with everything else. Everything is ultimately one. This means that my mind shares the same quantum sea as my computer. Hence my mind and my computer can resonate through the vacuum and become an A-B system too. Since my computer is designed to be a highly stable system, its resonance with my mind will be limited. However, if we look closely enough we will find some evidence of shared electronic resonance.

Utilizing the Princeton Engineering Anomalies Research (PEAR) Laboratory computerized "random event generator" (REG), Lonnie Nelson, Linda and I have witnessed this kind of sharing first-hand in our Human Energy Systems Laboratory at the University of Arizona. The REG device measures quantum fluctuations of electrons and feeds this information into a computer.

It is possible to examine very tiny shifts away from "randomness" when our minds "share" the same space with the device. The random event generator/computer/software system makes it possible for us to look very closely at the behavior of the device.

Metaphorically and statistically, when we smile, the REG smiles with us. SMILE takes on a second meaning (Systemic Manifestation of Intelligent Loving Energy). Such that one grand system, one universal mind, expresses its creative uniqueness in all of its parts. And at least one of its parts, labeled by us to be "human beings" has the capacity to envision, explore, and enable this grandeur to evolve.

What Are Some Implications for Ecology and Astrophysics?
(The wisdom of the earth, the evolving big bloom,
and the positive feedback expanding universe . . .)

If, as Lewis Thomas said in *The Lives of a Cell*, the earth can be thought of as a gigantic cell, then the systemic memory process applies and extends to the earth as a whole system—what British atmospheric scientist James Lovelock called the Gaia hypothesis.

Consider the following: Do you think that your individual brain, heart, muscle, skin, or bone cells, know that they are living inside a person? Do you think their individual consciousnesses are like the consciousness of you as a whole? How would we ask them, and how would we translate their info-energy response?

The systemic memory process requires that we hypothesize that the whole that makes you "you" is circulated to each and every cell in your body. Hence, each cell theoretically stores "you" in it. This is why each cell is like a tiny location in a huge hologram. In holograms, information about the "holo" is stored everywhere in the "gram"—the more of the "gram" you activate, the clearer the "holo" memory retrieved. However, although each cell may have information and energy about the whole, does it appreciate the whole? Can it consciously envision the whole? At this point, scientifically, we can't say one way or the other.

The truth is, in some deep way, we are like brain or heart cells in the organism called earth, and we have yet to even imagine what "its" consciousness is like as a whole.

Human awareness is just beginning to consider the possibility that we are something much greater than ourselves, and that we live inside a huge organism that may have a life, and purpose, that we as yet do not know. The idea of universal living memory helps us envision this possibility.

Returning to ecology, we need to search actively for the wisdom of the earth as expressed in global feedback loops, in the same manner as Dr. Walter Cannon, the Harvard physiologist, searched for *The Wisdom of the Body*, the title of his book, as expressed in physiological feedback loops.

We must remember that we leave our wastes not only physically, but informationally and energetically as well. We are creating a dangerous sea of electromagnetic energy pollution, as Dr. Robert Becker reminds us in *Cross Currents: The Perils of Electropollution, the Promise of Electromedicine*. The systemic memory process makes the challenge of pollution even more complicated. As a dynamical system, the planet is theoretically learning and remembering, and we may be making it sick. If earth is designed like we are to have a functional immune system, the earth may be learning to recognize the danger we are imposing with the goal of inactivating or destroying us.

The grandest of implications addresses the grandest of questions: the origin and evolution of the universe. There are two basic views about the origin of the universe, the big bang and the big bloom. There are others such as the steady state, for example, and there are mixtures of these, such as the big bang followed by the big "crunch" (when the universe potentially collapses back on itself, a hypothesis no longer in fashion in light of the discovery of the increasingly expanding universe).

If the universe is truly a system, and its components at all levels are connected energetically and informationally, then the universe system cannot expand randomly (from photons to super clusters of galaxies), it must unfold in a "recurrent feedback" and hence circulating manner.

The systemic memory process per se does not speak to the original "seed," the plan before the material expression of the all. However, the systems vision, that leads to the systemic memory process, requires that we hypothesize that some sort of original seed (design, plan, implicate order) must be there. Otherwise, there could be no organized galaxies containing millions and millions of stars, and no organized super-galaxies containing millions and millions of galaxies.

What the systemic memory process suggests is that as cosmic history unfolds over billions of years, and universal systemic memories accrue, these cosmic memories further shape the universe's destiny and everything contained within it. The cosmic systemic memories influence how the universe "swings" so to speak, just as systemic memories influence how the child "swings" in the playground (recall chapter 6). The quantum sea, the living vacuum, can be thought of as an infinitely huge, swinging wave, accumulating history as it waves and waves and waves.

It follows that if the universe is evolving, its "energy" is evolving too. The evolution of the universe is the evolution of everything, including energy itself. What we call the evolution of matter is an expression of the evolution of energy as well. The universe may be first and foremost a living energy universe. The big bloom may have begun with a big bang, and the whole thing may be eternal, alive, creative, and evolving. The systemic vision of *and* rather than *or*.

If Robert Krishner and colleagues at Harvard University are correct, the rate of cosmic expansion has been accelerating "recently." These findings hold such significance that *Science* magazine designated them the "scientific breakthrough of the year" for 1998. Must science search for a new "dark" force, or is the answer to be found in applying the systemic memory process to the universe as a whole. If the universe is a gigantic positive feedback loop of incalculable complexity, it may be waving and swinging, creating and evolving its information, energy, and matter into a new ultra-structure beyond anything yet imagined. Could it be, metaphorically, transforming itself into a rainbow-colored butterfly universe of indescribable beauty? If we do not look, we will not see.

There is reason to look at the extensive scientific data available, and ponder the origin and evolution of the overwhelming order apparent in the cosmos as a whole. The scope of this universal living memory vision ends up sounding remarkably spiritual. The evolving Stage E in religion and science is leading toward their reconnection in a way that is revising our vision of everything, both material and spiritual.

What are Some Implications for Spirituality and Religion? (Why we must all revise our old stories.)

If science must evolve, then religion should probably do so as well.

Thoughtful persons have a responsibility to ask: If Moses and the Buddha and Jesus and Mohammed had been born in the year 2000, and they had the accumulated history of scientific knowledge available to them as we do today, would they create the same religious stories as they did in their time? If Pythagoras and Aristotle and Newton and Darwin had been born in the year 2000, and they had the accumulated history of scientific knowledge available to them as we do today, would they create the same science stories as they did in their time?

A safe bet is probably "no" and "no." These luminaries of science and religion would, in all likelihood, come to the vision of an evolving God in an evolving transformational universe. The logic and data speak for themselves.

Can twenty-first-century science and religion learn the same lesson? Our contemporary leaders of both science and religion are ultimately in the same boat. They were raised as children to accept certain stories as dogma, and it hurts them, like it hurts us, to revise these cherished stories. Too often we make the mistake of defining ourselves by our histories, by our past systemic memories, and by the stories we ultimately accepted and the stories we ultimately rejected. We live a storybook life, and often, we are not very reliable storytellers.

Fortunately, we are not the mere history of our stories. *We have the energy and information to create new stories.* We should not be defined merely by what we have learned, but by our potential, including our potential goals and dreams. This seemingly simple point has deep implications for how we think about spirituality.

All religious stories, throughout recorded history, are ultimately stories in various stages of evolution. As Catholic-turned-Episcopalian theologian Matthew Fox describes it, we need to create a "Creation Spirituality," a spirituality that is as creative and evolving as the universe itself, a spirituality that not only keeps up with science, but informs and inspires it as well.

155

We all must learn to be humble about the religious stories we were spoon-fed (and sometimes forced to "swallow") as children. In the same way that humans have to learn to ingest things that make them sick in order to develop health damaging habits such as smoking, drinking, and drugs, many of us have had to learn to "stomach" religious beliefs that made us sick and that ultimately were not in our best interests, individually or collectively.

The fact is, religion as an institution has failed to inspire unconditional love and acceptance. Despite Moses and Jesus in distant times, and the Dalai Lama and Mother Theresa in modern times, we have still not received their collective message of life nor learned the fundamental lesson of love. However, our failure to receive the message of LIFE (Loving Intentions Faithfully Expressed), and learn the lesson of LOVE (Listening, Observing, Valuing, Empowering), is neither their fault nor ours.

Their respective scientific worldviews and implicit world hypotheses, as well as ours, have encouraged most of us to experience nature as being primarily a reflection of Stage M (the reductionistic stage). As we discussed in chapters 3 and 4, the reductionistic scientific model has diluted the implicit spiritual model reflected in Stage I, as modeled historically by Moses, and particularly Stage L, as modeled historically by Buddha and Jesus.

What excites Linda and me about the systemic memory process and the vision of universal living memory is that it inspires humankind to think anew, to look more closely at everything, and to see life and love as a wondrous blessing. As was envisioned 6,000 years ago in the Indian Sutras, Shiva's Heart (the God of Love) was the universe. The universe may be more than bubbling with life and love, it may be the very essence of it, and twenty-first-century systems science may facilitate our knowing it.

If living systems theory in general (Stage L), and the systemic memory process in particular (Stage E), turn out to be true, then there will be scientific justification to posit a creative and caring cosmic process, expressed as an intelligent and loving force in the universe. Everywhere connected, organized and whole, eternal and evolving, it is beyond our most comprehensive and creative conceptualizations.

"May the Force be with you" takes on new, living and loving meaning. Historically this loving process has been called many things, from Jahweh and the Great Spirit, to Universal Chi and God. All are visions of an Omniscient Nurturing Energy, all expressions of the ONE. This is why we claim that unless our systemic memory hypothesis is rejected, there is logical, scientific reason for believing in the existence of a GOD.

This is the big idea that more than justifies the years of study behind this book. But there is more. If the systemic memory process turns out to be true, then there will be scientific justification to posit the idea that personal consciousness continues after death, and that the history of our love relationships can continue to unfold, potentially forever.

According to the systemic memory process, the info-energy systems that comprise our personal histories, both the good and the bad, continue unconditionally, but this does not mean that we must be forced to relive them, over and over. This is because the stories, as info-energy systems, can evolve as new information is uncovered and added to them.

The history of humankind tells us that we are an evolving species who live on an evolving planet that is an integral part of an evolving universe. Remember, a mere hundred years ago, humans still dreamed of flying, and today we take jet flight for granted. The history of science tells us that dreams can be translated into technology that extend our bodies, minds, and spirits accordingly. Who is to say that in the future, we will not be able to speak on the phone with the living info-energy systems of our loved ones who have physically departed? Probably the same people who said that humans will never be able to fly.

Some Implications for Education—
Teaching Children to Think Dynamically and Openly

If systemic memory is true, children should be taught to think systemically from a very early age. There may be critical periods when the human mind and brain may be especially open to learning how to think and feel systemically.

There are many creative ways to teach children systemic thinking and to demonstrate the idea that everything may be eternal, alive, and evolving. Computer animation, with interactive multimedia, can bring all this to life. This empirical-spiritual perception encourages openness and humility, and it discourages dogma and arrogance. For the theory to "walk the talk," it must be open to its own revision and transformation.

Can you imagine a culture of our children's children's children that was actually open-minded, flexible, responsible, and humble? It is not impossible. All humans have the capacity to learn, grow, love, and care. If we are to continue to wish that our children will have better lives than we did, it behooves us to envision the possibility of an evolving and responsible future, and live it before it is too late.

Linda and I have seen firsthand that children, in particular, smile when they think about sharing heart information with the people and pets that they love. One wonders how the lives and visions of children might change if they came to envision their bodies as integrative energy systems extending into space. Would they feel more interconnected, more part of the world and the cosmos? Would they become more sensitive to the feelings of others, and become more responsible in terms of their effect on others and on the environment? Would they become more heart-focused, more heartfelt, more loving? And would they be better able to appreciate the wonder and mystery of nature and the universe?

The history of science suggests that we should not underestimate the power of creative and caring evolution.

Chapter 12

Searching for Invisible Rainbows

From Levels of Life to Energy Theology

> *The future is bound to surprise us,*
> *but we need not be dumbfounded.*
>
> Kenneth Boulding

> *There will be some who will understand.*
>
> The Buddha

When I was a young assistant professor of psychology at Harvard in 1972, I read a paper published in *Science* that forever changed my vision of rainy days and my envisioning of rainbows.

The paper reported that invisible rainbows were actually present in the infrared spectrum. Since our eyes do not register infrared light, we do not normally see infrared rainbows, so we naturally assume they do not exist. However, with the invention of sensitive infrared cameras that convert the infrared spectrum of frequencies of photons we can't see into the narrow spectrum of frequencies of photons we can see, it became possible to discover the existence of invisible rainbows.

Someone had to first ask the question whether there might be an infrared rainbow before someone could purposely point an infrared camera into a rainy sky and look for an invisible rainbow.

The invisible rainbow might have been just an imaginary rainbow, or it could have been a real though seemingly invisible rainbow. The camera confirmed that invisible infrared rainbows were real. The systemic memory process encourages us to look for "invisible rainbows" of memory in all systems at all levels. If the logic of systemic memory is correct, many of these questions will turn out to reflect invisible rainbows of energy and information.

Are you open to the possibility of invisible rainbows? What about an invisible universe teeming with invisible rainbows? As we did in chapter 11, let's consider the possibility that the systemic memory process is real, and that it applies to all systems, at all levels. Some of the most controversial questions of our times are addressed below.

If There Are Levels to Systems, Does This Imply That There Are Levels to Life?

Yes and no.

As you can see below, it is possible to organize the entire universe in terms of "nested" levels of systems, from the micro to the macro. Nested means that one level is inside another level. We have identified eleven levels, but you could create fewer or more.

ELEVEN LEVELS OF SYSTEMIC ORGANIZATION

Level 11	Universe
Level 10	Galaxies
Level 9	Solar System
Level 8	Earth
Level 7	Groups
Level 6	Individuals
Level 5	Organs
Level 4	Cells
Level 3	Molecules
Level 2	Atoms
Level 1	Energy/Information

Every level includes the levels below it. Everything begins with energy and information (Level 1). Atoms (Level 2) contain energy and information (Level 1). Molecules (Level 3) contain atoms (Level 2),which contain energy and information (Level 1). Cells (Level 4) contain molecules (Level 3), which contain atoms (Level 2), which contain energy and information (Level 1). The pattern repeats, over and over, with ever increasing complexity and emergent properties, as one progresses higher and higher.

We can show this graphically as follows:

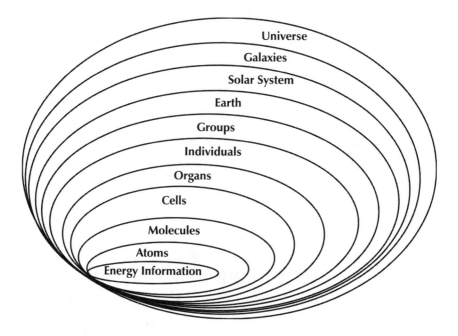

At every level, living systemic memories emerge. Since the higher levels contain all the lower levels, integrative systemic memories at the higher levels "trickle down" to the lower levels. Hence, all the information, to various degrees, is stored everywhere. The logic is straightforward.

161

If memory begins at the very beginning, extending from the micro to the macro, and systems are always dynamic and evolving (Stage E), then everything at every level is "living." Hence, universal living memory. But are they living to the same degrees, at the same levels? This is a big question. Are they conscious to the same degrees, at the same levels? This is also a big question.

As far as we know, humans are more conscious than dogs, dogs are more conscious than butterflies, and butterflies are probably more conscious than photons. We presume that brains are more conscious than individual neurons, that individual neurons are more conscious than the individual microtubules contained within each neuron, and that the individual microtubules are more conscious than the individual water molecules contained in each microtubule.

If the systemic memory process is true, levels of life, and levels of consciousness, will be expressed in more complex ways depending upon the complexity of the system. Though the universal living memory may exist at all levels, the complexity of its expression will change from level to level.

Note that if all memory is ultimately stored "everywhere," the potential for the highest complexity will still be found in the very simplest. Hence, though a simple water molecule obviously cannot "speak," it may have access to every language that was ever spoken.

As we mentioned in chapter 6, you may wish to use the following acronym to help you remember all this:

SYSTEM = SYnchronized (or SYmpathetic) Storing of Time, Energy and Motion

Are Most Water Molecules "Old Souls"?

In a deep sense, yes. Water has been around a long time, and water, like everything else, accumulates history to various degrees. Virgin water can be created in the laboratory, and it will not have the history of water that has been around for millions of years. Virgin water, though pure, may be lacking the "soul" of water that has been around a long time. Does the age of water influence the level of life expressed through it? Maybe. It is worth remembering that physical life, as we know it, requires water.

When We Physically Die, Do Our Living Energy Systems "Dissolve" and "Disappear" into the Vacuum of Space?

The obvious answer appears to be yes, but the systemic memory vision is most definitely no.

Yes, in that our info-energy is always extending into space and "dissolving" into the "vacuum." And when this occurs, it "looks" as if the info-energy has "disappeared." It looks as though our souls have vanished. No, because the obvious observation of "disappearance" does not require the inference that the info-energy has lost its identity, its "soul." Though the soul is extended, it is not extinguished. Dis-solving does not require dis-identifying. It just looks that way, until we look more closely.

Here's a simple way to look more closely: If we take a teaspoon of sugar, and dissolve it in water, it looks as if the sugar has disappeared. The water may taste sweet, but the sugar crystals appear to have vanished, as if by magic. However, the key question is, have the sugar crystals actually lost their identity? Are they really gone? According to systemic memory theory, the answer is clearly no. The sugar crystals not only still exist, but they have evolved to include info-energy about water!

Can we prove this? Easily. All we have to do is allow the water to evaporate. As the water "disappears," what do we see? The sugar crystals "reappear," again as if by magic. This experiment is completely replicable; the implications are both reassuring and revealing. The sugar crystals that reappear tell us that the sugar was never lost, the sugar was simply extended in the water temporarily. The sugar's integrity was never challenged. Systemic memory further suggests that the reemerging sugar crystals include the history of having been extended (dissolved) in the water. Also, the water that has evaporated includes the history of having shared space and time, and hence energy and information, with the sugar.

Wouldn't it be wonderful if our loved ones, as expressed in their living info-energy systems, maintained their integrity and identity as they extended into space and became an integral part of the fabric of eternal life? Like the light of distant stars, their "dissolving" souls were still unique and whole, entangled with us dynamically and eternally? This is a sweet vision indeed.

What About Claims of People Seeing "Ghosts"?
(Living energy systems in all things, the potential of "PIP," and the creation of energy zoology)

If the systemic memory process (the heart and soul of systems) exists, then "ghosts" of everything potentially exist. Theoretically, if all material systems contain info-energy systems, then everything has the potential to be a "ghost." But most ghosts are invisible.

This applies even to gravity. Paul Pearsall suggested that "When it comes to believing in ghosts, gravity is right at the top of the list." The truth is, gravity is an invisible, all-pervasive universal attractive force that scientists infer holds the universe together. The gravity hypothesis is used by physics to explain what makes the universe become and remain as one integrative system. It follows that if the universe functions as a system, then it can have systemic memories too.

It is important to understand that we do not actually "measure" gravity; we infer it. What we actually do is measure objects falling, or we observe needles on scales move when objects are placed on them, and then we infer an invisible force. The inference (the story) is not the observation. The map is not the territory. No one has ever seen the ghost of gravity. And no one has seen the ghost of living energy systems, at least not scientifically yet.

However, the technology for envisioning living energy system entities and revealing "ghosts" may be within our grasp. If Harry Oldfield is correct, his PIP system (which stands for "polycontrast interference photography") has revealed living energy systems affectionately titled "Snoopy—the crystal entity life-form," and "Angelos," a so-called "collector of souls" who may help "guide" the recently departed to "another place."

If the extraordinary claims in Jane and Grant Solomon's book, *Harry Oldfield's Invisible Universe*, are confirmed in future research, the PIP procedure may reflect a quantum leap in the evolution of human sight, from telescopes and microscopes to living energy systems scopes.

Systemic memory suggests that we keep our eyes open for such extraordinary possibilities. If living energy systems exist, we will ultimately need to catalogue them as living energy "species" as we have catalogued living biological species. Will we see the birth of Energy Zoology in the twenty-first century?

As Pearsall explained to us, the first definition of "ghost" in *Webster's New Third International Dictionary* is "the life principle or vital spark" and "the spirit of man." Ancient Hawaiian *kahuna* (ka means "to keep" and huna means "secret") taught that everything and everyone is a representation of *manna* (eternal energy). The universal living memory process can be thought of as a Western theory for the most ancient Polynesian wisdom: everything is and will always be, invisible evolving *manna* with information.

No wonder the Hawaiians (and most ancient cultures) believed in invisible ghosts that sometimes became visible. They intuitively understood the ghostly implications of living energy systems theory and the systemic memory process.

If the Universe Is a Living Energy System, Why Does It Create Living Material Systems?

This is a deep question. If the logic of living energy systems theory is correct, the creation of ever more complex physical systems includes the evolution of ever more complex energy systems. The $E=mc^R$ process literally takes place inside physical systems. What we experience as "physicality," so to speak, may be the "scaffolds" that help build ever new and more beautiful living energy systems. Only when the scaffolds are removed can we witness the full beauty of the buildings.

The purpose of physical systems may be to shape the evolution of living energy systems. From this perspective, the purpose of matter may be to evolve information and energy, the soul and spirit of the universe.

Speaking of Soul and Spirit, What About "Reincarnation"?

If the systemic memory process is true, then what has been called "reincarnation" is not only plausible, its potential is required.

However, a deeper question arises: How do we know if what we experience as "our" past life is actually "a" past life that we have retrieved from the larger pool of systemic memories that we can resonate with? How do we know if "a" memory is "our" memory? Being open to the universal living memory process, we can imagine that we have the potential to experience many "past" lives, which may or may not be "our" past lives.

Some individuals, as documented by Dr. Ian Stevenson and his colleagues at the University of Virginia, show biological evidence (for example, scars) that seem to corroborate the past lives they report remembering. However, even these special cases do not prove that "they" lived before; only that they are deeply connected to people who have lived before. We may all connect, to various degrees, with a family of souls that go back hundreds or thousands of years or more. We may have a spiritual family history, an expression of spiritual DNA.

The systemic memory process requires that we entertain such questions. However, the systemic memory process also requires that we entertain the possibility that "we" have not necessarily lived before—that these are not "our" past lives, but the past lives of people with whom we resonate. Can science address this challenging question? Linda and I would not be surprised if the answer turns out to be yes.

What About "Karma"? (The natural law of circulation)

Another controversial question. Karma is an ancient word that speaks to the idea that one's past history, including one's presumed past lives, affects the present. One cannot, so to speak, escape one's past history.

The systemic memory process is very clear. What goes around comes around.

Circulation is circulation. And it creates memories. Karma is a simple integrative systems theory (Stage I), recognized implicitly thousands of years ago. When we added living systems theory (Stage L) and evolving systems theory (Stage E), then karma becomes an eternal, living, and evolving process itself.

Karma makes me smile because it suggests that the universe is designed with responsibility and justice. If we knew in our heart of hearts that everything was eternal, alive, and evolving, we might live our lives on earth with more love, appreciation, and responsibility. We might feel more connected to the past and the future, and see that the possibilities far exceed our imagination.

It would be comforting indeed to believe that the universe had a flexible wisdom that encouraged us to continually grow and evolve. The concept of universal living memory, derived from the logic of systems theory, encourages this kind of thinking.

Are There Two Kinds of Destiny, Original Source and Systemic Memory?

Probably. As we described in chapter 10, Stage I alone requires that we entertain the idea that some ultimate design, a GOD (Grand Organizing Design) seems to be required to make sense of the order of the universe.

However, the systemic memory process adds a second kind of destiny, the kind that evolves with time. As history unfolds, the history remains, so the past can influence the present. The systemic memory process is one way that the past can live in the present. Similar models have been voiced from time to time throughout recorded history. What people call karma, described above, is this second kind of destiny.

Can We Communicate with Jesus? And How Does This Relate to Jung's Notion of Archetypes?

According to the systemic memory process, it is possible that people can communicate with Jesus, especially if his living info-energy system wishes to communicate with us.

But can we be sure we are speaking with the "original" Jesus? If millions of people create stories about a version of Jesus who never lived, this "story" can become a "living story"—a living idea that can have a life of its own. The concept of a shared story, existing as an identity template or archetype, is the foundation of one of Carl Jung's deepest insights. You may wonder, how could we tell if we were communicating with the original Jesus or a Jesus created by the minds of women and men? Unfortunately, there is no simple answer here.

Let us consider a more personal example. Imagine that someone disguised his voice as Henry's, and called Linda on the phone tomorrow claiming to be her deceased father? How could she tell if this was her original father or an imposter? Now, imagine that a medium in trance spoke in a voice that sounded like Henry's? How could Linda tell if this was her original father or an imposter? Finally, imagine that Linda heard a voice in her head, and it sounded just like Henry's? How could Linda tell if this voice was her father's or an imposter's (let alone a creation of her own imagination or memory)?

Linda would say that science needs to create a "TEFA"—a device that performs a "Total Energy Frequency Analysis" of the voice and its systemic memory history. We should remember that the science fiction envisioned today is the scientific technology created tomorrow. This is a deep challenge for the future.

Does the Same Logic Apply to Claims of Alien Abduction?

Yes. It is difficult to know what are "our" memories, what are "shared" memories, and what are "created" memories. However, it is possible that people are literally connecting with the living memories of intelligent beings from other parts of the cosmos. The truth is, the systemic memory hypothesis opens our minds to the plausibility of connecting with living energy systems from here and there and everywhere.

What About Memory for Evil?
(The power and responsibility of intention and choice)

If the systemic memories of the original Jesus, as well as the alternative Jesus created by the human mind, continue to live as evolving info-energy systems, then the systemic memories of the original Hitler, as well as the alternative Hitlers created by the human mind (for example, invented by certain hate groups), potentially continue to live as well.

As far as we know, starlight continues regardless of the "personalities" of the individual stars in the sky. Hence, the potential for us to resonate with the most horrific aspects of the past exists side by side with our potential to resonate with the holiest aspects of history. Memory is memory. It is therefore our choice, and responsibility, to foster in consciousness, the most loving and caring info-energy systems of our collective histories.

Linda often reminds me that it is hypothesized by many spiritual/energy healers that people who live their lives with love generate a higher frequency of energy/vibration than people who live their lives with hate. Future research can determine if loving energy is in fact a more coherent, powerful, and higher frequency vibration.

The interesting prediction that unfolds from the loving energy hypothesis, when reinterpreted in terms of living energy systems theory, is the idea that loving energy systems may live on in a higher frequency spectrum (shorter wavelength) of the living energy universe. And higher frequencies can be "stepped down" to interact with lower frequencies (longer wavelength). What some people have described as higher "dimensions" of consciousness may reflect higher spectrums of existence and experience.

The human species has the potential to determine which spectrum of the living energy universe it wishes to resonate with. Stated somewhat more poetically, each of us can make the conscious choice concerning which colors of the visible and invisible rainbow universe we wish to experience and evolve. As a theory, the systemic memory process addresses the total frequency of the living energy universe, both the visible and the invisible. As a species, we have the potential to recognize any or all of it. The choice is ours.

Does It "Take One to Know One"? (The heart of recognition)

The reason why tuning fork B can resonate with tuning fork A is because A and B share a similar history of structure and design. It is

169

hard to retrieve information if you cannot recognize it. Recognize means re-cognize, that is, to cognize again. The systemic memory process, on a grand scale, provides the information freely. Hence, to the extent that one is open to the information, more information can be retrieved. At least that is the inference.

Does this mean that we could, conceivably, understand a language we had never learned? That we could not only re-cognize true versus fictional languages, but even grasp their meanings? It should be possible, in principle, to do such things to various degrees. What mathematicians call "wavelets" (little wave patterns, what might be called "wave alphabets") may be a key to unlocking this mystery.

How Do We Get Rid of Old Memories?

We sweat, we excrete. We even replace all of our cells. Why do we do this? Just to get rid of the "material" toxins? Or, do we release all this material because it all contains systemic memories, and we need to get some space from all this information and energy in order to remain fresh and open to new information and energy? Are chronic diseases expressions of clogged systemic memories? Does healing require flexible, open systems? Is "old" age a side effect of being unable to release excessive information and energy that bogs us down?

It is claimed that it is healthy to drink many glasses of water each day. Have people who live to be a hundred or more, learned how to engage in a larger process of sharing and releasing information and energy?

Can Energy and Information Be "Intelligent"?
(The emergence of energy theology)

As energy and information become info-energy systems, they can function just like you and me. Can I find my way to the university? Of course. If I send my "thoughts" to the university, can "they" find their way too? Why not? If the dynamical energy systems theory is true, the process is the same.

The ancient Chinese believed in the concept of *Qi*—an intelligent force that enlivened the whole universe. What most people do not like to think about is that this imagined energy is indeed presumed to be intelligent—it may be smarter than we think or have even imagined. When Linda and I wrote our "energy cardiology" paper, we defined living systems, paraphrasing Miller, as being "dynamic organizations of intelligent information expressed in energy and matter." We spent days coming to the final wording of this definition.

What Linda and I term "living energy" is "intelligent information expressed in energy." Intelligent information? Intelligent energy? From a dynamical evolving systems perspective, of course. Does this suggest a new scientific vision for theology, an evolving "energy theology"? From a dynamical evolving systems perspective, yes.

Can Intelligent Information Look to the Future and Back? (Time as the first dimension, revising "spacetime" to "timespace")

Some contemporary physicists, as well as some ancient mystics, believe that memory for everything, including the "future," exists in the "now" and can, through a feedback-like process, influence the present. Not only is the past present, but the future is present too. Can the systemic memory process be applied to these truly extraordinary ideas? Of course. Should we consider them? Only if we wish to be complete.

One way to reenvision this is to reconsider Einstein's notion of spacetime. Maybe Einstein had it backwards. Maybe it is actually "timespace."

When I was a professor at Yale, the thought came to me that in order to have three dimensions of space, or even just one dimension of space, one needed to have "time" first. If space did not continue to exist over time, there would be no space. Space exists in time, over time.

If time is the first dimension, before space—not the fourth dimension, after space—then potential futures can exist along the time dimension. These implicate orders would simultaneously exist along a sequential dimension, waiting to be potentially manifested in space. Extending John Wheeler's quote at the beginning of this book, maybe God invented time not only so that everything that

171

was possible wouldn't happen all at once, but also so that everything that was possible could potentially exist in the first place.

What About Spirit-Assisted Medicine?
Spirit-Assisted Movement? Spirit-Assisted Mind?

What we affectionately term the SAM hypothesis (Spirit-Assisted Medicine/Movement/Mind) becomes a required possibility. If everything is eternal, alive, and evolving, then the living and evolving history of the past can help us in the present to go into the future. Spiritual healers have claimed this for thousands of years. Modern spiritual healers, as portrayed in Diane Goldner's book *Infinite Grace*, almost take this for granted. Are there really doctors in the afterlife? Teachers on the other side?

These are beautiful thoughts, wonderful wishes, and they cannot help but make us smile. Once you understand the logic of the systemic memory process, these kinds of questions become scientifically plausible. How we deal with these profound possibilities is up to us, and ultimately it will define us as a self-evolving or self-destructing species.

How Do We Connect with SAM? The Answer May Be DNA

If universal living memory is ultimately everywhere, spanning out into the vacuum of space, then the possibility exists for everything to potentially register everything.

A metaphor most of us can grasp is the modern development of cell phones. As I write these words at my computer, I can imagine receiving a call on my cell phone. It is sitting next to my desk. Phone calls from hundreds of thousands, if not millions of people, are streaming down from satellites, going here and there and everywhere, including to my desk. But I do not hear any of them. However, my phone is tuned so that it can register a certain pattern, start ringing, and initiate communication. It serves as an antenna, tuner, and amplifier.

If the Grand Organizing Designer is everywhere, spreading his or her Supreme Agape Memory everywhere (another meaning for

SAM, where "agape" refers to a selfless, giving love), making it possible for us to have a Spirit-Assisted Mind (if not a Source-Assisted Mind), then how can we tune into all this information? We need a Dynamic Noetic Antenna (if not a Divine Noetic Antenna).

Linda has suggested that this may be DNA. Each and every cell, from the single celled organism to the sixty-plus trillion cellular organism called homo sapiens, has a brilliant molecular structure in the nucleus that has the code for its very existence. The sixty-four trillion dollar question is, how does this code work? Does it "have" the information, or does it "tune in" to the information? Linda suggests the latter, and she may be right. Linda further suggests that the meridian and acupoints system of acupuncture may reflect a complex energy antenna system that "tunes in" to information as well. In terms of the jargon of acupuncture, this connection is known as "celestial stems and branches," denoting subtle energy connections between meridians and the cosmos.

As homo sapiens conceptually evolve into homo spiritus, deoxyribonucleic acid may conceptually evolve into the divine noetic antenna. SAM may only be a DNA away.

Is the Universe Intentional? Is God Evolving?
Does This Hypothesis Make You Smile?

This depends on whether you are open to SMILE.

If our four stage analysis has some basis in fact, and if Stage E is genuine, then we must reentertain the idea that the universe is an expression of an intentional, ultimately loving energetic process, and that GOD, or the ONE, or the Source, or SAM are potentially not only the basis of it all, but part of the evolution of it all as well. If the all includes the "All," and the all is the Supreme Agape Memory, then the "All" is evolving too. What we call the divine is actually a remembering Divine.

Hence, not only is the big plan potentially evolving, but the Grand Planner may be evolving as well. As Henry was fond of saying to Linda, God may be "the great experimenter," the supreme discoverer. And humankind may be playing a role in helping God revise and evolve the plans.

There is an old saw in science called Ockham's Razor—which says, if the simpler hypothesis works, use it. It is sometimes called KISS—Keep it Simple, Sweetheart. Well, if we wish to KISS and to SMILE, the simplest hypothesis to entertain is the universal living memory hypothesis.

- It incorporates and integrates a host of observations that fall outside the current paradigm.
- It makes new predictions that can be confirmed or disconfirmed in future research.
- It helps us understand our place in the universe, as well as our potential.

The systemic memory process is a big idea because it extends a big idea—systems thinking. The idea of a system is one of the biggest ideas that has ever come to the human mind. Linda and I sit on the shoulders of the gentle (and not so gentle) giants who have envisioned these possibilities, and from this new height, we look out with children's minds.

We would love to believe that the vibrant ideas of these giant guardians live on inside us, and that our minds are serving as gardens for them, helping them to bloom. That "t-here" really includes "here." That "over t-here" is really "in here." That systemically, we are ultimately all One—not only physically, but info-energy spiritually as well.

However, Linda's and my wish that the universe is designed for living energy systems and eternal living memories ultimately doesn't matter here. Similarly, our hope that the ONE is actually an expression of Ominiscent Nurturing Energy is ultimately immaterial (no pun intended). What matters, plain and simple, is whether the concept of a universal living memory process reflects a truth in nature, a map that accurately helps science and humankind navigate and appreciate the evolving territory.

As scientists, our goal is not to create imaginary stories about nature but to learn how to listen to nature's unfolding story. Much work needs to be done. Someday we will know. It's just a matter of time. Meanwhile, we can remember invisible infrared rainbows, and Harry Oldfield's invisible PIP universe, and continue to dream.

Chapter 13

Eternal Memories and Eternal Love

A Reason to Hope and a Reason to Dream

The love of learning rules the world.
Phi Kappa Phi plaque,
University of Arizona

Our separation from each other is an optical illusion of consciousness.
Albert Einstein

We believe that what twenty-first-century science is searching for is a rational excuse to believe in and to experience life and the universe as Wonderful, Entertaining, Inspirational, Revisable, and Designed—a revised vision of WEIRD.

Can science quench our thirst for finding meaning and purpose in life, and even help point the way? If the logic of the systemic memory process is true, and science discovers that universal living memory operates in all systems at all levels to various degrees, then life is more wonderful, entertaining, inspirational, revisable, and designed than any of us can yet imagine.

Science and society are approaching a fork in the road. The choice between the "dead" vision and the "living" vision, the non-systemic and the systemic vision, is not just one more fork in the road. It is the definitive fork. If we choose the correct hypothesis, systems science may enable humans to rediscover a living divinity,

175

and in the process enable us to honor the gift of gifts—our capacity to know and empower love, everywhere and in everything.

The inspiration that led to the discovery of the universal living memory process arose because of a love of learning that was fostered by my parents, and their parents.

Howard and Shirley Schwartz encouraged me to ask not only "what" questions, but "why" questions as well. Their philosophy was that any question, properly framed, could be asked in such a way that it could be discussible, and ultimately researchable. This passion for possibility, this love of questions, was a gift that they gave naturally. The love of learning was in their blood, and they passed this love on to me.

Over the years I have tried to share the love of learning they gave me with my students at Harvard, Yale, and the University of Arizona. Mark Rosekind, one of my Ph.D. students at Yale University once called it an "overdeveloped sense of wonder." It was the love of knowing, the openness to ask "what" and "why" that ultimately led to my stumbling upon the logic of systemic memory at Yale, and to share it briefly then with my students in the seminar.

However, my fears about the hypothesis and its implications led me to suppress the theory. Had it not been for Linda and her quest to know whether her father was still alive, the systemic memory process would have stayed relatively buried in the back of my mind. The hypothesis would never have resurfaced and evolved into what it has become today.

Linda was also raised in a home that fostered a love of learning. Her parents encouraged her not only to ask "what" and "why," but to ask "why not" as well.

Her "why not" questions have taken the hypothesis far beyond its original, more limited vision, and transformed it from being a caterpillar concept hiding in a coccoon to a butterfly theory exploring the universe.

The logic of the systemic memory process leads inexorably to ideas about eternal life and evolution that have the power to expand our vision so we may, as Marcel Proust said, "see with new eyes." As I look back on this journey, the path has continually been about love. The systemic memory process gives us a reason to believe that everything is eternal, alive, and evolving, and therefore our love will remain eternal, alive, and evolving. That universal living memory = life eternal.

This is, of course, a wonderful thought, as well as entertaining, inspiring, revisable, and designed. The systemic memory process provides a framework that takes general systems theory (Stage I) and living systems theory (Stage L) and enlivens and evolves them even further (Stage E).

However, does living systems theory address the origin of love itself, or the origin of organized "systems" themselves? Does the systemic memory process explain the infinite origin of order, and the love that engenders this order? Clearly no. Though universal living memory is a huge story, it is not the whole story. We need additional concepts, and we must be open to imagine other possibilities.

Waves Waving and Enformy

Two of our current favorite possibilities reflect the seminal ideas of two senior physicians who also embody a love of learning. Interestingly, both of their theories bridge science and spirituality.

The first theory is Dr. Irving Dardik's hypothesis of "waves waving." Dardik is a former Olympic Team M.D. consultant who developed cardiac exercises and an entire health program based on cardiac rhythms in dynamic relationship with biological and global rhythms. His vision is that the universe is one unified rhythm or wave, and that everything that we witness in nature, from the micro to the macro, is an expression of waves upon waves upon waves. The idea of a wave, of course, precedes the idea of a system. The very first "wave" is the first:

- up and down
- in and out
- yin and yang
- forward and backward
- give and receive

The first wave is not only the universal glue that holds everything together but it is the original attractive force. It is the abstract idea of energy. It is also the abstract idea of love as the attractive force. Giving and receiving, the heart of love, can be viewed as a pulsation which is a universal wave that beats throughout the cosmos.

Dardik's vision goes from the general to the specific, and he applies his model to cycles of health and healing. If waves reflect the universal energy of attraction, the force that enables all things to evolve and express themselves, then waves become a scientific expression of love.

Dardik's vision is an eternal vision. When we add the systemic memory process to Dardik's vision, the combined vision becomes that much more powerful because it becomes alive and evolving. We can envision the concept of "wave systems" (which is another way of saying "energy systems"), and conceive of living systemic memories in the dynamics of waves waving.

But where did the very first wave come from? Who or what established the capacity to create waves, and wave systems, from which everything else unfolds? Are waves and systems a reflection of an implicit generic loving and creating process in the universe? A Grand Organizing Designer? An Omniscient Nurturing Energy?

We must reach back, even further, and this takes us to Dr. Donald Watson's work. Watson is a brilliant neuroscientist and psychiatrist, now retired, who has worked on the problem of the origin of order for most of his professional life. Watson has taken possibly the greatest of conceptual leaps by positing the existence of a creative ordering process he terms "enformy." The term enformy combines "energy" and "form." However, as Watson continually reminds us, enformy, which creates "enformation," precedes the creation of time and space, and therefore precedes the creation of information, energy, and waves. Enformy is posited to actually create the dimensions of time and space, then information and energy, and finally wave systems.

Enformy reflects the tendency to order—to create, organize, evolve. It is the organizing intention that precedes everything. It reflects the "plans," and planning capability, that precedes actual expression in information and energy.

Watson, Schwartz and Russek, in a highly technical paper, call these "quanta" of enformation, "enformed systems." Now if you were saying to yourself, "This sounds a lot like GOD," you would be

right. Watson's vision incorporates all levels of the tendency to organize, from the physical to the theological. His vision provides a
framework for envisioning the origin of the loving impulse as a fundamental property of everything. Theoretically, enformy creates
enformed systems that transcend time and space; enformed systems
create living energy systems that evolve in time and space, and living energy systems create material systems that we experience as the
emerging physical world. It follows that with physical "death," the
emergent info-energy continues to evolve not only as a nonmaterial
living energy system within time and space, but also as an enformed
system that transcends time and space.

Waves waving and enformed systems are two visionary ideas.
When the systemic memory process is added, the theoretical trinity
is awesome.

A Reason to Hope and a Reason to Dream

You may be wondering, why do we choose to end this visionary
book with visions that go beyond it? The reason is partly for conceptual integrity, and partly for conceptual inspiration.

As we have said, as big as the universal living memory story is, it
is not the whole story. The future challenge will be to integrate the
concepts like enformed systems and waves waving with the concept
of universal living memory. Though the expanded picture will be
undoubtedly more complicated, it will also be more complete.

However, there is a deeper, more spiritual reason for ending this
book with visions of enformed systems and waves waving in the context of universal living memory and the living energy universe. This
book is about the challenge, as James Taylor wrote it, to "look up
from our lives," and see life with new eyes.

If the universe turns out to be as wonderful, entertaining, inspirational, revisable, and designed as most of us hope it is, it will be because at its core—its inception—is the incentive to love. As we
learn about the systemic memory process, enformed systems, and
waves waving, we can look up from our lives, and in the process
reenvision the highest goal—the evolution of LOVE (listening, observing, valuing, empowering).

Someday we may learn, as Linda put it, that in the beginning, and before the beginning, there was love. This has been the vision of the greatest mystics throughout recorded history. If universal living memory is true, their histories live on eternally and energetically. By merging our intuitions and reason we may be able to resonate with them, and grow accordingly. Our discovery in the thirty-five and forty-two-year follow-up research to the Harvard Mastery of Stress study that perceptions of parental love and caring in college are powerful predictors of long term physical and emotional health in mid-life, takes on new meaning when viewed in terms of living energy systems theory.

By understanding eternal memories and the evolving universe, we may be able to move toward envisioning eternal relationships and the loving universe. The living energy universe becomes the loving energy universe.

Enformed systems, waves waving, and universal living memory—evolving concepts in contemporary science—provide Linda and all of us with a reason to hope, and therefore a reason to dream. We are finally ready to return to Linda's original question, "Is my father, Henry, still alive?"

Chapter 14

Is My Father Still Alive?

Resurrecting the Reputation of God

When dreams of youth shattered by schemes of men
ignite the aging heart to dream again
alas, 'tis worth the toil and strain, my friend
if but to glimpse the fleeting rainbow at the shower's end.
Dr. Henry I. Russek

How could God have allowed him to die like this?
Stardust Johnson

Henry, Linda's father, loved rainbows. They were a source of hope and dreams for him and his family. Henry also loved the raising of questions and the process of searching for answers. The deep and sacred significance of the systemic memory process was raised by Linda's question about her father's death, and answered by Mrs. Johnson's question about her husband's death.

Mrs. Johnson, known to her friends as "Dusty," was a guest lecturer in professor Robert Wrenn's inspiring course, The Psychology of Death and Loss. Bob Wrenn has been teaching one of the most popular and oversubscribed courses at the University of Arizona for more than twenty years. I was there because Patti Harada, then an honors student at the University of Arizona, said, "Gary, I believe that it would help Linda and you conduct research on the possibility of survival of consciousness after death if you audited Dr. Wrenn's course." Dusty was there because she was sharing with the class her painful experiences of death and loss following the recent murder of her husband, Roy D. Johnson, a renowned and cherished professor of music and an organist at the University of Arizona.

After Dusty shared some of her heartfelt story with the class, I raised my hand and asked her, "Do you believe in the possibility of survival of consciousness after death?"

She said, "I would like to."

I then asked, "Have you received any communication from your husband since he died?"

Dusty recounted some remarkable "coincidences" both during the time that Roy was being murdered, and afterwards, while she and her friend were searching for him when he had not returned home. For example, she experienced hearing his voice in her head telling her, clearly and convincingly, that he was dying.

After class, I shared with Dusty that Linda and I were conducting research on the possibility of survival of consciousness after death, and if she would like to meet with me, I would be happy to tell her about the research. Dusty called my office that very afternoon, with an urgency in her voice that led me to reschedule one of my appointments the next day to make time to see her. My meeting with her changed my life, forever.

Dusty is not only a *religious* person, she is *spiritual* as well. However, when her husband was taken from her, totally unexpectedly, and seemingly for so little purpose, her faith in a loving God was shaken to its core. She became profoundly angry at a God that could allow such horrors to happen to such loving people.

We talked about the idea that the price humans pay for the gift of freedom is that freedom can be abused, sometimes horrendously. However, this was not what was really hurting Dusty in her soul.

Dusty was afraid to think about whether her husband might still be with her or not, because if he was not, and death was merely "dust to dust, ashes to ashes," then her feelings toward God would go beyond anger. The kind of God that could allow people to love and be loved deeply, and then not only have this love tragically taken away, but have it be taken forever, was too cruel to be imagined.

I wondered, what kind of God would allow the light of stars to continue to exist forever, and not allow the same for deeply loving souls? I experienced her spiritual and existential crisis, and I felt it in my core.

I then asked Dusty, "Would it matter to you if science had a good reason to believe that survival of consciousness after death was possible, and that science could actually prove that this hypothesis was valid?"

Dusty replied, "If science could do this, it would give me a reason to hope, and to live."

I proceeded to tell her about Linda's question, my Vancouver experience of Light Remembering, the evolution of the systemic memory hypothesis, and our current research on after-death communications and the survival of consciousness after death.

Dusty left my office with a new dream and a smile on her face.

The following day, I shared with Linda the lessons I had learned through Dusty's experience. This was the day that the words came from my lips, "If the systemic memory hypothesis is true, science may resurrect and revise the reputation of God."

The Lindas and Dustys of the world can envision a Grand Organizing Designer who is also a Giving Open Designer, one who not only gives the gift of love, but gives it forever.

Just as the energy and information of distant star systems travel in space forever, if the universal living memory process is true, our personal info-energy systems—literally composed of photons of visible and invisible "light"—have the potential to travel, to journey and explore, and to evolve. This is the vision of *The Living Energy Universe*. If this vision is true, then the kind of loving intelligence that created such a process has given all of us both freedom and eternity. This is the kind of God that can make all of us smile.

So I think about Linda's question, and its healing effect on Dusty, and I say in my heart, "Thank you, Henry" to my late father-in-law, a man I never met.

You see, if the universal living memory process turns out to be true, scientific integrity requires that we entertain the hypothesis that not only is Henry's consciousness alive and evolving, but that he may even be part of the process of writing this book.

AFTERWORD

What's Wrong with the Hypothesis?
Points/Counterpoints/Circles

We must bear in mind that the scientific or science-producing value of the efforts made to answer these old standing questions is not to be measured by the prospect of ultimately obtaining a solution, but by their effect in stimulating men [and women] to a thorough investigation of nature.

James Clerk Maxwell

The logic passes muster.

Lynn Nadel

I think your theory is quite amusing.

Heinz Pagels

We have written the afterword for those of you who have serious concerns about the hypothesis of universal living memory in all dynamical systems, and would like a reasonable list of possible arguments to question the hypothesis, if not dismiss it all together. Since Linda and I are scientists, we have an ethical responsibility to entertain all hypotheses, both pro and con, and consider them seriously.

The process itself can be entertaining. As the great scientist Richard Feynman said of his own discipline, "Physics is play." So let us play with the points and counterpoints, and see if we come full circle. Obviously, we would not have written this book if we didn't think that the systemic memory process not only deserved serious consideration but had a serious chance of being true. Though the hypothesis may be "amusing," we have come to the firm conclusion that the hypothesis is definitely worth thinking about.

As you examine the detailed logic expressed in these pages, we hope you will remember Henry Russek and Roy Johnson. The reason to resist dismissing the systemic memory theory without first studying the arguments is not only for the sake of scientific integrity, it is also for the memories of your loved ones as well.

A Prelude to Controversy—Why Did the Skeptics Scoff?

On July 4, 1997, the *Tucson Citizen* published a feature article titled "Hypothesis: Objects Have Memory," with the subheading, "2 at UA say cells and even jewelry may be able to remember. Skeptics scoff."

On the positive side, the article cited Roger Edwards from Harvard University, who was then a senior member of the editorial board of the peer-reviewed journal *Alternative Therapies in Health and Medicine* that published one of our articles on the systemic memory hypothesis. He was quoted as saying the Schwartz and Russek hypothesis "is quite plausible in the sense that it helps explain some phenomena that we cannot explain now . . . They took a lot of information that was out there and said, 'Let's take it one step forward on the theory side.'"

On the negative side, they cited Larry Squire, from the University of California at San Diego, a distinguished neuroscientist who studies the neurobiology of memory.

According to the *Tucson Citizen*, Squire compared the hypothesis to a flying saucer report. "There's no way it could be right," he said. "It's preposterous." The *Citizen* went on to say that Squire was so disgusted that anyone was writing a story on the theory that he declined to be interviewed further. "The scientific paper doesn't bother me," Squire said. "It bothers me that you're interested in it."

How can two intelligent scientists have such diversely different opinions about the hypothesis? It is important to realize that whereas Edwards had read and studied the paper, Squires never read the paper. Squires was apparently content to make a definitive judgment without reading the published scientific papers and carefully examining the logic for himself.

It is worth remembering that in Copernicus's time, there were those who refused to look through the telescope and simply dismissed Copernicus and his ideas. Apparently, this unfortunate lesson in the history of science has yet to be fully appreciated.

The *Tucson Citizen* also interviewed Lynn Nadel, professor and head of the University of Arizona's department of psychology; Nadel is considered to be a distinguished neuroscientist who studies the neurobiology of memory. Nadel was quoted as saying, "I think what you'll get from most people is that this is flaky nonsense."

However, as reported in the article, Nadel went on to say that he had read the article and that "the logic passes muster."

"The logic seems sound, and therefore it's worth exploring," Nadel said. "The scientific method needs to be done on these types of issues. . . . The mere fact that to our minds it sounds implausible, doesn't mean it's wrong."

If ever there was a hypothesis that justifies close scrutiny by scientists in all fields of study and fully deserves the label "controversial," it is the systemic memory hypothesis. This book has highlighted only a sample of possible implications of the hypothesis, and we anticipate that some of you will have envisioned implications that have not occurred to us.

What kinds of arguments can be used to "scoff" at the hypothesis and conclude that it is "preposterous"? Here is a partial list of nine major categories of critique, accompanied by our responses:

Category 1—The hypothesis is preposterous. It can't possibly be true.

The same critique was applied to the idea that the earth is round, that the earth revolves around the sun, that germs cause disease, that electrons can be waves at one time and particles at other times. These are just a sample of ideas that were once thought to be preposterous. Nadel put it quite well when he said, "The mere fact that to our minds it sounds implausible doesn't mean it's wrong."

The history of science, over and over, has re-humbled the human mind. If there is one single lesson to learn here, it is for us to be humble and remain open.

Category 2—The hypothesis is too abstract, vague, general, and metaphorical to be taken seriously, and it cannot be disproven.

Yes, the hypothesis is decidedly abstract. Moreover, the hypothesis is currently "vague" in the sense that we have not laid out all the complex mathematics that unfold when the logic is modeled mathematically. A's and B's are abstract symbols, and complex interactions that emerge over time need to be expressed mathematically. This task is for the mathematically inclined.

The hypothesis is most definitely general. The logic is unconditional. A and B can be anything. However, we must remember that the ideas of system, feedback, and interaction are also general, and hence universal. So too are the ideas of energy and information. What Linda and I have done is added one more potentially universal idea to a growing list of universal ideas that are taken seriously, and generally accepted, in contemporary science.

Since it is easy for people to lose the forest for the trees, we have attempted to focus on the forest in this book, and give you a vision of the big picture first.

Ultimately, it is possible that the hypothesized systemic memory process of today will evolve into the established systemic memory principle of the twenty-first century.

We have sometimes used metaphors to express the ideas of the theory. For example, our playful rendition of $E=mc^R$ (evolution equals memory times circulation that is recurrent/repeating) is not meant to express a strict numerical calculation but rather a deep conceptualization in the form of a mathematical metaphor. Our metaphors are used in the spirit that other well known metaphors such as the "big bang" or the "big bloom" are used in science. The reader should understand that our purpose in using metaphors from time to time is not to dilute the hypothesis but to rather enliven your vision of the hypothesis. The metaphor is not the hypothesis.

As for potentially disproving the hypothesis, this is actually quite easy to do in principle. In order to disprove the prediction that the theory is universal, science need only find *one exception* to the general rule. To disprove the prediction that gravity is universal, for example, science need only find one mass that does not have gravity. Similarly, if science proves in the future that there is a class of positive feedback loops that do not accumulate information over time—they do not dynamically grow over time as predicted by feedback theory—the universal claim can be discarded.

If science proves in the future that the dynamic behavior of positive feedback loops do not actually involve the storage of information and energy as predicted by the logic of the systemic memory process, then the entire systemic memory claim must be discarded as well.

In our role as scientists, we keep searching and researching for negative evidence that can disprove the theory of positive feedback, recurrent resonance, and the explanation of systemic memory. Try as we might, thus far we have found none.

Because systemic memory makes specific predictions, it is decidedly researchable. It is not like current string theory, which Alan Lightman, an MIT professor writing in the July-August 1999 issue of the *Harvard Magazine*, likened to "a hundred-dollar bill in a laundromat." One wonders what would happen if a few great minds knowledgeable in string theory spent some time pondering predictions from systemic memory. Would a "systemic string theory" become researchable too?

Category 3—The hypothesis seems inconsistent with certain current theories and observations.

This is true. It is an inherent consequence of the hypothesis that cannot be avoided. The systemic memory hypothesis stretches our minds to

- reconsider our assumptions and theories,
- reevaluate what we have previously observed, and
- reenvision what we have yet to observe.

For example, the systemic memory hypothesis seems inconsistent with certain aspects of living systems theories (including chaos and complexity theories) that accept, as a given, that self-organization and memory primarily occur at cellular levels and higher. Interestingly, the concept of memory is minimally addressed in current books on living systems and complexity such as Fritz Capra's *The Web of Life: A New Scientific Understanding of Living Systems*, and Stuart Kaufmann's *The Origin of Order: Self-Organization and Selection in Evolution*. The systemic memory hypothesis extends both living systems and self-organization by focusing on the process of recurrent *resonance*, showing how it leads to recurrent *revision*, which ends up creating recurrent *remembering*—a systemic revision of the "three R's." What we call "transformational evolving systems theory" (TEST) includes this inherently revisionistic "Three R's" vision. Systemic memory, as an expression of TEST, is itself a process of inherent self-revision, occurring to various degrees in systems of all shapes and sizes, over and over and over.

It is important to remember that just because a new theory seems inconsistent with certain current theories does not necessarily make the new theory wrong. The new theory may simply be more inclusive, revising and extending the earlier theories in the process. TEST as a Stage E (evolving) theory incorporates, revises, and extends Stages M (multiple), I (Integrative) and L (Living) theories. In fact, transformational evolving systems theory is a natural evolution of complexity and chaos theories, since they each have, at their root, the concept of a dynamical system.

This inclusive/revisionistic phenomenon has often occurred in the evolution of science. Newton's classical physics was conceptually revised and extended by the seemingly inconsistent quantum physics. Quantum physics is currently being conceptually revised and extended by the seemingly inconsistent superstring physics (which hypotheses, for example, the existence of 10 or 11 dimensions, a proposal that stretches most mortal minds beyond their personal experience and comprehension).

The challenge, as Iris Bell reminds us fondly, is to integrate the different levels of seemingly inconsistent theories. We could not agree more.

It is also important to remember that just because a new theory may seem inconsistent with certain observations, this does not necessarily make the new theory wrong. The new theory may lead us to look more closely at phenomena in nature, and not only include observations that have previously been interpreted as "anomalies," but make new discoveries as well. If the systemic memory hypothesis turns out to be true, there is an abundance of new observations waiting to be uncovered that is nothing less than awesome.

Category 4—The systemic memory hypothesis goes far beyond the available data.

This is also true. However, there is absolutely nothing we can do about this since it reflects the inherent universal scope of the hypothesis itself. Like the concept of feedback, which applies universally to all systems at all levels, the concept of systemic memory applies universally to all systems at all levels that involve recurrent feedback interactions. Since Linda and I posit that all systems at all levels contain recurrent feedback interactions, we are logically required to offer an unconditional systemic memory hypothesis—universal living memory—that must go beyond the available data.

Category 5—The second law of thermodynamics "proves" that the hypothesis must be false.

Do you remember the Humpty Dumpty story? Physics tells us that it is easier to break Humpty Dumpty than it is to put him back together again. It is also easier to break Humpty Dumpty than it is to create him in the first place.

The truth is, classical physics and reductionistic science (Stage M) has never been able to explain how Humpty Dumpty got built in the first place! General and living systems theories (Stages I and L) have added structures like DNA and observations like self-organization, but they still revert to "random selection of the fittest" to somehow build an evolving egg.

The hypothesis that everything can form through "randomness" ultimately does not "hold water." It can't even predict water. As we explained in chapter 10, randomness requires independence of action, and systems, by definition, are interdependent, not independent.

The logic of the randomness argument as an explanation for evolution (or simply the creation of Humpty Dumpty) is ultimately faulty, and in the absence of an implicit ordering process, the complex emergents we observe in the universe could never have formed. The understandable wish of Stages M, I, and L science (including chaos and complexity theory) to rely on the randomness hypothesis turns out to be both conceptually and empirically inconsistent with an interconnected energy universe.

If all things in the universe inter-resonate energetically to various degrees, then our theoretical models must take this into account and be revised accordingly. The systemic memory hypothesis is one of the few contemporary theories (for example, Sheldrake's morphic resonance and Laszlo's interconnected "fifth" field in the vacuum) that envisions this organizing, transformational, evolving potential (Stage E) and calls for its inclusion in science. The scientific rationale for a Grand Organizing Designer Hypothesis is emerging.

The highly replicable observation that it is genuinely difficult to put Humpty Dumpty back together again can be reinterpreted from the perspective of the systemic memory process.

It is wise to remember that we cannot put our feet in the same stream twice. What has been called the second law of thermodynamics (called "entropy"), that things tend to wear out, may prove to be evidence for the accumulation of information and energy beyond a particular system's capability to contain it. Remember, the components of so-called "worn out" systems still engage in complex resonant interactions, and they still contain, in theory, living energy systems.

Hence, "entropy" may actually be very complexly ordered—the challenge for future science will be to uncover it. It is worth remembering that the order of digits in "pi" has been precisely defined to millions of digits, and yet no one has discovered the "formula" for revealing its replicable order . . . yet (and if the mathematician Gödel is correct, we may never be able to calculate certain very complex ordering processes). Our inability to find the hidden order in pi should remind us to be humble about concluding that "entropy" lacks order. Of course, entropy "looks" disordered, but that does not make it so; to our everyday senses, the earth looks flat, and the sun looks like it revolves around the earth, but that does not make them so either.

It is also wise to remember that if the second "law" truly applied to everything, we would never be able to see the billions of stars and galaxies in the sky, or discover the organized information and energy present from the presumed beginning of the big bang or big bloom, which is termed the background radiation. Nature would never have existed, and science would not be possible.

Category 6—Even if the logic is true, nature may not work this way.

This is a theoretical possibility. Having learned the lesson of the once flat earth, which turned out to be round, who are Linda and I to claim that nature works precisely the way the systemic memory process predicts it should? Science is constantly revising its stories. Humility should be science's first rule.

However, what we can conclude at this point in the history of science is that positive feedback loops seem to abound in nature. We can also conclude that positive feedback loops seem to express the logic of the systemic memory process. If these conclusions turn out to be valid, then the wisdom in considering the implications seriously is self-evident.

Category 7—The observations purported to be consistent with the hypothesis can all be explained by other theories (including the theory that they are mistaken observations in the first place).

This is a good point. Yes, one may wish to try to explain the heart transplant observations in chapter 7 for example, as statistical coincidences, side effects of the drugs, or the stress of surgery. Yes, one may wish to try to explain the homeopathy observations in chapter 8 for example, as self-deceptions of the clinicians.

Yes, one may wish to try to explain the claims for survival of consciousness after death in chapter 9 as mistaken false memories of mediums and grieving people who desperately wish that their loved ones continue to be alive.

For each "anomaly" we should consider alternative hypotheses comprehensively, and to be responsible scientists we must do this faithfully and with integrity. However, standard scientific procedure mandates that all things being equal, one should seriously consider the simpler of the hypotheses. This is Ockham's Razor. When we take this mandate seriously and apply it to all these phenomena, which hypothesis

- turns out to be simpler,
- makes more predictions, and
- explains more of the variance;

the systemic memory process hypothesis, or an idiosyncratic selection of diverse hypotheses required to explain the multiplicity of the observed anomalies?

Category 8—The logic is circular, so it must be wrong, and here is why.

As you know, Linda and I have not found a flaw in the conceptual or mathematical logic, and as we revise these concluding words in the final editing process, neither has anyone else.

We used two basic types of reasoning in chapter 6: (1) reasoning by analogy (similarity of structure), and (2) reasoning by causality (similarity of process). Analogical reasoning refers to the question of "what"; causality reasoning refers to the question of "how."

Reasoning by analogy ("what") uses conceptual categories or "sets." One reasons that things in a given category or set will have similar properties. The "what" in systemic memory is the category, "feedback system," or "feedback network." Reasoning by causality ("how") focuses on mechanisms or "processes." One reasons that due to specific mechanisms, a system functions in a certain way. The "how" in systemic memory is the process of "recurrent feedback interaction," while the mechanism is "circular causality."

It is much easier to understand "what" reasoning than "how" reasoning. The "what" reasoning is elementary:

- If all feedback networks store memories, learn, and evolve,
- and "X" is a feedback network (where "X" can be anything that is a feedback network),
- then "X" will store memories, learn, and evolve.

Systems theory proposes that all things in nature, from the micro to the macro, exist as dynamical feedback network systems to various degrees. Hence, analogical categorical/structural similarity reasoning leads to the prediction that since all dynamical systems exist as feedback network systems, they all store memories to various degrees.

The "how" logic required to understand the feedback process is decidedly circular and, historically, circular logic was to be avoided at all costs by Stage M reductionistic theorists. However, feedback systems are, by definition, intrinsically circular. Information, energy, and matter circulate in complex ways in dynamical systems. We can not understand the process of feedback and circulation without engaging in logic and mathematics that is decidedly circular. What was once ignored at all cost is now too costly to ignore.

Linda puts it this way: Circulation is a Natural Law. Circulation is the heart of systems, the essence of life, the recurrent flow of all. Linda's concept of a Natural Law of Circulation (called in our technical papers "circular causality") is one of the fundamental take-home messages of this book. This is why we metaphorically summarize it as

Evolution = memory multiplied by circulation^{Repeating}.

Of course, if a fundamental flaw were found in the logic in the future, this would be an obvious and essential reason to reject the hypothesis, and we would be the first to do so. One astute reader, Bill Gladstone, our editor, thought he found what he called a "flawless flaw"—the theory demands the acceptance of linear or sequential time. Since the denial of sequential time on a deep level would eliminate the logic that leads to the hypothesis (that it takes time for information and energy to travel from A to B and back again), Bill has acknowledged that this conceptual "flaw" did not invalidate the hypothesis from the perspective of science, which also requires a belief in linear or sequential time.

Even if in some deeply abstract way time is not linear or sequential (some pioneering "post-quantum" physicists posit such a state), the indisputable fact is that it has taken a substantial amount of sequential time for Linda and me to conceive and write this book, for Bill to edit it, and for you to read it! The systemic memory process applies to this kind of time, the time that defines our physical lives.

Of course, if the process of circulation ultimately applies to all phenomena in the evolving universe, then Linda's prediction applying the process of circulation to time itself also deserves consideration. Though this deep insight is quite mind-boggling, it is implicit in systemic memory theory, and we include it for the sake of completeness.

Here's the bottom line:

- If we had found a flaw, or
- Lynn Nadel and our team of original friendly devils' advocates had found a flaw, or
- The many reviewers of various scientific manuscripts had found a flaw, or
- The many readers of various published papers had found a flaw, or
- The thousands of scientists who have now heard us present the basic systemic memory hypothesis at meetings had found a flaw, then

we would have been the first to tell you "the hypothesis is wrong for this reason—let's forget it, and move on."

As Linda's father was fond of saying, "Time is what a life is made of." When you reach our age (fifty-plus) time becomes ever more precious. Why should we waste our time, and yours, pursuing fiction in the name of science? Although Linda and I both enjoy science fiction from time to time—and personally, Yoda is one of our favorite fictional characters—it is neither our avocation nor dedication.

There are those who genuinely believe the logic is fundamentally wrong, but they can't say how. They believe some of the implications are definitely wrong, but they can't say why. A distinguished professor of applied mathematics at a major university believes that the logic of the systemic memory process may well apply to living systems, even heart cells, but he is thoroughly convinced that the logic can't possibly apply to what he calls "inanimate" objects. It is his firm belief that water cannot have memory, and therefore the many years of research on homeopathy must somehow be in error.

When we ask him, "What's wrong with the logic?" he simply says, "The logic must be wrong somewhere." However, he can't specify where. Similarly, when we ask him, "What's wrong with the double-blind controlled research on homeopathy?" he again simply says, "The research must be wrong somewhere." Will his as yet inexplicable belief that there must be an error in the logic and the research ultimately turn out to be correct? At this point we tend to doubt it, but he could be right.

Of course, even if the specific logic turns out to be wrong, the general idea of systemic memory may prove to be valid in some form. Linda's intuition that everything has universal living memory may prove to be correct, even if our current reasoning turns out to be wrong. However, for Linda and me it is the unyielding persistence of the reasoning and the math that keeps us following our intuition which suggests that something really amusing if not weird is going on in the universe, and has been doing so for a very long time.

Category 9—Even if systemic memory and the natural law of circulation are true, their effects are too subtle in many areas to need to be taken into account by contemporary science.

On the face of it, this would appear to be a valid point. The truth is, what does it matter if the watch we wear everyday is able to store a version of the personal history of our life? Isn't the primary purpose of a watch to keep time? As long as it keeps good time, we are happy. Why should science take systemic memory into account here, or a myriad of other places? We can practice science as usual, can't we?

The answer is yes and no. Yes in some cases, no in other cases. The "no" cases, the exceptions to the rule, prove the more expanded rule. Just as Einstein's theory of general relativity need not be used to predict the path that a baseball will take on earth, systemic memory theory need not be used to predict how a baseball functions as it sits in the pitcher's glove waiting to be thrown. Newtonian reductionistic (Stage M) physics "works" to explain much of what a baseball does, in and out of the pitcher's glove.

However, Newtonian physics turns out to be a special, and more limited, case of Einstenian physics. Hence, conceptually, Newtonian physics is fundamentally "incorrect." Similarly, if the thesis of this book is true, "dead" universe physics (Stage M) will ultimately turn out to be a special, and more limited, case of systemic, living, and evolving physics (Stages I, L, and E). Conceptually speaking, "dead" science may turn out to be fundamentally "incorrect."

In this book, we have illustrated many phenomena (such as emergent properties of water or the documented effects of homeopathy) that non-systemic science is unable to explain or predict but that dynamical energy systems theory can explain and predict. To address these phenomena, research must adopt an expanded vision.

An expanded vision of science can help us appreciate how and why a gifted psychic can sometimes retrieve information from a person's watch; this method is called psychometry and refers to retrieving information of past use and associations from potentially any physical object. Also, the actual time-keeping of watches may reveal subtle systemic effects that will only be discovered through careful and sensitive observation. Watches may be more than "dead" time keepers; they may be living watchers of time as well.

Practically speaking, since the mathematics of recurrent feedback interactions are complex, it is understandable why scientists ignore systemic statistics, and why they will continue to do so as long as they can. One must be practical, in science and everyday life.

However, it has often been said, "There is nothing as practical as a good theory." Wouldn't it be curious if science someday discovered that the systemic memory history of a particular baseball played a subtle role which, every now and again, made the difference between the strike, ball, or hit that won the game?

More important, an expanded vision of science integrates aspects of human life that define who we are and what we can become as a species. For example, love can certainly be researched reductionistically, and science can explore the biochemical, neurophysiological, and psychological correlates of love using classical theories. However, the kind of love that inspires the Lindas of the world to look beyond "dead" material to living energy systems as they search for continued connection with their deceased loved ones, needs to be considered if not fostered by a living, evolving science. Is it time for science to open its eyes and heart and experience the fullness of life?

Chaos theory predicts that under special circumstances a butterfly in Kansas can affect the weather in Florida. It may be time for science to stop funtioning with its "eyes wide shut" and revise itself so that it can embrace the wide variety of seeming anomalies that enable us to envision the evolving majesty of a living energy universe.

"You don't know what I mean by the word amusing." A reason to SMILE

The original technical paper that described the systemic memory process that is reprinted in appendix A of this book, was dedicated to the memory of Linda's father, Henry, and also to the memory of Heinz Pagels, a distinguished physicist at Rockefeller University who wrote *The Cosmic Code: Quantum Physics as the Language of Nature*.

Thanks to Pagels and *The Cosmic Code*, I was able, in my mind, to enter the minds of some of the major quantum physicists. The year was 1983, and I was preparing to give my presidential address to the Health Psychology Division of the American Psychological Association. The need to connect energy and systems was clear to me, and I wanted to illustrate some of the potential implications of their conceptual marriage to the emerging scientific and clinical marriage of psychology and medicine.

I never planned to talk about the systemic memory hypothesis, it was clearly too controversial. But I did want to consider a less controversial implication, an extension of Einstein's theory of relativity as applied to stress management. I termed this the general relativity/general relaxation hypothesis. However, I was not sure if my logic was correct, and I decided that the best person to examine the logic was Professor Pagels. So I called Pagels at Rockefeller University, and asked him for his evaluation and counsel. I told him that I was a psychologist, not a physicist, and that I had deeply enjoyed his book, *The Cosmic Code*.

I shared how if I correctly understood his explanation for how Einstein came to derive the theory of special relativity, and if my reasoned extension of Einstein's logic held water, then a controversial new bridge between quantum physics, physiology, and psychology was ready to be built and put to scientific test. I also explained that I was very nervous about coming "out of the closet," about my deep interest in the applications of quantum physics to psychology and medicine. Hence, I wanted his professional advice about this choice of topic for my presidential address.

After listening for over a half hour to my understandings and extensions, Pagels replied, "Gary, I think your theory is quite amusing."

I replied, "What? Here I am, struggling to make a decision that could cost me my reputation, if not my career, about presenting a hypothesis and vision that many of my colleagues will find weird to begin with, and your conclusion is that my theory is quite amusing?"

He said, "Gary, you don't understand what I mean by amusing."

Pagels then told me a story about how when he was a graduate student at Princeton University, he learned an important perspective about the nature of scientific theory from his advisor, the late luminary Eugene Wigner. According to Pagels, Wigner was fond of saying that there were two kinds of theories in science, "interesting theories" and "amusing theories." Wigner said, "Interesting theories, though often true, are often not worth remembering. However, amusing theories, though often wrong, are absolutely worth thinking about!" It was then that I smiled.

Thanks to Pagels and Wigner, I decided to give my address on the implications of quantum physics for the future of health psychology and, as I expected, I lost serious credibility with some of my colleagues. As the introduction to my address, I shared with my audience the struggle I faced as I attempted to make a decision about the topic of my address, and the good fortune I had to speak with Professor Pagels. I then told them the Wigner story and said: "My purpose, ladies and gentlemen, is to share with you some amusing theories about potential implications of quantum physics for psychology and medicine."

What Linda and I hope is that the universal living memory hypothesis is both interesting and amusing. In ending this book, our collective journey to explore the hypothesis has just begun.

We hope you will write to us at the Human Energy Systems Laboratory, The University of Arizona, Department of Psychology, PO Box 210068, Tucson, Arizona 85721-0068, with your own experiences which either validate or cast doubt on this hypothesis of universal living memory. You may also reach us at our website, www.livingenergyuniverse.com.

We thank you for participating with us in this noble scientific exploration. If you are curious about the technical language of the systemic memory hypothesis, we encourage you to explore appendixes A and B. They are there for your interest and amusement

If you would like to learn about our latest discoveries involving video feedback systemic memory, we invite you to read the Authors' Note at the end of the book.

Selected Readings

The following books were referenced in the text
or contributed to the writing of this book:

Achinstein, P. 1991. *Particles and Waves: Historical Essays in the Philosophy of Science.* New York: Oxford University Press.

Armstrong, K. 1993. *A History of God: The 4,000-Year Quest of Judaism, Christianity, and Islam.* New York: Ballantine Books.

Bateson, G. 1972. *Steps to an Ecology of Mind.* New York: Ballentine Books.

Becker, R. O. 1990. *Cross Currents: The Perils of Electropollution, the Promise of Electromedicine.* New York: Jeremy P. Tarcher/Perigee.

Becker, R. O., and G. Selden. 1988. *The Body Electric: Electromagnetism and the Foundation of Life.* New York: Quill, William Morrow.

Bergson, H. 1988. *Matter and Memory.* New York: Zone Books.

Brown, C. 1998. *Afterwards, You're a Genius: Faith, Medicine, and the Metaphysics of Healing.* New York: Riverhead Books.

Burr, H. S. 1972. *Blueprint for Immortality: The Electric Patterns of Life.* London, England: Neville Spearman Limited.

Cannon, W. B. 1932. *The Wisdom of the Body.* New York: Norton.

Capra, F. 1996. *The Web of Life: A New Scientific Understanding of Living Systems.* New York: Anchor Books.

Cheney, M. 1981. *Tesla: Man Out of Time.* New York: Dell.

Cobb, J. B., and D. R. Griffin. 1976. *Process Theology.* Philadelphia: The Wesminster Press.

Coveney, P., and R. Highfield. 1995. *Frontiers of Complexity: The Search for Order in a Chaotic World.* New York: Fawcett Columbine.

Davidson, M. 1983. *Uncommon Sense: The Life and Thought of Ludwig von Bertalanffy, Father of General Systems Theory*. Los Angeles: J. P. Tarcher.

de Chardin, T. 1959. *The Phenomenon of Man*. New York: Harper and Row.

Denton, M. J. 1998. *Nature's Destiny: How the Laws of Biology Reveal Purpose in the Universe*. New York: The Free Press.

de Rosnay, J. 1979. *The Macroscope: A New World Scientific System*. New York: Harper and Row.

Dossey, L. 1993. *Healing Words: The Power of Prayer and the Practice of Medicine*. San Francisco: HarperSanFrancisco.

Ebert, J. D. 1999. *Twilight of the Clockwork God: Conversations on Science and Spirituality at the End of an Age*. Tulsa: Council Oaks Books.

Feynman, R. 1965. *The Character of Physical Law*. Cambridge: MIT Press.

Fox, M. 1979. *A Spirituality Named Compassion*. San Francisco: Harper and Row.

————. 1992. *Sheer Joy: Conversations with Thomas Aquinas on Creation Spirituality*. San Fransicso: HarperSanFrancisco.

Goswami, A. 1995. *The Self-Aware Universe: How Consciousness Creates the Material World*. New York: Jeremy P. Tarcher/Putnam.

Goldner, D. 1999. *Infinite Grace: Where the Worlds of Science and Spiritual Healing Meet*. Charlottesville, VA: Hampton Roads Publishing Company.

Greene, B. 1999. *The Elegant Universe: Superstrings, Hidden Dimensions, and the Quest for the Ultimate Theory*. New York: W. W. Norton.

Jahn, R. G., and B. J. Dunne. 1987. *Margins of Reality: The Role of Consciousness in the Physical World*. New York: Harcourt Brace-Jovanovich.

Jung, C. G. 1953. *Psychology and Religion: West and East. Collected Works, vol. 11*. Princeton: Princeton University Press.

Kauffman, S. 1993. *The Origins of Order: Self-Organization and Selection in Evolution*. New York: Oxford University Press.

Kraft, R. W. 1983. *A Reason to Hope: A Synthesis of Teilhard de Chardin's Vision and Systems Thinking*. Seaside, CA: Intersystems Publications of the Systems Inquiry Series.

Koestler, A. 1978. *Janus: A Summing Up*. London: Hutchinson.

Kuhn, T. 1970. *The Structure of Scientific Revolutions*. Chicago: University of Chicago Press.

Laszlo, E. 1987. *Evolution: The Grand Synthesis*. Boston: Shambhala.

————. 1995. *The Interconnected Universe: Conceptual Foundations of Transdisciplinary Unified Theory*. Singapore: World Scientific Publishing.

————. 1996. *The Whispering Pond: A Personal Guide to the Emerging Vision of Science*. Rockport, MA: Element Books.

Lovelock, J. 1979. *Gaia: A New Look at Life on Earth*. New York: Oxford University Press.

Martin, J., and P. Romanowski. 1997. *Love Beyond Life: The Healing Power of After-Death Communications*. New York: HarperCollins Publishing.

McMoneagle, J. 1997. *Mind Trek: Exploring Consciousness, Time, and Space through Remote Viewing*. Charlottesville, VA: Hampton Roads Publishing Company.

Miles, J. 1995. *God: A Biography*. New York: Alfred A. Knopf.

Miller, J. G. 1978. *Living Systems*. New York: McGraw-Hill.

Moreland, J. P., ed. 1994. *The Creation Hypothesis: Scientific Evidence for an Intelligent Designer*. Downers Grove, IL: InterVarsity Press.

Narby, J. 1998. *The Cosmic Serpent: DNA and the Origins of Knowledge*. New York: Jeremy P. Tarcher/Putnam.

Newton, R. G. 1997. *The Truth of Science: Physical Theories and Reality*. Cambridge: Harvard University Press.

O'Murchu, D. 1997. *Quantum Theology: Spiritual Implications of the New Physics*. New York: The Crossroad Publishing Company.

Ornish, D. 1997. *Love and Survival: The Scientific Basis for the Healing Power of Intimacy*. New York: HarperCollins Publishing.

Pagels, H. R. 1983. *The Cosmic Code*. London: Joseph.

Pearsall, P. 1998. *The Heart's Code*. New York: Broadway Books.

Peat, F. D. 1996. *Infinite Potential: The Life and Times of David Bohm*. Read, MA: Helix Books, Addison-Wesley.

Pepper, C. S. 1942. *World Hypotheses: A Study in Evidence*. Cambridge, England: Cambridge University Press; rev.ed. Berkeley, CA: University of California Press, 1961.

Pert, C. B. 1997. *The Molecules of Emotion*. New York: Scribner.

Peterson, I. 1998. *The Jungles of Randomness*. New York: John Wiley and Sons.

Popper, K. R., and J. C. Eccles. 1977. *The Self and Its Brain*. Berlin: Springer International.

Potak, C. 1990. *Wanderings*. New York: Fawcett Books.

Poundstone, W. 1985. *The Recursive Universe: Cosmic Complexity and the Limits of Scientific Knowledge*. New York: William Morrow and Company.

Pribram, K. 1991. *Brain and Perception: Holony and Structure in Figural Processing*. Hillsdale, NJ: Lawrence Erlbaum Associates.

Pribram, K. H., ed. 1998. *Brain and Values*. Hillsdale, NJ.: Lawrence Erlbaum Associates.

Prigogine, I. 1980. *From Being to Becoming*. San Francisco, CA: W. H. Freeman.

Radin, D. 1997. *The Conscious Universe: The Scientific Truth of Psychic Phenomena*. San Francisco: HarperCollins.

Raymo, C. 1998. *Skeptics and True Believers: The Exhilarating Connection Between Science and Religion*. New York: Walker and Company.

Richardson, G. P. 1992. *Feedback Thought in Social Science and Systems Theory*. Philadelphia: University of Philadelphia Press.

Riley, G. J. 1997. *One Jesus, Many Christs: How Jesus Inspired Not One True Christianity, but Many*. San Francisco: HarperSanFrancisco.

Salk, J. 1983. *The Anatomy of Reality: Merging of Intuition and Reason*. New York: Columbia University Press.

Satinover, J. 1997. *Cracking the Bible Code*. New York: William Morrow and Company.

Schroeder, G. L. 1998. *The Science of God: The Convergence of Scientific and Biblical Wisdom*. New York: The Free Press.

Scott, A. 1995. *Stairway to the Mind: The Controversial New Science of Consciousness*. New York: Springer-Verlag.

Sheldrake, A. R. 1981. *A New Science of Life: The Hypothesis of Formative Causation*. London: Blond and Briggs.

———. 1988. *The Presence of the Past: Morphic Resonance and the Habits of Nature*. New York: Times Books.

Smith, H. 1958. *The Religions of Man*. New York: Harper and Row.

Smith, S. 1964. *The Mediumship of Mrs. Leonard*. New Hyde Park, NY: University Books.

Solomon, J., and G. Solomon. 1998. *Harry Oldfield's Invisible Universe*. Hammersmith, London: Thorons.

Stevenson, I. 1996. *Reincarnation and Biology*. New York: Praeger.

Sylvia, C., with W. A. Novak. 1997. *Change of Heart*. New York: Little Brown and Company.

Targ, R., and J. Katra. 1998. *Miracles of Mind: Exploring Nonlocal Consciousness and Spiritual Healing*. Novato, CA: New World Library.

Taylor, E. 1996. *William James on Consciousness Beyond the Margin*. Princeton: Princeton University Press.

Templeton, J. M. 1997. *Worldwide Laws of Life*. Philadelphia: Templeton Foundation Press.

Tiller, W. A. 1997. *Science and Human Transformation: Subtle Energies, Intentionality, and Consciousness.* Walnut Creek, CA: Pavior Publishing.

Tipler, F. J. 1994. *The Physics of Immortality: Modern Cosmology, God and the Resurrection of the Dead.* New York: Doubleday.

von Bertalanffy, L. 1968. *General System Theory.* New York: Braziller.

Weiner, N. 1961. *Cybernetics. Second Edition.* Cambridge: MIT Press.

Weiss, P. 1939. *Principles of Development.* New York: Holt.

Westfall, R. S. 1980. *Never at Rest: A Biography of Isaac Newton.* Cambridge: Cambridge University Press.

White, S. E. 1940. *The Unobstructed Universe.* New York: E. P. Dutton and Company.

Whitehead, A. N. 1925. *Science and the Modern World.* New York: Macmillan.

———. 1929. *Process and Reality.* New York: Macmillan.

Wilber, K. 1996. *A Brief History of Everything.* Boston, MA: Shambhala.

Wolf, F. A. 1996. *The Spiritual Universe: How Quantum Physics Proves the Existence of Soul.* New York: Simon and Schuster.

Zukav, G. 1979. *The Dancing Wu Li Masters: An Overview of the New Physics.* New York: William Morrow and Company.

The following selection of materials by the authors and colleagues were referenced in the text or contributed to the writing of this book: Starred [*] articles include coverage of systemic memory.

*Bell, I. R., C. M. Baldwin, G. E. R. Schwartz, and L. G. S. Russek. 1999. Integrating Belief Systems and Therapies in Medicine: Application of the Eight World Hypotheses to Classical Homeopathy. *Integrative Medicine.* 1(3):95-105.

*Pearsall, P., G. E. R. Schwartz, and L. G. S. Russek. 1999. Verbatim Reports from Heart Transplant Patients that Parallel Certain Characteristics of the Donors. (Submitted for publication.)

Russek, L. G., and G. E. Schwartz. 1994. Interpersonal Heart-Brain Registration and the Perception of Parental Love: A 42 Year Follow-up of the Harvard Mastery of Stress Study. *Subtle Energies.* 5(3):195-208.

*————. 1996. Energy Cardiology: A Dynamical Energy Systems Approach for Integrating Conventional and Alternative Medicine. *Advances: The Journal of Mind-body Health.* 12(4):4-24.

*————. 1996. The Heart, Dynamic Energy, and Integrated Medicine. *Advances: The Journal of Mind-body Health.* 12(4):36-45.

————. 1996. Narrative Descriptions of Parental Love and Caring Predict Health Status in Midlife: A 35-year Follow-up of the Harvard Mastery of Stress Study. *Alternative Therapies in Health and Medicine.* 2(6): 55-62.

————. 1997. Perceptions of Parental Caring Predict Health Status in Midlife: A 35-year Follow-up of the Harvard Mastery of Stress Study. *Psychosomatic Medicine.* 59(2):144-149.

————. 1997. Feelings of Parental Caring Predict Health Status in Midlife: A 35-year Follow-up of the Harvard Mastery of Stress Study. *Journal of Behavioral Medicine.* 20(1):1-13.

Russek, L. G., G. E. Schwartz, I. R. Bell, and C. M. Baldwin. 1998. Positive Perceptions of Parental Caring Are Associated with Reduced Medical and Psychiatric Symptoms. *Psychosomatic Medicine.* 60:654-657.

Russek, L. G. S., G. E. R. Schwartz, E. Russek, and H. I. Russek (hyp). 1999. A Possible Approach for Researching Purported Spirit Communication: An Empirical-Anecdotal Investigation. *Advances in Mind-Body Medicine.*

Schwartz, G. E. 1972. Voluntary Control of Human Cardiovascular Integration and Differentiation Through Feedback and Reward. *Science.* 174: 90-93.

————. 1979. The Brain as a Health Care System: A Psychobiological Framework for Biofeedback and Health Psychology. In *Health Psychology*; ed. C. Stone, N. Adler, and F. Cohen. San Francisco: Jossey-Bass.

————. 1984. Psychobiology of Health: A New Synthesis. In *Psychology in Health: Master Lecture Series Volume III*; ed. C.J. Scheirer, and B. L. Hammonds. Washington, DC: APA Books.

————. 1987. Personality and the Unification of Psychology and Modern Physics: A Systems Approach. In *The Emergence of Personality*; ed. J. Aronoff, A. I. Robin, and R. A. Zucker. New York: Springer.

————. 1990. Psychobiology of Repression and Health: A Systems Approach. In *Repression and Dissociation*; ed. J. E. Singer. Chicago: The University of Chicago Press.

————. 1997. Energy and Information: The Soul and Spirit of Mind-Body Medicine. *Advances: The Journal of Mind-body Health.* 13(1):75-77.

Schwartz, G. E., L. Nelson, L. G. Russek, and J. J. B. Allen. 1996. Electrostatic Body-Motion Registration and the Human Antenna-Receiver Effect: A New Method for Investigating Interpersonal Dynamical Energy System Interactions. *Subtle Energies and Energy Medicine.* 7(2):149-184.

Schwartz, G. E., L. G. Russek, and J. Beltran. 1995. Interpersonal Hand-Energy Registration: Evidence for Implicit Performance and Perception. *Subtle Energies.* 6(2):183-200.

Schwartz, G. E., and L. G. Russek. 1996. Neurotherapy and the Heart: The Challenge of Energy Cardiology. *Journal of Neurotherapy.* 1(4):1-11.

————. 1997. Information and Energy in Healthy Systems: The Soul and Spirit of Integrative Medicine. *Advances: The Journal of Mind-Body Health.* 13(4): 25-29.

*————. 1997. Dynamical Energy Systems and Modern Physics: Fostering the Science and Spirit of Complementary and Alternative Medicine. *Alternative Therapies in Health and Medicine.* 3(3):46-56.

*————. 1997. The Challenge of One Medicine: Theories of Health and 'Eight World Hypotheses.' *Advances: The Journal of Mind-body Health.* 13(3):7-23.

*————. 1998. Do All Dynamic Systems Have Memory? Implications of the Systemic Memory Hypothesis for Science and Society. In *Brain and Values*; ed. K. H. Pribram. Hillsdale, NJ.: Erlbaum.

————. 1998. Family Love and Life-long Health? A Challenge for Clinical Psychology. In *The Science of Clinical Psychology*; ed. R. Derubeis, and D. K. Routh. Washington, DC: APA Books.

*Schwartz, G. E. R., and L. G. S. Russek. 1997. Testing the Surivival of Consciousness Hypothesis: The Goal of the Codes. *Journal of Scientific Exploration.* 11(1):79-88.

*————. 1998. The Origin of Holism and Memory in Nature: The Systemic Memory Hypothesis. *Frontier Perspectives.* 7(2):23-31.

*————. 1998. The Plausibility of Homeopathy: The Systemic Memory Hypothesis. *Integrative Medicine.* 1(2):53-59.

*————. 1999. The Century of the Heart. Forward to *The Heart's Code*; P. Pearsall. New York: Broadway Books.

*————. 1999. Can Physics and Physical Chemistry Explain the Workings of Homeopathy: A Systemic Memory View. *Journal of Alternative and Complementary Medicine.*

————. 1999. Registration of Actual and Intended Eye Gaze: Correlation with Spiritual Beliefs and Experiences. *Journal of Scientific Exploration.* 13(2):213-230.

*Schwartz, G. E. R, L. G. S. Russek, S. L. Shapiro, and P. Harada. 1999. Loving Openness as A Meta-World Hypotheses: Expanding Our Vision of Mind and Medicine. *Advances in Mind-Body Medicine.* 15(1):5-19.

Schwartz, G. E., L. G. Russek, Z. S. She, L. Z. Y. X. Song, and Y. Xin. 1997. Anomalous Organization of Random Events During an International Qigong Meeting: Evidence for Group Consciousness or Accumulated Qi Fields? *Subtle Energies and Energy Medicine.*

*Schwartz, G. E. R., L. G. S. Russek, I. R. Bell, and D. Riley. 1999. The Plausibility of Homeopathy and Conventional Chemical Therapy: The Systemic Memory Resonance Hypothesis. *Medical Hypotheses.*

Schwartz, G. E. R., L. G. S. Russek, D. E. Watson, L. Campbell, S. Smith, E. H. Smith (hyp), W. James (hyp), H. I. Russek (hyp), and H. Schwartz (hyp). 1999. Potential Medium to Departed to Medium Communication of Pictorial Information: Exploratory Evidence Consistent with Psi and Survival of Consciousness. *The Noetics Journal.*

Shapiro, S. L., G. E. Schwartz, and G. Bonner. 1998. Effects of a Mindfulness-based Stress Reduction on Medical and Pre-Medical Students. *Journal of Behavioral Medicine.*

Shapiro, S. L., and G. E. Schwartz. 1999. The Role of Intention in Self-Regulation: Toward an Intentional Systemic Mindfulness. In *Handbook of Self-Regulation*; ed. M. Boekaerts, P. Pintrich, and M. Zeidner. New York: Academic Press.

Song, L. Z. Y. X., G. E. R. Schwartz, and L. G. S. Russek. 1998. Heart-Focused Attention and Heart-Brain Synchronization: Energetic and Physiological Mechanisms. *Alternative Therapies in Health and Medicine.* 4(5):44-63.

*Watson, D. E., G. E. R. Schwartz, and L. G. S. Russek. 1999. The Theory of Enformed Systems: A Paradigm of Organization and Holistic Systems. *The Noetic Journal.* 2(2):159-172.

APPENDIX A

Do All Dynamical Systems Have Memory? Implications of the Systemic Memory Hypothesis for Science and Society[1]

Gary E. R. Schwartz, Ph.D.
Linda G. S. Russek, Ph.D.

ABSTRACT

Memory is one of the most fundamental and valued phenomena in nature. Memory technology is currently evolving at a rapid rate, improving our ability to store not only information but energy as well. However, is the process of memory unique and selective, limited to nervous systems, immune systems, and storage systems of modern technology? Or, is the storage of information and energy an essential and ubiquitous process in nature, inexorably tied to the very process of the existence of objects as dynamical systems? When a dynamical energy systems approach is used to examine the process of interaction (especially recurrent feedback interaction) in systems, the logic leads to the systemic memory hypothesis which posits that all dynamical systems store information and sustain memory. The chapter outlines the fundamentals of systems theory, information and energy, and illustrates the profound implications that

---

1   From Pribram, K. H., ed. "Brain and Values: Is a Biological Science of Values Possible." Hillsdale, NJ: Lawrence Erlbaum Associates, 1998.

follow when these concepts are integrated. Using resonance between and within two tuning forks as a model system, the logic of how recurrent feedback interaction generates dynamic memory is explained. Recurrent feedback interaction was anticipated by William James (1890), was implicit in the writings of Warren McCulloch (1951), is implicit in the holonomic brain theory of Karl Pribram (1991), and is implicit in the neural network concept of the recurrent feedback loop. Recurrent feedback interactions not only occur between neurons in neural networks, but occur within all cells and molecules. Heretofore unexplained observations reported in homeopathy, kinesiology, aromatherapy, organ transplants, and parapsychology can be understood in terms of the systemic memory hypothesis. One of science's greatest challenges is to develop mathematical models for the retrieval of holistic information inherently stored in dynamical systems. Future research can confirm or disconfirm the wide ranging predictions of the systemic memory hypothesis for science and society.

The real voyage of discovery consists not in seeking new lands but in seeing with new eyes.
Marcel Proust, 1871-1922

In this regard I would caution the reader to adhere to a maxim once issued by Warren McCulloch: "Do not bite my finger; look where I am pointing."
Pribram, in Laszlo, 1995

Introduction and Overview

Memory is clearly one of the most valued characteristics of a system. Moreover, systems tend most easily to retrieve information that is valued and used on a regular basis. The capacity for memory is a prerequisite for a system not only to have values, but to sustain values as well. Since memory is both deeply valued and value-laden, it is not surprising that memory is one of the most fundamental and far-reaching phenomena in nature. The thesis of this chapter is that memory may be ubiquitous in nature.

The human brain has the extraordinarily advanced ability to store highly diverse and complex forms of information. It also has the remarkably creative capacity to invent new electronic, chemical and mechanical systems for storing ever increasing amounts of information. Memory technology is currently evolving at a rapid rate, improving the capacity to store energy as well as information.

In lay usage, the term memory refers to the conscious retrieval of information as well as the storage of information. Historically, the term memory came from the Latin *memoria*, which meant "the faculty of remembering" (Webster, 1977). However, this use of the word memory (which in psychology is termed explicit memory) is only one form of memory. Substantial research on memory without awareness, termed implicit memory, documents that information can be stored in the absence of conscious awareness, and evidence for memory storage can be found in behavior in the absence of explicit recall (Schacter, 1996). Implicit memory refers to the demonstration that information has been stored per se, even if the information can not be retrieved consciously. The modern use of the term memory in computer science (e.g., hard disk memory) and electrical engineering (e.g., battery memory) also refers to the storage of information per se. In this chapter, we use the term memory in the generic sense to refer to the storage of information per se, regardless of whether the information can be retrieved consciously.

Is the process of memory unique and selective, limited to the nervous system, the immune system, and storage systems invented through technology? The purpose of this chapter is to outline the logic that leads to the far-reaching hypothesis that all dynamical systems generate and sustain memory, and to consider some of the implications of this hypothesis, termed the systemic memory hypothesis, for science and society. As will become clear, implicit (unconscious) storage of information and energy may be the rule, rather than the exception, in all levels of nature—explicit memory, the conscious retrieval of information and energy, may be a special case of implicit memory.

The systemic memory hypothesis occurred to the first author while he was a professor at Yale University in the early 1980s working on applications of systems theory to behavioral medicine and modern physics (e.g., Schwartz, 1984, 1987). In the process of attempting to explain to a seminar of students the basic mathematics of how feedback interactions worked (both negative and positive), he unexpectedly came to the realization that feedback interactions, especially cyclic, repeated feedback interactions (termed here recurrent feedback interactions), inherently involved the dynamic storage of information. Because he considered the systemic memory hypothesis too controversial to communicate at that time, he did not publish the hypothesis.

However, inspired by the second author's understanding and extension of the hypothesis to the storage of energy in energy medicine (Russek and Schwartz, 1996a,b), the decision was reached to publish the logic and implications of the hypothesis with the hope that this will stimulate thoughtful debate and research designs to test the hypothesis.

The systemic memory hypothesis addresses a persistent mystery in modern science, the origin of holism and emergent properties in dynamical systems. The simple dictum "the whole is greater than the sum of its parts, and its corollary," "the whole depends upon the interaction of its parts for its unique properties" together express the foundation of general and living systems theory (von Bertalanffy, 1968; Miller, 1978) and modern complexity and chaos theory (Kauffman, 1993) as they are employed in the physical, biological, behavioral, social, and environmental sciences. The problem of the origin of holism in dynamical systems is potentially resolved when circular feedback is viewed as recurrent feedback interactions that inexorably lead to the storage of information and the creation of dynamical systemic memories in all dynamical systems at all levels. The complex linear and non-linear interactions that naturally accumulate through the circulation of information and energy turn out to be holistic memories that reflect the evolving identity of systems as emerging wholes.

As will become clear below, the logic used to generate the systemic memory hypothesis is relatively simple and straightforward. The logic has been evolving over the past 100 years, and inexorably follows from modern systems theory. We will describe how the systemic memory hypothesis was anticipated by William James in 1890, how it was implicitly recognized by Warren McCulloch in

1951, how it is implicit in the holonomic brain theory of Karl Pribram (1991), and how it is the explanation for the creation of memory in neural networks. The concept of the recurrent feedback loop in neural networks (e.g., Lisberger and Sejnowski, 1992) turns out to be a special case of the general principle of recurrent feedback interaction. Though the term feedback implies recurrent (hence the term recurrent feedback will seem redundant to some), recurrent feedback is the term used in the neural network literature. We add the term interaction to emphasize that recurrent feedback involves interaction, and systemic memory involves the storage of interactions.

In addition to explaining the origin of dynamic memory and the expression of holism and emergent properties in systems, the logic of recurrent feedback interaction also provides an explanation for self-organization, self-awareness, and evolution in systems. As will become clear, some of the predictions that follow from the concept of recurrent feedback interaction prove to be novel, and some prove to be very controversial. This is unavoidable. Conceptual integrity and logical completeness requires that the deep and challenging implications be entertained openly and addressed seriously.

Our current ideas about memory explicitly shape science and society, especially concerning our openness to phenomena that challenge our current beliefs because they appear inexplicable. We logically dismiss controversial claims for the clinical effectiveness of homeopathy and well-controlled double-blind studies documenting significant effects of selective homeopathic preparations (reviewed in Bellavite and Signorini, 1995), because our theories lead us to hypothesize that while neurons and immune cells can have memory for molecules, water per se cannot. We logically dismiss historical claims of native populations and well-documented psychics (e.g., Smith, 1964) that detailed information about persons and situations can sometimes be retrieved from ancient artifacts and personal effects, and explain these claims as due to coincidence or superstition, because our theories lead us to hypothesize that while neurons can have detailed information about persons and situations, material artifacts cannot. We logically dismiss emerging reports from certain organ transplant patients that their memories and values have changed in surprising ways since receiving their new organs (e.g.,

Sylvia with Novack, 1997), and explain their post surgical symptoms as side effects of immunosuppressant drugs or stress, because our theories lead us to hypothesize that the donor's personal history is only stored in his or her central nervous system, and not in his or her donated organs (for example, the heart or the lungs).

How would science and society change if a theory, already well-accepted within modern science, turned out to predict that the dynamic storage of information and energy was an essential and ubiquitous process in nature, inexorably tied to the very process of the existence of objects as dynamical systems? How would the practice of basic science change if such a theory predicted that electromagnetic energy and information, expressed for example as organized patterns of visible light, was continuously stored in all objects to varying degrees, especially in objects that were black in color? How would the practice of medicine change if such a theory predicted that sensory and perceptual information was continuously stored in all biological tissues, including the heart and lungs, or that natural medicines such as herbs and aromatherapy could sometimes be superior to synthetic drugs because of the systemic information and energy stored in the molecules? How would the practice of our religious institutions and rituals change if such a theory predicted that personal information historically termed "spiritual" was stored in the personal effects of our loved ones?

Prelude to the Systemic Memory Hypothesis: The "White Crow" of Cellular Memory?

A particularly remarkable implication of the systemic memory hypothesis concerns predictions about organ transplants, especially heart transplants. As described in Russek and Schwartz (1996a,b), the heart can be viewed as a dynamical energy generating system. Of all the organs within the body, the heart is preeminent in terms of the centrality of its location, the richness of its connections to all the cells within the body, and particularly relevant here, the intensity of its energy transmission. This energy aspect of the heart does not receive much attention. But just as the heart not only pumps patterns of biochemical nutrients to every cell within the body through the circulation, it also "pumps" patterns of energy and information to every cell within the body through the circulation as well. For example, it is well-known that the electrical potential generated by the heart, identified by the electrocardiogram, can be recorded from any site on the body because of volume conduction, a mechanism that is well known in physics and biology and is not, in and of itself, controversial (Malmivuo and Plonsey, 1995).

A common phrase is that we learn things "by heart," and that we know things "by heart." Is this simply a misplaced metaphor, or is there some deep significance to this particular choice of words? If all cells store information (a prediction from the systemic memory hypothesis), if the heart is especially involved because of the centrality of its location and connections, and if the heart is especially involved in emotion, then memories (in particular, implicit emotional memories), may literally involve the heart in addition to the brain (Russek and Schwartz, 1996a,b).

If the heart of one person is transplanted into another (something that does not happen naturally in nature), some aspects of the history of the donor (as processed and stored by the heart) will be potentially accessible (implicitly if not explicitly) to the recipient. Since the recipient's body typically treats the donor's heart as foreign matter to be rejected, drugs are required to suppress this natural reaction. Is it possible that the rejection response is not simply the rejection of the matter comprising the heart, but the rejection of stored energy and information contained in the heart as well?

It would take a special recipient, indeed, to possibly retrieve the hypothesized information stored in the donor's heart. However, sporadic reports have surfaced suggesting that strange changes in recipient's perceptions and preferences sometimes occur (e.g., Siegel, 1995). The critical question is, do the recipient's new perceptions and preferences correspond to the donor's known preferences?

We recently learned of the experiences of a former dancer, Claire Sylvia, who received a heart/lung transplant in Boston. Hers was the first successful heart/lung transplant in New England. According to her book, A Change of Heart (Sylvia with Novak, 1997) Sylvia (and other unique transplant recipients) report that their lives sometimes change in strange ways after their transplants. For example, Sylvia purportedly remembered that six weeks after her transplant, when she was allowed to drive again, she had driven straight to the nearest Kentucky Fried Chicken, a place she had never been before, and this former dancer and fit, thin person had ordered chicken nuggets. She later learned that the eighteen-year-old-person whose heart and lungs now lived inside her had a fondness for fried chicken nuggets. Moreover, at the time of the young man's death, uneaten chicken nuggets were found stuffed inside the pocket of his leather jacket.

Claims such as these are typically and understandably treated as nonsense—that is, they do not make any sense—from a traditional non-systemic perspective. They are explained as coincidences or misperceptions, side effects of the immunosuppressant drugs, or the expression of preexisting psychopathology interacting with the stress of surgery. However, when systems are viewed not only as material systems, but as informational and energy systems as well, claims such as these from select transplant patients begin to make sense.

As William James put it, "If you wish to upset the law that all crows are black . . . it is enough if you prove one single crow to be white." It is possible that Claire Sylvia may be the "white crow" of systemic memory. Claire Sylvia may be a special case because she is artistic, a skilled dancer, in touch with her body and emotions, open-minded and spiritual. Maybe her experiences do not simply reflect her creative consciousness and/or effects of the drugs, but reflect actual information retrieval (explicit or implicit) from the essential organs she has inherited. Whether this information is truly episodic and cognitive in nature, or is more stylistic and emotional/motivational in nature, it is a completely open question that can and should be addressed in future research.

This chapter begins with a brief overview of systems theory and the concepts of information and energy. The logic of dynamical recurrent feedback interaction is then analyzed, and the emergence of the systemic memory hypothesis is explained. Various implications of the hypothesis for science and society are then outlined. The relationship of dynamic memory to values and valence is discussed in this context. Though neurons are clearly especially gifted in storing sensory and psychological information (because neurons are so highly interconnected, creating profoundly complex recurrent feed-back interactive networks), it may be time to evolve our intellectual heritage and reenvision the brain as being a marvelously special case of a ubiquitous dynamic systemic (holistic) memory process in nature.

What Is Systems Theory? The Key Is Dynamic Interaction

Historically, systems theory, including general systems theory (Von Bertalanffy, 1968) and living systems theory (Miller, 1978), was developed as a conceptual tool to organize and integrate knowledge within and across disciplines, from the physical and biological sciences to the behavioral and social sciences (Schwartz, 1982; 1984; 1987; 1989). Some recent advances stemming from systems theory include information theory (Abu-Mostafa, 1957), self-regulation theory (Mithaug, 1993), complexity theory (Flood, 1988), self-organizing theory (Yates, 1987; Kauffman, 1993), and chaos theory (Cambel, 1993). Chaos theory has been applied to both classical and quantum physics (NATO, 1985), an example of its integrative capacity. The further use of systems theory as a conceptual framework for integrating classical and quantum physics in the psychobiology of personality and health is illustrated in Schwartz (1984; 1987). The integration of systems theory with modern concepts of energy reflects the continued evolution of these ideas (Russek and Schwartz, 1996a,b).

As described by Miller (1978, page 9):

"General systems theory is a set of related definitions, assumptions, and propositions which deal with reality as an integrated hierarchy of organizations of matter and energy. General living systems theory is concerned with a special subset of all systems, the living ones."

The meaning of "system" is often confused and is used differently in different contexts. A "system" of measurement units (e.g., the measurement of energy, see below) simply means "structure" (static information), whereas a "system" of cells comprising an organ means much more—"interactions," "relationships," "non-linear summations" (dynamic information). Hence, whereas the "structural" meaning of system is static and closed, the "interactions" meaning of system is dynamic and open. Note that the term interaction is used broadly here—the concept of interaction in statistics (e.g., analysis of variance) reflects a special (limited) case of the concept of interaction in systems.

The root meaning of the word "system," which derives from the Greek synhisanai ("to place together") is the concept of an integrated whole whose essential properties arise (emerge) from the relationships between its parts.

A classic example of holism in a system is how atoms of hydrogen and oxygen, each with their own unique set of holistic properties, can combine to form H_2O, a molecule created by particular bonds or valences, whose resulting unique (holistic) properties are qualitatively different from the individual properties of hydrogen and oxygen, and only emerge when hydrogen and oxygen interact recurrently. The same logic applies to the atoms of hydrogen and oxygen themselves. Electrons, protons, and neutrons each have their own unique set of properties. They can combine to form hydrogen, an atom whose unique (holistic) properties are qualitatively different from the individual properties of the subatomic particles, and only emerge when the particular combination of the subatomic particles interact recurrently and create hydrogen.

In systems theory, a system is defined as follows (Miller, 1978, page 16):

> A system is a *set* of *interacting units* with *relationships* among them. The word 'set' implies that the units have some *common* properties. These common properties are essential if the units are to interact or have relationships. *The state of each unit is constrained by, conditioned by, or dependent on the state of the other units.* The units are *coupled.* Moreover, there is at least one measure of the sum of its units which is *larger than the sum* of that measure of its units. (italics added)

These ideas, so to speak, are the heart of systems theory. Table 1 illustrates some core concept differences between a non-systemic and systemic approach to nature.

Table 1: Comparison of Non-Systemic and Systemic Concepts	
Non-Systemic Concepts	Systemic Concepts
Independence	Interdependence
Separation	Relationship
Static	Dynamic
Closed	Open
Active	Interactive
Disconnected	Connected
Linear summation	Non-linear as well as linear summation
Linear prediction	Emergent (non-linear) as well as linear prediction
Linear action	Circular (recurrent) interaction
Randomness	Complex order
"Either-or" logic	"And" logic as well as "either-or" logic
State independent	State dependent
Parts	Wholes
Fixed	Flexible, creative

Living systems theory (Miller, 1978; Capra, 1996) adds functional units which generate and process information, including memory, decoder, and reproducer subsystems, that operate at multiple levels (from cells to societies). Paraphrasing Miller (1978), we have defined living systems as dynamic organizations of intelligent information expressed in energy and matter (Russek and Schwartz, 1996a). Because systems theory is deliberately general (i.e., it is not unique to any discipline or sub-discipline) it might more appropriately be called a meta-theory or meta-framework. In any case, we have taken these general ideas, applied them to the concept of energy, and reframed them as dynamical energy systems hypotheses. However, we must first review what is meant by the terms information and energy before we can explain how systems theory revises our vision of memory in nature.

What Are Information and Energy?
Energy Does the "Work" of Information.

Information is one of the most mundane yet complex concepts in modern psychology. In one sense, everyone knows what information is. We use everyday language such as the "Information Highway" and the "Information Age." According to Miller (1978), information in systems refers to the abstract concept of patterns (literally, to give form). Information may be simply descriptive (structure and mathematical order), it may reflect complex knowledge, or it may convey deep wisdom. Information is the heart, so to speak, of the concept of mind, and is the foundation of consciousness and intention (Chalmers, 1996).

Everyday language reminds us that there is much more to information than just the "surface" pattern, form or order. For example, the pattern of letters *"bon jour"* is explicitly different from the pattern of letters "hello" even though both patterns of letters implicitly mean the same thing (e.g., warm greeting). Patterns can have "depth" or layers of meaning—which is, of course, the essence of language. Language involves the translation of intended meaning into sequences of words (encoding by the sender) and pattern recognition and interpretation of the sequences of words (decoding by the receiver). Systems theory emphasizes that components "process" information—information is "interpreted," and interpretation influences "memory." Since the behavior (functioning) of systems is influenced by both the physical and interpreted aspects of information, the systemic (holistic) memories that are stored will reflect a complex integration of pattern and meaning.

Energy is one of the most mundane yet mysterious concepts in modern physics. In one sense, everyone knows what energy is. We use everyday language such as "the sun generates energy." Electricity, magnetism, sound, pressure, temperature; these common terms all involve energy in some way. The reader not familiar with the measurement of energy, force and fields, especially as they are applied to biological systems, will find a clear introduction in *The Body Electric* (Becker and Selden,1988) and *Cross Currents* (Becker, 1990). The sophisticated reader will find a detailed review in *Bioelectromagnetism* (Malmivuo and Plonsey, 1995). Research on the effects of electromagnetic energies on cellular and organ function are regularly published in the journal *Bioelectromagnetics*.

The concept of energy addresses the fundamental question of how things move in space. Classically, energy is defined as the "ability to do work," (Miller, 1978, page 11). Physics speaks of two general types of energy: (1) kinetic energy, the energy that is expressed when an object accelerates, and (2) potential energy, the energy that is potentially available. In classical physics, quantities such as force and energy are usually measured either in meters, kilograms, and seconds (termed the "MKS system") or in centimeters, grams, and seconds (termed the "CGS system") (Orear, 1962). Note that the term "system" was used here by a physicist (Orear, 1992) simply to mean "structure"—in a static sense—not to mean "interactive units"—in a dynamic sense—as is used by systems theorists.

Though the measurement of energy may be defined precisely, the interpretation of energy is abstract and is difficult to comprehend (even by seasoned physicists). The inherent difficulty in understanding energy can not be understated. The abstract nature of energy may be one reason why the concept of energy, though appreciated by certain early scholars of psychology and medicine (e.g., Freud and Jung), has yet to make its way into the mainstream of modern psychology, neuroscience, and medicine (Russek and Schwartz, 1996a,b).

In this chapter, we use the term energy in the most general sense to reflect any process that has the "ability to do work" and therefore can influence the motion, and hence functioning, of objects (or systems). Examples of objects or systems include atoms, molecules, cellular processes, physiological functioning, consciousness, and overt behavior at the level of the organism. We will speak of biological systems as being energy "generating" systems, and we will speak of electrostatics (stationary charge), electricity (the flow of electrons), magnetism, sound, temperature, and pressure as examples of "energies" since they all have the ability to do work.

However, systems theory reminds us that what we measure is the functioning of systems. Energy and force are concepts we invent to make sense of the observation that iron particles do jump through space to a permanent magnet, and we use this observation to explain how, for example, the heart can be observed to contract when an electromagnet is placed near the chest (Ragan, Wang, and Eisenberg, 1995).

In summary, we can think of information as the form or structure of a system—and energy as the force or function that moves the system and enables it to emerge and evolve. In living systems, information and energy typically go hand in hand—energy contains information, and information is expressed through energy. Not only does energy convey information, in a deep sense energy does the work of information. It follows that organized energy both expresses and actualizes information (Schwartz, 1997; Russek and Schwartz, 1996a). As will become clear below, information and energy are both stored in systems as memory.

Conservation of Information and Energy

Classical physics reminds us of a profoundly important yet little appreciated fact—*information contained in energy, once produced, does not spontaneously vanish* (Orear, 1962). For example, the discipline of astrophysics is based on the assumption that the energy and information from stars, once released, travel at the speed of light indefinitely. This assumption explains the well-known fact that the visual experience of the stars at night reflects the electromagnetic history of stars at different ages depending upon their distance from the earth.

It logically follows that the visual pattern created by light reflected from a person's face, though obviously very weak compared to the energy of stars, also travels into space and continue indefinitely. Similarly, the electromagnetic pattern generated by a person's organs (e.g., the electrocardiogram, generated by the heart, which is the largest electromagnetic signal generated by a single organ in the body), also travels into space and continues indefinitely.

The idea that electromagnetic energy and information have a kind of immortality is not, per se, controversial. However, what becomes controversial is the realization of what happens when energy and information interact with dynamical systems.

Dynamical Energy Systems—Resonance as Interaction

When the essence of the mechanics of dynamic interactions is understood, the emergence of the systemic memory hypothesis becomes self-evident. We illustrate the logic using a simple two element system—the interaction of two tuning forks.

Consider the phenomenon of resonance between two tuning forks (A and B) that vibrate at similar rates. If one tuning fork (A) is struck, a second tuning fork (B) some distance from A will begin to "resonate" (make a sound), especially if B is identical in shape, size and substance to A.

How is this phenomenon explained? The classical, non-systemic interpretation is to say that tuning fork A generates sound "waves" which reach tuning fork B, and if B naturally vibrates at a frequency similar to the frequency generated by A, B will begin to move in synchrony with A. B therefore responds to A. A acts on B, hence B reacts to A.

It is worth noting that radar, a common measurement device, requires resonance. Waves are emitted (by A), travel to B and resonate with it, waves from B return to C (the receiver), and the waves that return are compared with the waves that left. However, *radar is designed to be minimally interactive in the sense that the purpose here is to hold A relatively constant, regardless of changes caused by B that might in turn cause changes in A.* The tuning fork example is more complex because *tuning forks have the potential to interact—A can react to B just as B can react to A.*

A dynamical energy systems interpretation requires that we reinterpret the relationship between tuning forks A and B as interactive, dynamically coupled, and cyclically connected. A does not simply act on B, A interacts with B. A and B are connected through the air (they are also connected electromagnetically, but we will ignore this for the time being). Since A and B are connected (coupled) when the energy from A begins to move B (cause vibration in B), B begins to generate a sound (energy), which returns to A. Therefore, *B begins to cause vibration in A shortly after A begins to cause vibration in B.* This implies that the functioning (behavior) of A (e.g., measured by the sound A emits) will be modulated in some complex ways by the functioning (behavior) of B (e.g., measured by the sound B emits).

To observe these predicted interactive effects, it becomes necessary to measure the sound coming from both A and B simultaneously. Using highly directional microphones, one microphone can be focused on A—pointed away from B—the other microphone can be focused on B—pointed away from A. The sounds must be monitored simultaneously and displayed over time. Data need to be collected striking A in the absence of B and striking A in the presence of B. *The dynamical energy systems prediction is that we should observe that A's behavior is quantitatively and qualitatively different (e.g., more complex) when struck in the presence of B as compared to when A is struck in the absence of B.* Conversely, we should observe that B's behavior is quantitatively and qualitatively different (e.g., more complex) when struck in the presence of A as compared to when B is struck in the absence of A.

This seemingly trivial interaction is not so simple to mathematically model over time. Complex phase interactions (dynamic interference patterns) need to be calculated over time and distance, and as will become clear below, the interaction will naturally evolve over time due to the circulation and sharing of energy and information between A and B.

Tuning forks A and B can be shown to be interdependent and interactive, processing information generated by each of them as they interact. From a dynamical energy systems perspective, since all systems are open to varying degrees at various times, it follows that all systems should interact energetically in complex and sometimes powerful ways.

What Happens between A and B Also Happens within A and B

Tuning forks A and B are obviously material objects, they are each material systems. As illustrated above, when tuning forks A and B resonate, they become a two tuning fork system. Each tuning fork functions as a subsystem in the two tuning fork system (or we can say each tuning fork is a system in the two tuning fork suprasystem—the principle is the same).

Tuning forks A and B each contain molecules. Molecules are subsystems within each tuning fork (or we can say each molecule is a system within a single tuning fork suprasystem—the principle is the same). Hence, it follows that resonance not only can occur between tuning forks A and B, resonance can occur within tuning forks A and B. In fact, tuning forks A and B cannot vibrate as individual tuning forks unless their molecules can vibrate (resonate) as a whole system. In other words, the logic of what happens between tuning forks A and B applies to what happens within tuning forks A and B as well.

Modern quantum physics tells us that even at the temperature of absolute zero, matter vibrates, and hence, resonates. As described by Forward (1996) in his tutorial on quantum mechanics (pages 328- 329):

"Matter is quantized. A block of matter, although seemingly a continuously divisible substance, is ultimately found to be made of 'quanta' called atoms. An atom consists of a small massive nucleus surrounded by a large cloud of electrons. The electron cloud acts as a 'spring' suspension for the mass of the nucleus, and suspends it in its place in the block of matter. This mass-spring system can vibrate. . . . These vibrational quanta have been named 'phonons.' . . . Now here comes the interesting part. When the equations of quantum mechanics are used to determine the 'average energy' $<E>$ of the vibrations of the atoms, the answer is $<E> = [n(T) + 1/2]hf$, where the number of phonons $n(T)$ is a function of temperature such that when $T=0$ K, $n(T)=0$. Thus, even at zero temperature, quantum mechanics predicts that each of the atoms will have an average residual energy of $<E>=hf/2$. This residual energy is an average. It is not that the energy of each atom is a 'half a phonon' but that roughly half the atoms have one (perhaps more) vibrational quanta or phonons, while the others have no phonon. *The phonon distributions rapidly change with time as the phonons are passed back and forth*

225

between the many atoms. This residual energy at zero absolute temperature predicted by the equations of quantum mechanics is the so-called 'Quantum Mechanical Zero-Temperature Vibrational Fluctuations of Matter.'"

Forward (1996) goes on to say (page 329):

"This quantum mechanical fluctuation energy of the atoms in matter has been measured by measuring the vibrations in a crystal as the temperature of the crystal is lowered. The experimental data agree with the predictions of the equations of quantum mechanics, so the quantum mechanical zero-temperature vibrational functions of atoms in matter is real. It is this residual quantum mechanical vibrational energy that keeps liquid helium from freezing even when it is cooled to within microdegrees of absolute zero temperature."

When matter is viewed from a dynamical energy systems perspective, logic dictates that interactive resonance not only occurs *between* material systems (e.g., between tuning forks A and B), but also occurs *within* material systems (e.g., within tuning fork A and within tuning fork B) as well. For this reason, the logic that leads to the hypothesis outlined below, that recurrent feedback interaction creates dynamic memory between tuning forks A and B, also requires that we entertain the hypothesis that recurrent feedback interaction simultaneously creates dynamic memory *within* tuning fork A and within tuning fork B as well, and this intra-tuning fork memory is sustained, even after tuning forks A and B have been separated. In psychological terms, the "short term" memory of the interaction between A and B may be sustained as a "long term" memory by the interactions within A and B.

From Interaction to Dynamic Memory—Recurrent feedback Interaction and the Systemic Memory Hypothesis

The interaction between tuning forks A and B (or between any A's and B's—e.g., photons, subatomic particles, atoms, molecules, cells, organs, organisms, groups of organisms, etc.) contains a profound implication. As A and B interact with each other, they literally create a dynamic memory of their interaction over time through the circulation of their information and energy. In fact, this dynamic memory is part of the expression of their interactions as a whole, and is a natural requirement for them to interact. The dynamic memory is the relationship. The relationship information is systemic information, and systemic information is an expression of the whole. Moreover, it follows that the information of the whole of a system is stored dynamically within each of the parts comprising the system to varying degrees.

This idea, surprisingly, is not well appreciated, even by seasoned systems theorists. However, the logic is relatively simple and straightforward, and inevitably follows when feedback interactions are analyzed systemically. If A and B do not interact (the classic non-systemic approach), dynamic memory between A and B is not an issue. However, if A and B do interact, and interact recurrently, logic dictates that dynamic memory processes must unfold over time naturally. We illustrate this point by considering memory from the point of view of tuning fork A. The logic is displayed in figure 1.

At time 0, before A is struck, A is vibrating dynamically as predicted by quantum dynamics (e.g., its electrons, protons and neutrons are vibrating and moving in complex, interacting, resonating ways as mentioned above). When A is struck at time 1, it vibrates with a frequency "a1." Now, frequency "a1" moves (at the speed of sound) to tuning fork B. B begins to vibrate at time 2, which is some complex product of "a1" (we will, for the sake of simplicity, assume for the moment that "a1" has not changed much as it travels to B) and B's state at time 2. We will call this complex product "a1b2."

As B vibrates, the sound now returns to A at time 3. The sound that returns to A at time 3 is a complex product of "a1b2" plus whatever interference occurs with the continued sound generated by A at time 3 (a3). This gives us the even more complex product "a1b2a3" that returns to A at time 3.

Now, let us hypothesize that A is influenced by this returned sound at time 3 to some degree, and starts to interact with A's vibration at time 4. Not only will A's vibration have changed spontaneously by time 4 (e.g., it might be decreasing—the simplest case), *but it will have further changed by the complex "a1b2a3" interaction reaching it.* The resulting sound will be "a4" modulated by "a1b2a3," or "a1b2a3a4."

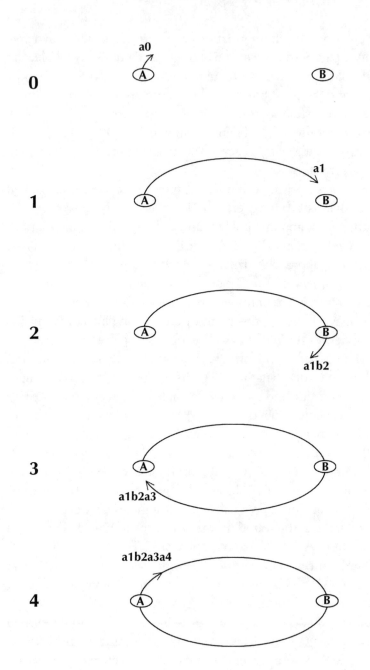

Figure 1: Graphic description of the logic of dynamic
(systemic) memory (see text for details)

In other words, in one complete "cycle" of A-B interaction (A influences B, B responds in part as feedback from A), the sound generated by A at time 4 contains *the complex history of the A-B interaction (their a1b2a3 relationship) over the cycle.* We see an "image" of a1, modulated by b2, interacting back with a3, returning to A, so that the vibrational pattern of A at time 4 includes the *history of the first A-B interaction in its next interaction.* Meanwhile, from the perspective of B, a somewhat parallel set of interactions is also simultaneously occurring.

Each cycle includes the previous information, hence the history (dynamic memory) continues to grow. *As long as the units are connected, the memory trace will be retained, albeit modified as time goes on.* All things being equal, the dynamic memory trace will "grow" with time.

Of course, the growth of dynamic memory will naturally occur in the context of what an anonymous reviewer termed the "3 D's"—dilution, dissipation, and decay. However, it is possible that the capacity of a system to sustain its organization and wholeness against the 3 D's (and therefore continue its negentropy) may actually involve the effective circulation of recurrent feedback interactions and the maintenance of dynamic memory.

Also of course, if recurrent feedback could be somehow perfectly reversed in phase, cancellation of the dynamic memory could, in theory, occur. However, it is highly improbable that perfect phase reversed recurrent feedback processes are created and sustained in complex systems in nature. Hence, complete cancellation of dynamic memory is virtually impossible in complex systems.

Now, if we take a dynamical energy systems approach, we realize that *systems are always interconnected to various degrees in various ways.* Hence, energy (and the information riding with the energy) is continually being exchanged to various degrees in various ways. As a result, the dynamic memories continue naturally.

The logic and simple mathematics of the two tuning fork example are obviously grossly oversimplified. We have chosen only four time points, and have described the complex interaction only from the perspective of tuning fork A. However, the essence of the idea should be self-evident. Any time two (A + B) or more (A + B + n) things interact, information concerning their history accumulates in some form over time. A and B can be an electron and a proton, a thermostat and a furnace, the two strands of DNA, the heart and the brain, a mother and a fetus, even the planets and the sun. From a dynamical energy systems perspective, *at whatever levels the systems are interacting, the interactive history of the energy and information should be contained in a complex way.* Simply stated, all memory is dynamic (systemic) memory.

As described in the previous section, every system is, by definition, composed of multiple subsystems, and these subsystems normally are in constant interaction with each other. *Therefore, it logically follows that after tuning forks A and B have interacted, tuning fork A and tuning fork B will have each stored information about their A-B interactions.* This information will continue to circulate within each tuning fork, even if the tuning forks are separated from each other. In fact, if quantum mechanics is correct, this information will continue to circulate within each tuning fork, even if the tuning forks were cooled to absolute zero.

Of course, outlining the logic that dynamic memory is intrinsically created and stored in systems does not imply that this information, once stored, can be accessed and retrieved (at least in human consciousness). *The deep question of retrieving dynamic memory, once stored, will be briefly addressed later.*

Some Implications for Basic Science—
Recurrent Feedback Interactions and Dynamic Memory
in Neurons, Neural Networks, Cells, DNA, and Water.

The concept of recurrent feedback interaction has been emerging for at least the past 100 years. The concept of recurrent feedback interaction was anticipated at the neural level by William James (1890). In chapter 16 of James Psychology (Briefer Course), James stated:

> "When two elementary brain-processes have been active together or in immediate succession, one of them, on reoccurring, tends to propagate its excitement into the other."

When the word "subsystems" is substituted for "brain-processes," the systemic memory hypothesis is anticipated.

"When two subsystems have been active together or in immediate succession, one of them, on reoccurring, tends to propagate its excitement into the other."

McCulloch (1951), in his seminal paper "Why the Mind is in the Head," not only proposed the idea of "reverberatory memory," but pointed out that:

"The reverberating activity patterned after something that happened retains the form of the happening but loses track of when it happened. Thus it shows that there was some time at which such and such occurred. The 'such and such' is the idea wrenched out of time."

He went on to state:

"It is an eternal idea in a transitory memory wherein the form exists only so long as the reverberation endures. When that ceases, the form is no longer anywhere."

McCulloch did not extend his logic to physical and biological systems other than neurons. Had he done so, he would have discovered that "reverberation" (circulating interaction) in systems is the rule, not the exception, and that according to modern quantum dynamics, reverberation persists, even at absolute zero temperature. In fact, recurrent feedback resonance would be predicted to occur in its most "effortless" (frictionless) form in "super-conducting" states of matter. Only in the case of presumed complete entropy would it be predicted that dynamic memory should be eliminated completely (note that entropy is a concept derived from classical physics—systemic physics would predict that recurrent feedback interactions would likely continue in the entropic state). Note also that the psychological distinction between "short" term and "long" term memory blurs when a dynamical energy systems perspective is taken (e.g., "short" term memory may differ from "long" term memory in terms of the difficulty of retrieving the "short" term memory rather than the presumed lack of the storage of the short term memory per se).

The concept of recurrent feedback interaction is implicit in the writings of Karl Pribram (e.g., Pribram, 1991) in his holonomic brain theory of perception and language. His writings are replete with descriptions such as "local circuit interactions," "ensembles" with "iterations," "spatial interactions," "back propagations," and "cooperative interactions." For example, Pribram writes:

> "A microprocess is conceived in terms of ensembles of mutually interacting pre- and postsynaptic events distributed across limited extents of the dendritic network. The limits of reciprocal interaction vary as a function of input (sensory and central) to the network—limits are not restricted to the dendritic tree of a single neuron. In fact, reciprocal interaction among pre- and postsynaptic events often occurs at a distance from one another." (Pribram, 1991, page 16).

It is this capacity for "reciprocal interactions" to occur between highly interconnected, distributed, "mutually interacting" dendritic processes that allows for the emergence of holographic-like information to be stored throughout complex dendritic (network) systems. At the end of the appendix (Pribram, 1991), Yasue, Jibu, and Pribram note that information "comes to be stored in the new neural channel between the units A and B. The inference process thus has a procedure for enlarging the scope of inference." Though not emphasized by Pribram, the logic he has used to explain dynamic memory formation in an interconnected, mutually interacting neural network system can be applied to dynamic memory formation in *any highly interconnected, mutually interacting dynamical network system.*

It is well known that recurrent feedback loops in neural networks foster dynamic memory and learning in neural networks (e.g., Lisberger and Sejnowski, 1992). Neural networks are mathematical models that reflect our attempt to envision how recurrent neural interactions allow for memory to occur in the brain. It has not been appreciated that the logic used to explain recurrent feedback loops in neural networks can be equally applied to recurrent feedback networks in all dynamical systems at all levels. However, the reasoning is fundamentally the same. Moreover, the insight that circulating recurrent feedback interactions provide an explanation for holism in all dynamical systems has not been previously explicated.

Hence, information should be stored dynamically not only in neurons, but in all biophysical systems, from the very small (e.g., electron-proton interactions in the atom) to the very large (e.g., atmosphere-ground interactions in the planet). The systemic memory hypothesis clearly stretches and challenges our capacity to envision the dynamical interactive nature of systems (e.g., do recurrent feedback interactions occur between the moon and the earth? Do recurrent feedback interactions occur between the earth and the sun?). By definition, the mathematics of dynamic recurrent feedback interactions is not limited to a subset of scientists in a subset of disciplines studying a subset of systems. For this reason the hypothesis is termed the systemic memory hypothesis and the memory is termed dynamic memory.

Certain molecules may be particularly good at storing complex information. DNA, the profoundly complex double-helix, may be especially designed to store informational and energetic interactions between its two strands. However, all cells, theoretically, should store information—not just neural cells and immune cells, but heart cells and lung cells as well. Because individual neurons are so extensively interconnected with other neurons, and because there are literally billions of extensively interconnected neurons, neurons are exquisitely designed to generate profoundly rich and complex parallel recurrent feedback interactions, which may be why they are especially successful in the storage of rich and complex information.

Of course, each cell can only store the information it receives, and it will process this information in its own way. Systems can potentially store only what they are capable of responding to (and hence processing). Technology reminds us, for example, that photographic plates store visible light patterns much better than they do audible sound patterns. It logically follows that the nature of information stored between subatomic particles, for example, will be of a different order than the nature of information stored between neurons. Also, the more reliable and flexible the components of the system (and hence, the more complex the system), the more reliable and flexible should be the storage of information.

It logically follows that the more rapidly recurrent feedback interactions occur in a given system, the more rapidly a stable holistic history should emerge. For example, atoms vibrate billions of times a second. Therefore, although it would be predicted that it should take a finite amount of time for a molecular holistic history to form when hydrogen and oxygen come together as H_2O, the time it actually takes may be a few nanoseconds.

Of course, the fact that information is theoretically stored does not necessarily mean that the information can be retrieved, at least consciously. Everyday experience and substantial empirical research (Schacter, 1996) reminds us that our ability to recognize information is typically far greater than our ability to recall information. For example, the senior author's recall of basic chemistry is minimal—yet his recognition of chemistry, particularly in the textbooks he studied as an undergraduate minor in chemistry—is substantial.

Failure to show recall does not necessarily imply that dynamic memory has not occurred. Forgetting, therefore, does not necessarily imply that dynamic memory has been erased—the process may involve an alteration in retrieval. This point is emphasized by Pribram (1991, page xxvvii):

> "By using primes and probes, Fergus Craik in an elegant program of experiments (Craik, 1988), has shown that disturbances of remembering are almost always due to interference with the process and not with a loss of stored items. Neuropsychological evidence (e.g., Pribram, 1986; Weiskrantz, 1986) has also repeatedly demonstrated that 'engrams' are not 'lost' as such as a result of brain damage. Rather engrams are reconstructions that can appear as intrusion errors when amnesiacs are examined in a systematic fashion; that is, during recall, reconstruction of an engram occurs but in an inappropriate context."

The systemic memory hypothesis predicts that information, once received, is retained in some form forever, so long as the system remains intact and recurrent feedback interactions (cycling) continue. Not only will the information continue, but it potentially will evolve over time. In fact, in a deep sense, it may be impossible to ever erase information completely in an intact system. Theoretically, if the experiment is sensitive enough, evidence for savings (see Schacter, 1996) or other subtle measures of change in functioning (behavior) should be demonstrable in all systems as a function of the evolution of the hypothesized dynamic memory process.

It is generally assumed that psychosocial information is not stored in the genes, and therefore it is not transferred biologically from parents to fetus. This assumption is consistent with the empirical observation that rats, for example, do not show obvious transfer of maze learning across generations, though not all scholars interpret the data in this way (Sheldrake, 1981). Failure to show transfer of learning does not necessarily imply that information has not been *transferred—it could equally be the case that the information had been transferred in some form but was not retrieved.* This conceptual distinction is very important, because the systemic memory hypothesis requires that we seriously entertain the hypothesis that recurrent feedback interaction involves dynamic memory to some degree. Data that are inconsistent with the hypothesis that the information is stored (dynamic memory), therefore, may require an alternative interpretation (failure to retrieve). As will be seen, understanding how information is retrieved, especially the complex kind of information accumulated through the process of recurrent feedback interaction, is one of science's greatest challenges.

As mentioned earlier, the concept of recurrent feedback interaction provides us with a new approach to understanding the phenomenon of emergent properties (Scott, 1995). The classic example is how two molecules, hydrogen and oxygen, invisible gases at room temperature, combine to create a unique molecule, water, which is clearly visible at room temperature. No other combination of atoms is known to form a molecule with the identical properties of water. Water is one of the few molecules that increase in size when it solidifies. Also, water is one of the few molecules that in the process of freezing creates a seemingly infinite number of beautifully complex structures termed snowflakes. The capacity for water to form such unique combinations of order is challenging for science to understand.

Life as we understand it requires water. Although all molecules have unique, emergent properties—water may be especially unique. From a systems perspective, water as a liquid may function as a complex dynamical system (e.g., the whole ocean can be viewed as a gigantic dynamical system—the circulation of blood in organisms can also be viewed as a large dynamical system) and it may have a special capacity to store information and energy.

When a dynamical energy systems approach is applied to quantum mechanics, and these concepts are applied to water, questions can be raised about the storage of information not only in water as a system, but in the individual molecules comprising the water system (e.g., the recurrent dynamic interactions between hydrogen and oxygen—see Jibu, Pribram, and Yasue, 1996). Moreover, the logic requires that we entertain the possibility that if hydrogen and oxygen are subsequently separated after having existed in the water molecule, the hydrogen and oxygen will each retain some information about their history (due to recurrent feedback interactions between the electrons and the nuclei) that may be expressed in terms of increased dimensional complexity. Though clearly controversial, the systemic memory hypothesis requires that we posit the possibility of recurrent feedback resonance and dynamic memory between and within atoms.

Emergent properties (i.e., novel properties of the whole) may reflect a recurrent feedback interaction process—through dynamical recurrent feedback interaction, unique, creative, holistic memories can emerge and be expressed.

It is worth noting that the systemic memory hypothesis has implications for understanding normal and pathological aging. It is conceivable that systems can only accumulate so much information/complexity. It is possible that certain systems (e.g., living systems) ultimately "collapse under the weight," so to speak, of too much information (e.g., complex vibrations that destroy the integrity of the system to function as a whole). Moreover, if a system is unable to sustain dynamic circulation, it will not be able to sustain its holistic memories, and therefore, theoretically, it should "die."

Implications for Predicting and Explaining Certain Heretofore Unexplained Observations and Claims—Homeopathy, Kinesiology, Aromatherapy, and Parapsychology

The concept of recurrent feedback interaction, and the systemic memory hypothesis, provide a possible explanation for a host of heretofore unexplained observations and claims. In the emerging field of alternative medicine, two areas that challenge our traditional models are homeopathy and kinesiology. Homeopathy involves treatments using dilutions of substances in water that are so weak that virtually no molecules of the substance dissolved in the water can be detected. However, double blind studies (reviewed in Bellavite and Signorini, 1995) show that certain homeopathic dilutions can have statistically and clinically significant effects in reducing certain symptoms and treating certain diseases. Proponents of homeopathy claim that water contains a memory for the molecules. The systemic memory hypothesis provides a rationale for predicting and explaining these observations.

Kinesiology (e.g., Diamond, 1979) involves diagnoses and treatments that presume that the muscles and organ tissues store information and energy, for example, about traumas. Since traditional models presume that memories are stored only in the central nervous system, the observations and interpretations of kinesiologists are interpreted as being in error. However, the systemic memory hypothesis suggests that all cells may indeed store information, and therefore this information can be potentially retrieved from muscles and organ tissues. Having a patient "tune into memories stored in specific bodily regions" may be more than just a metaphor—organs may store patterns of information that are unique and can be added to information stored in the brain.

Aromatherapy involves the distillation of plants and diffusing the resulting "essential oils" in the air, rubbing them on the skin, and/or ingesting them. Claims for medical, psychological, and spiritual applications have existed for thousands of years. A basic premise is that the essential oils reflect the "essence" of the plants, and that the "soul" and "spirit" (information and energy) (Schwartz, 1997) of the plant as a whole is retained in the essential oils. Non-systemic physics and chemistry would predict that distillation removes the structure of the plant, leaving behind a soup of molecules whose properties are no different from a collection of molecules created synthetically in the laboratory. However, systemic physics and chemistry, and hence systemic memory, would predict that distilled molecules still retain core aspects of the information and energy of the plants they composed. Natural mixtures may sometimes be more potent than synthetic mixtures because even though both mixtures may have the same physical "structures," they will have different functional properties due to their different systemic (informational and energetic) histories.

Probably the most controversial heretofore unexplained observations involving memory and memory retrieval are reported in parapsychology. It is commonly claimed in parapsychological folklore as well as some well documented case studies (e.g., Smith, 1964) that "sensitives" and "psychics" can "read" information about a person from personal effects, including photographs. Claims for "psychometry" truly challenge our traditional theories of memory. However, quantum physics, viewed from a dynamical energy systems perspective, provides a possible systemic explanation for these effects.

Consider what happens when an object (such as a person) spends time in front of a surface such as a black wall, or the black pupils of someone else's eyes. Physics tells us that objects appear black because they "absorb" the visible spectra of light (Orear, 1962). Complex patterns that comprise the organization of visible light (the visual portion of the electromagnetic spectrum) are "absorbed" by the wall, the pupil (or any black surface). Complex patterns comprising the organization of invisible light (e.g., infrared that is related to heat) are also "absorbed."

Once these energy patterns are "absorbed," where do they go? Do the dynamic patterns of information simply disappear? This is the assumption of classical, non-systemic physics. But a dynamical energy systems approach, accepting recurrent feedback interaction and resonance as common and natural, and accepting the storage of information in "A-B" situations as similarly common and natural, would hypothesize that the patterns become part of the ongoing systemic energetic (recurrent) interactions occurring within the wall or eye system, and therefore will be "stored" (i.e., become part of the wall's or pupil's systemic history).

A black wall, for example, being a less complex system than the pupil of the eye, should "store" this information in a less complex (and potentially physically more "pure") manner. Theoretically, however, people interact with walls in a manner that is similar to the way people interact with eyes (though obviously less complexly). People may vary in their ability (or desire) to "resonate" with walls or pupils, and, therefore, resonate differently with the stored information in the walls or pupils. Since the storage of information (the "membering" part of re-membering) is not the same as the retrieval of information (the remembering), the task of retrieving all of this hypothetically stored information remains a major challenge for future science.

It is challenging to raise the question about whether electromagnetic information, at least in the visible spectrum, is "stored" in a black object. It would be predicted, for example, that black objects should store more patterned light information than white objects. It is even more challenging to raise the question about whether such information, once stored, is "living." When systems are viewed as energetic and dynamic, each comprised of continually interacting subsystems (e.g., recall that water is comprised of billions of continually interacting water molecules) creating recurrent information (a water system), the simple distinction between non-life and living becomes blurred. Though beyond the scope of the present paper, it is clear that the criteria we use to determine whether information and energy are "living" or not (Miller, 1978; Capra, 1996) needs to be specified in order to address this question.

A logical extension of these hypotheses applies to the ancient idea that spaces and settings store information and energy, even over centuries. For example, some people claim that certain places of worship (e.g., St. Patrick's and St. John the Divine Cathedrals in New York City) accumulate very different information and energy (e.g., love and compassion), compared with certain places of transportation (e.g., tension and frustration in the Port Authority Terminal and Grand Central Station in New York City) (Brennan, 1993).

These hypotheses may also help explain Jung's controversial concept of archetypes and the so-called "collective unconscious" stored in the so-called "quantum sea" (see Laughlin, 1996). The systemic memory hypothesis encourages us to be open to the possibility that some aspects of parapsychological folklore may, in part, reflect a genuine dynamic memory phenomenon.

Some Implications for Society—The Information Bomb and the Survival of Consciousness Hypothesis

If future research were to establish that some version of the systemic memory hypothesis were true, the implications for society would be far-reaching. One profound implication is the possibility that the past really exists in the present, and that this information is potentially accessible. The amount of information potentially stored is extraordinarily challenging to envision. However, what would happen if someone figured out a procedure for retrieving this information?

To the extent that knowledge is power, access to this information could not only be potentially very useful, it could also be potentially abused. In the same way that the discovery of $E=mc^2$ led to the development of atomic power and atomic destruction, the discovery of a parallel formula for information and memory retrieval could have both positive and negative effects.

For example, most of us are not flooded with all the implicit information we have stored in our lifetime. Is it possible that systems evolve to keep most of this implicit information in check? Is it critical for human consciousness that we not be flooded with past information? Are some disorders of mental illness the breakdown of inhibitor mechanisms that keep implicit information out of awareness? What would happen if someone discovered a drug that removed the capacity to keep information in check? Could this become a new method of chemical warfare, leading solders and citizens to be swamped literally by their own information? What is science fiction today sometimes becomes the science of tomorrow. The hypothesis that information is continually stored and is potentially retrievable has many potential science fiction implications, some of which may turn out to be tomorrow's science.

Probably the most controversial implication of the systemic memory hypothesis concerns the survival of consciousness after death. Throughout recorded history, people have entertained the hypothesis, and the wish, that some aspects of consciousness continue after physical death. Interest in the bridge between science and spirituality continues to grow, and scholarly books addressing the psychology of consciousness at all levels in systems (Chalmers,

1996) and the physics of immortality (Tipler, 1994) are appearing. If it were the case that the history of people's lives, their information and energy, is not only stored in their brains and bodies, but is to some degree dynamically stored in all systems (especially in their living loved ones and objects with which they have spent significant time), and if consciousness is a fundamental aspect of information (Chalmers, 1996), then the survival of consciousness hypothesis after physical death becomes a greater possibility. The systemic memory hypothesis provides an unusually challenging and intimate bridge between science and spirituality.

The Power of Logic and Its Limitations: The Answer Lies in Future Research

Who would have guessed (except with hindsight) that in the process of attempting to understand the logic of circular feedback (recurrent interactions) from the perspective of information, that the logic would inevitably lead to the systemic memory hypothesis? As we attempt to explicate in this chapter, when the implications of dynamical recurrent feedback interaction are understood, some surprising and far-reaching predictions follow that can be confirmed or disconfirmed in future research.

In a review of a recent paper (Russek and Schwartz, 1996a) outlining some dynamic energy systems implications for cardiology, mind-body medicine, and alternative medicine, Puthoff (1996), a physicist, noted that "On this trail we are led inexorably to consider not only hypothesized deep connections between brain and heart, consciousness and cardiovascular activity, but between the whole organism and its environment, including others, by means of patterned energetic mechanisms." Puthoff's selection of the term "inexorably" seems well chosen. When a systems approach to energy and information is taken, and the process of interaction is analyzed, a series of novel and controversial predictions do follow inexorably.

One could argue that the logic of systems theory is circular, and that the reasoning of recurrent feedback interactions is circular. Interestingly, this turns out to be literally and unavoidably true. In fact, the essence of the meaning of the word "circular" (and the concept of a circle) is "ending in itself" (the fifth definition of the word "circular" in *Webster's Unabridged Second Edition Dictionary*).

Capra (1996), in his book on living systems, emphasized that feedback is in fact circular feedback, that relationships are circular relationships, and that organization is circular organization. Though Capra (a seasoned systems theorist) emphasized that circular organization is involved in self-organization, self-awareness, and evolution, and he implicitly recognized that self-organization, self-awareness, and evolution require the storage of information and energy, he apparently did not take the logic far enough to discover that circular feedback involves recurrent (circular) interaction which naturally creates dynamic memory—the systemic memory hypothesis (see Schwartz and Russek, 1997, for further discussion of circular causality in science and medicine).

Recurrent feedback interaction means cyclic, repeated interaction (the word recurrent comes from the word "recur," which means to "return"), and this implies "circulation." It turns out that the hypothesis of the storage of information and energy as dynamic memory (e.g., the preserving of order) was historically understood in the concept of circulation. According to Webster, the obsolete definition of the word circulation is "a series in which the same order is preserved, and things return to the same state." When the concept of dynamical interaction is added to Webster's historic description of the concept of circulation, logic leads to the hypothesis of dynamical (evolving) order (storage of evolving information and energy) in systems—the systemic memory hypothesis.

Circular logic also suggests that the emergence and expression of holism in systems may be a natural result of dynamical interactive circulation of accumulating relationship information and energy. Dynamic systemic memory, then, is holistic memory.

Of course, this does not mean that the logic is correct, or that the predictions are valid. Though the authors have been unable to discover an obvious flaw in the logic, the logic may still be misplaced or mistaken. Even if the logic turns out to be correct, nature may not work the way logic predicts, suggesting that the basic assumptions are in error. For example, though general systems theory makes the assumption that systems in nature are always open to various degrees, and therefore interact recurrently with other systems to various degrees, the openness assumption could be wrong, and therefore systemic memories should not form.

However, it is possible that the logic has not been taken far enough. Is it possible that energy interacts with energy in the absence of matter? For example, do organized patterns of light/electromagnetic waves interact in a vacuum? Do these "packets" or "quanta" of energy in a vacuum combine and create pure energy systems? If pure energy systems do in fact exist, is information stored in these systems too?

New quantum mechanical predictions about electromagnetic fluctuations of the vacuum suggest that some version of this hypothesis is tenable. According to Forward (1996, page 330):

> "Now comes the real problem, and the major reason why we need to carry out experiments to verify that the quantum mechanical electromagnetic fluctuations of the vacuum behave as the equations of quantum mechanics predict. The block of matter has a large, but finite, number of atoms and therefore a finite total quantum mechanical vibrational fluctuation energy. The region of vacuum, however, can support an infinity of electromagnetic vibrations. . . ."

It is conceptually challenging to ponder that between every "particle" of "matter" is a "space" (a "region of vacuum") that is potentially teaming with energy and information. If the region of the vacuum can support an "infinity of electromagnetic vibrations" (the quantum mechanics hypothesis) and electromagnetic vibrations can function as pure energy systems, then an "infinity of recurrent feedback interactions" can occur as well (the systemic memory hypothesis). Since the vacuum (V) theoretically exists between components A and B in the simplist, two component system, V may serve as a dynamic mechanism allowing stored information and energy to leave the particular A-B system selectively and enter the larger V suprasystem (that includes A and B). It follows that all subsystems, systems, and suprasystems, are ultimately interconnected by V.

Using the concept of "quantum vacuum interaction" to explain the formation of memory, Laszlo (1995) provides a new explanation for the wave/particle paradox observed in the well-known single slit/double slit quantum physics experiment. (Page 54, italics by Laszlo, 1995).

> "It appears, then, that photons successively emitted by a given light source pass through only one of the slits and then interfere with each other. This suggests that not self-interference, but *memory* is at work. The previously emitted photons are no longer physically 'there,' but their *traces* can be: the most reasonable interpretation is that the successively emitted photons interfere with the traces of the photons that were emitted previously. But how are these traces registered and conveyed? For a realistic interpretation a physical medium carrying the traces is required: a medium that transcends the limitations of relativisitic spacetime . . . the indicated medium in the guise of the scalar-mediated spectrum of the quantum vacuum."

It is possible that the systemic memory hypothesis, integrated with modern quantum dynamics of the vacuum (Milonni, 1994; Laszlo, 1995), may help explain the profoundly challenging hypothesis about memory in the universe proposed by Sheldrake (1981). Sheldrake has proposed that information in the universe is continuously stored in so-called morphogenetic (i.e., form) fields, that systems emerge through morphogenetic resonance, and therefore, that the physical laws of nature are better understood to be evolving "habits" (Sheldrake, 1981) or memories of a dynamic universe rather than fixtures of a static universe. If modern quantum mechanics is correct, the vacuum may turn out to be the ultimate storage device for recurrent feedback energy systems interactions and the "habits" of nature.

The logic that leads to the conclusion that the vacuum may be the ultimate storage device for recurrent feedback energy systems interactions is implicated in Bohm's recurrent process explanation of Sheldrake's morphogenetic resonance hypothesis (Sheldrake and Bohm, 1982). After Bohm published his seminal book on wholeness and the implicate order (Bohm, 1980), Bohm went on to employ the circular concepts of "reinjection," "reprojection," and "recurrent actuality," to explain the origin of memory and wholeness in nature. Simply stated, Bohm hypothesized that implicate memories emerge through "repeated cycles of reinjections and reprojections." Repeated cycles of reinjections and reprojections described at the quantum level can be viewed as being a special case of the process of recurrent feedback interactions that occur in all systems at all levels—the implicit logic is the same. According to Bohm, our everyday concept of "actuality" (what we term "reality") should be reconceptualized as being a dynamical process, a *"recurrent* actuality."

However, the deep challenge still remains, how can implicate memories stored in dynamical systems become explicate? It is difficult enough to attempt to explain, conceptually and mathematically, how information, once stored as memory in neural systems, can be retrieved. It is even more difficult to attempt to explain, conceptually and mathematically, how information, possibly stored as memory in other organ systems, could be retrieved. It is extraordinarily difficult to attempt to explain, conceptually and mathematically, how information, potentially stored as memory in a vacuum (pure energy systems), could be retrieved. Though this chapter has not addressed the profound challenge of the retrieval of systemic memory, it seems possible that the solution to the retrieval of systemic memory will involve an even deeper understanding of recurrent feedback resonance in systems, integrating harmonic resonance and stochastic resonance (e.g., Astumian, Weaver, and Adair, 1995) from a recurrent feedback interaction perspective. To "re-member" may be to "re-resonate" in some deep systemic way.

Pribram (personal communication) has suggested that valence (the foundation of value) patterns recurrent feedback interaction and hence the creation of systemic memory. His suggestion is consistent with dynamical energy systems theory. The concept of a system requires that the components be connected energetically with a variety of valences. Energetic connections implicitly involve the concept of valence. In humans, emotions (in particular, love) function as valence, and emotions (in particular, love and loving relationships) foster memories. Valence in turn fosters the creation and maintenance of relationships. Thus the capacity to "re-resonate" with systemic memory may involve patterns of valence as well.

The purpose of this chapter has been to raise fundamental questions about dynamical recurrent feedback interaction, to encourage open discussion about the storage of information and energy and the creation of dynamic memory, and to stimulate empirical research to determine whether dynamic memory exists in all systems at all levels. As mentioned in the beginning, though neurons are especially gifted in storing sensory and perceptual information (because neurons are so highly interconnected, creating profoundly complex recurrent interactive networks), it may be time to evolve our intellectual heritage and reenvision the brain as being a marvelous special case of a ubiquitous dynamic (systemic) memory process in nature. It is our belief that in the process of addressing the question of recurrent feedback interaction, science will gain a deeper understanding of the essence of memory, emergent properties and holism, and self-awareness and evolution, and in the process, make better sense of heretofore unexplained observations in medicine such as homeopathy (Bellavite and Signorini, 1995), and in psychology such as parapsychology (Bem and Hornoton, 1994), that strain our current theories of how memory works.

Acknowledgments

Our sincerest thanks to John J.B. Allen, John P. Kline, Lynn Nadel, and Lonnie Nelson, from the University of Arizona, for their help in challenging and clarifying the thesis of this chapter, and to Karl H. Pribram, for his inspiration, insights and editorial suggestions. The chapter is dedicated to the memory of Heinz Pagels, the distinguished physicist, who encouraged the first author at Yale University to risk integrating concepts from modern physics and systems theory with psychology and neuroscience to foster both basic and applied science, to the memory of Howard Schwartz, a chemical engineer and pharmacist, who held a special appreciation for atoms and molecules and encouraged the first author to be open to the wonders of physics and chemistry, and to the memory of Henry I. Russek, M.D., the distinguished cardiologist, who encouraged the second author during their twenty year research and clinical collaboration to risk integrating biological, psychosocial, and spiritual concepts to foster both the art and science of clinical medicine.

References

Abu-Mostafa, Y. S. 1957. *Complexity in Information Theory.* New York: Springer-Verlag.

Astumian, R. D., J. C. Weaver, and R. K. Adair. 1995. Rectification and Signal Averaging of Weak Electric Fields by Biological Cells. *Proceedings of the National Academy of Sciences.* 92:3740-3743.

Becker, R. O. 1990. *Cross Currents.* New York: Jeremy P. Tarcher/Perigee.

Becker, R. O., and G. Selden. 1988. *The Body Electric.* New York: Quill, William Morrow.

Bellavite, P., and A. Signorini. 1995. *Homeopathy: A Frontier in Medical Science.* Berkeley, CA: North Atlantic Books.

Bem, D. G., and C. Hornoton. Does Psi Exist? Replicable Evidence for An Anomalous Process of Information Transfer. *Psychological Bulletin.* 115: 4-18.

Bohm, D. 1980. *Wholeness and the Implicate Order.* London: Routledge and Kegan Paul.

Brennan, B. A. 1993. *Light Emerging.* New York: Bantam Books.

Cambel A. B. 1993. *Applied Chaos Theory: A Paradigm for Complexity.* Boston: Academic Press.

Capra, F. 1996. *The Web of Life: A New Scientific Understanding of Living Systems.* New York: Anchor Books.

Chalmers, D. J. 1996. *The Conscious Mind: In Search of a Fundamental Theory.* New York: Oxford University Press.

Craik, F. I. M. 1988. On the Making of Episodes. In *Varieties of Memory and Consciousness: Essays in Honour of Endel Tulving;* ed. H. L. Roediger III, and F. I. M. Craik. Hillsdale, NJ: Lawrence Erlbaum Associates.

Diamond, J. 1979. *Behavioral Kinesiology.* New York: Harper and Row.

Flood, R. L. 1988. *Dealing with Complexity: An Introduction to the Theory and Application of Systems Science.* New York: Plenum.

Forward, R. 1996. Mass Modification Definition Study. *Journal of Scientific Exploration.* 10:325-254.

James, W. 1890. *Psychology (Briefer Course)*. New York: Holt.

Jibu, M., K. H. Pribram, and K. Yasue. 1996. From Conscious Experience to Memory Storage and Retrieval: The Role of Quantum Brain Dynamics and Boson Condensation of Evanescent Photons. *International Journal of Modern Physics*. 10:1735-1754.

Kauffman, S. A. 1993. *The Origins of Order*. New York: Oxford University Press.

Laszlo, E. 1995. *The Interconnected Universe: Conceptual Foundations of Transdisciplinary Unified Theory*. Singapore: World Scientific Publishing.

Laughlin, C. D. 1996. Archetypes, Neurognosis, and the Quantum Sea. *Journal of Scientific Exploration*. 10:375-400.

Lisberger, S. G., and T. J. Sejnowski. 1992. Motor Learning in a Recurrent Network Model Based on the Vistibulo-Ocular Reflex. *Nature*. 360: 159-161.

Malmivuo, J., and R. Plonsey. 1995. *Bioelectromagnetism*. New York: Oxford University Press.

McCulloch, W. S. 1951. Why the Mind is in the Head. In *Cerebral Mechanisms in Behavior*; ed. L. A. Jeffress. New York: John Wiley.

Miller, J. G. 1978. *Living Systems*. New York: McGraw-Hill.

Milonni, P. W. 1994. *The Quantum Vacuum: An Introduction to Quantum Electronics*. New York: Academic Press.

Mithaug, D. E. 1993. *Self-Regulation Theory: How Optimal Adjustment Maximizes Gain*. Westport, CT: Praeger.

NATO 1985. *Chaotic Behavior in Quantum Systems: Theory and Applications*. New York, NY: Plenum.

Orear, J. 1962. *Fundamental Physics*. New York: John Wiley & Sons.

Pribram, K. H. 1991. *Brain and Perception: Holonomy and Structure in Figural Processing*. Hillsdale, NJ: Lawrence Erlbaum Associates.

————. 1986. The Cognitive Revolution and Mind/Brain Issues. *American Psychologist*. 41:507-520.

Puthoff, H. E. 1996. Technological Problems, Bold Possibilities. *Advances: The Journal of Mind-Body Health*. 12(4):35-36

Ragan, P. A., W. Wang, and S. R. Eisenberg. 1995. Magnetically Induced Currents in the Canine Heart: A Finite Element Study. *IEEE Transactions on Biomedical Engineering*. 42:1110-1115.

Russek, L. G. and G. E. Schwartz. 1996a. Energy Cardiology: A Dynamical Energy Systems Approach for Integrating Conventional and Alternative Medicine. *Advances: The Journal of Mind-Body Health*. 12(4):4-24.

————. **1996b.** The Heart, Dynamic Energy, and Integrated Medicine. *Advances: The Journal of Mind-Body Health.* 12(4):36-45.

Schacter, D. L. 1996. *Searching for Memory.* New York: Basic Books.

Schwartz, G. E. 1982. Cardiovascular Psychophysiology: A Systems Perspective. In *Perspectives in Cardiovascular Psychophysiology;* ed. J. T. Cacioppo, and R. E. Petty. New York: Guilford Press.

————. **1984.** Psychobiology of Health: A New Synthesis. In *Psychology and Health: The Master Lecture Series. Volume 3;* ed. B. L. Hammonds, and C. J. Scheirer. Washington, DC: APA.

————. **1987.** Personality and the Unification of Psychology and Modern Physics: A Systems Approach. In *The Emergence of Personality;* ed. J. Aronoff, A. I. Robin, and R. A. Zucker. New York: Springer.

————. **1989.** Disregulation Theory and Psychosomatic Disease: A Systems Approach. In *Psychosomatic Medicine: Theory, Research and Practice;* ed. S. Cheren. New York: International University Press.

————. **1997.** Information and Energy: The Soul and Spirit of Mind-body Medicine. *Advances: The Journal of Mind-Body Health.* 13(1):75-77.

Schwartz, G. E., and L. G. Russek. 1997. The Challenge of One Medicine: Theories of Health and Eight World Hypotheses. *Advances: The Journal of Mind-Body Health.* 13(3):7-23.

————. **1997.** Dynamical Energy Systems and Modern Physics: Fostering the Science and Spirit of Complementary and Alternative Medicine. *Alternative Therapies in Health and Medicine.* 3(3):46-56.

Scott, A. 1995. *Stairway to the Mind: The Controversial New Science of Consciousness.* New York: Springer-Verlag.

Sheldrake, R. 1981. *A New Science of Life.* Los Angeles: Tarcher.

Sheldrake, R., and D. Bohm. 1982. Morphogenetic Fields and the Implicate Order. *ReVision.* 5:41-48.

Siegel, B.S. 1995. Exploring What Can't Be Explained. *Advances: The Journal of Mind-Body Health.* 11:2-3.

Smith, S. 1964. *The Mediumship of Mrs. Leonard.* New Hyde Park, NY: University Books.

Sylvia, C., with W. Novack. 1997. *A Change of Heart.* New York: Little, Brown.

Tipler, F. 1994. *The Physics of Immortality.* New York: Macmillan.

von Bertalanffy, L. 1968. *General System Theory.* New York: Braziller.

Weiskrantz, L. 1986. *Blindsight: A Case Study and Implications.* Oxford: Clarendon Press.

Yates, F. E., ed. 1987. *Self-Organizing Systems: The Emergence of Order*. New York: Plenum Press.

APPENDIX B

Ability of an Electric Current to Carry Information for Crystal Growth Patterns: Implications for Systemic Memory

Gary E. R. Schwartz, Ph.D.
Parmi Suchdev, B.A.
Linda G. S. Russek, Ph.D.

KEYWORDS: Systems theory, systemic memory, energy medicine, integrative medicine, cellular memory

ACKNOWLEDGMENT: We dedicate this paper to Donald Eldridge in Australia, who saw a reference to the systemic memory hypothesis, sent us a copy of Reid (1987), and encouraged us to explore the possibility of using the crystal growth experimental paradigm to test some of the predictions of the systemic memory hypothesis in alternative and complementary medicine. This research was conducted as part of Parmi Suchdev's honors thesis in the Department of Biochemistry at the University of Arizona. He is currently a medical student at the Northwestern University.

ABSTRACT

According to systems theory, interacting units of a dynamical system have specific relationships that lead to the emergence of the system as a whole. Taking the logic of systems theory further, the systemic memory hypothesis states that the recurrent feedback interactions of a system naturally store information and energy and generate "memory." Although the theory of dynamical energy systems and their ability to evolve has been explicated, and its potential to explain a wide range of seemingly anomalous observations in science and medicine, including homeopathy, cellular memory, and energy medicine diagnoses, has been documented, there is little empirical evidence specifically testing these predictions. Findings from a pioneer experiment by Reid (1987) suggest that electric current can carry information for crystal growth patterns. When current is passed through two beakers of 0.15 NaCl solution, the crystal pattern of the salt is of the usual cubic symmetry. However, when the first beaker contains added albumin protein, the NaCl crystal pattern of the second beaker may become more ornate, similar to a form found when albumin is present in NaCl solution. Replicating in a similar system that electrons can store and convey information, a model for demonstrating systemic memory is proposed, including some of its many implications for complementary, alternative, and integrative medicine. The need for conducting careful and systematic research in this area is emphasized.

INTRODUCTION

One of the most integrative conceptual models in contemporary science is systems theory, including general systems theory (von Bertallanffy, 1968), living systems theory (Miller, 1978; Capra, 1996), chaos and complex systems theory (Kauffman, 1993), and dynamical energy systems theory (Russek and Schwartz, 1996; Schwartz and Russek, 1997a).

Schwartz and Russek (1997a,b;1998a-c) have taken systems theory a logical step further. They have explicated the reasoning that leads inexorably to the prediction that recurrent feedback interactions in a system naturally generate "memory." Their proposed systemic memory hypothesis states that all dynamical systems, through their interactions and sharing of information and energy, inherently store and sustain memory to various degrees. Through the circulation of information and energy in semi-closed systems, informed-energy (reflecting dynamic interaction resonance patterns among the components) are stored, and the system naturally evolves as an emerging whole.

The systemic memory hypothesis was discovered accidentally in the early 1980s when the first author was a professor of Psychology and Psychiatry at Yale University. In an effort to explain to his students in a seminar on human psychobiology and systems theory how feedback in systems worked, in the process of deriving the logic of circular feedback mechanisms (using a simple resonating circuit, e.g., two tuning forks, as a model system), the implications of systemic memory were unexpectedly uncovered. He realized that the logic and resulting theory potentially explained a wide range of seemingly disparate, anomalous, memory-like phenomena reported in science, medicine, and spirituality, including homeopathy, kinesiology, cellular memory in certain transplant patients, morphogenetic resonance, energy diagnosis, distant healing, and even the plausibility of survival of consciousness after physical death. Given the inherently controversial nature of the theory, he withheld publication of it. However, with the development of dynamical energy systems theory (the integration of the concept of energy with dynamical systems theory–e.g., energy cardiology) in the mid 1990s (Russek and Schwartz, 1996), plus the emergence of alternative and complementary medicine, the time was appropriate to share the logic and the implications of the systemic memory hypothesis with the scientific community. More than fifty physicists, biologists, neuroscientists, psychologists, and physicians have examined the logic of systemic memory, and to date, none have discovered a flaw.

The scientific acceptance of many modalities in alternative and complementary medicine will hinge (in part) on discovering plausible theoretical models using contemporary science to explain their mechanisms. This paper presents a potential theoretical and experimental paradigm, plus new empirical findings, that address this scientific challenge.

The Reid Experimental Paradigm

There are various ways to empirically investigate the fundamental predictions of systemic memory and apply them to alternative and complementary medicine. A simple yet ingenious experimental paradigm was suggested by the pioneering research of Reid (1987,

1989, 1995). In a paper published in the *Journal of Biological Physics* entitled "The ability of an electrical current to carry information for crystal growth patterns," Reid claimed through a straightforward experiment with electrical current and salt solutions that aggregates of electrons could convey information. The authors became aware of the Reid experiment thanks to correspondence with Mr. Donald Eldridge, an Australian interested in memory processes in complementary and alternative medicine.

Reid (1987) passed a current from a 1.5V battery through two beakers—one containing a 0.15 M NaCl solution and the other a 0.15 M NaCl solution with the added protein, albumin. Crystal patterns of NaCl tend to have a simple, cubic symmetry, whereas the same NaCl solution with added albumin, has a fine-branched crystal pattern that is much more ornate. Drops of solution were drawn from each beaker and allowed to dry on slides. With time, the crystal pattern from the NaCl solution began to look more complex, similar to the crystal pattern from the drops taken from the NaCl + albumin beaker. From his results, Reid concluded that the electrical field, carrying information from the albumin, was responsible for the alteration in crystal pattern. Since his experiments had insufficient controls, the controversial findings were not considered seriously by chemists and physicists at the time.

Therefore, replicating Reid with the appropriate controls and demonstrating that aggregates of electrons can carry information, is an important stepping stone to studying the question of systemic memory. If replicable, the experimental paradigm Reid developed can be modified to address whether the information carried by the current is stored and leads to the evolution of the system.

Prior to describing the current experiments, it is valuable to review some of the concepts of crystallization and systems theory to further clarify the reasoning and methodology of the research and its applications to CAM.

Crystallization

Crystals, derived from the Greek "congealed by cold," are solids that have long-range order and regular periodicity in their structure

(Flint, 1971). The crystallization process occurs in the course of phase transitions (e.g., change from liquid to solid) and is accompanied by a release of energy in the form of heat.

We conducted preliminary studies in our laboratory to characterize the crystal patterns of NaCl and various NaCl + albumin solutions at numerous concentrations. NaCl crystals are typically characterized by a simple, cubic symmetry. Depending on concentrations and growing conditions, these crystals occur as isolated cubes, clustered cubes, or pieces of cubes of various sizes (figure 1). When mixed with albumin, there is a dramatic change in the NaCl crystal structure. At a concentration of 10 mg/mL of albumin dissolved in NaCl, a fine-branched crystal pattern is produced as in a fern leaf (figure 2). At 1 mg/mL of albumin there is instead, a pattern of circular rings as in a fingerprint (figure 3). Although it is uncertain how albumin dramatically changes the structure of NaCl crystals, previous studies have shown that the environment in which a crystal is grown affects its subdivision into specific patterns of finer structure. The energy needed to produce such structures may be present in an environmental form (Reid, 1987).

Looking at the dynamics of an albumin + NaCl solution, it is thought that during the solvation process, Cl$^-$ anions bind the albumin molecule. NMR analysis with Cl indicates 10 or less chlorides bind per albumin molecule at physiological pH (Halle and Lindman, 1978). Evidence is also suggested by the isoelectric point (the pH at which the net charge of a molecule, including any bound ions, is zero) of albumin in 0.15 M NaCl. The isoelectric pH is about 4.7, lower than the isoionic point of pH 5.2 when there are no adherent charges such as salt ions (Peters, 1996). This binding of ions presumably influences the resulting charge of albumin, thereby affecting the energetics of crystal formation.

Systems Theory, Complexity, and Systemic Memory

Systems theory was proposed in the 1940s by biologist Ludwig von Bertalanffy and others (reviewed in von Bertalanffy, 1968; Capra, 1996) as a paradigmatic response to reductionism in science. They emphasized that systems are open to, and interact with their

Figure 1
Photomicrograph of 0.15 M NaCl crystals dried on a
microscope slide. 200X magnification.

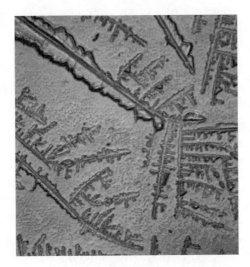

Figure 2
Photomicrograph of 0.15 M NaCl +10mg/mL albumin crystals.
400X magnification.

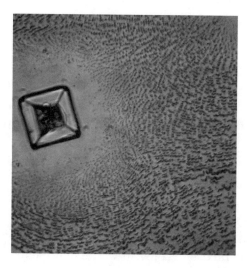

Figure 3
Photomicrograph of 0.15 M NaCl + 1 mg/mL albumin crystals.
400X magnification.

environments, thereby acquiring qualitatively new properties though emergence. According to Miller (1978), a system is defined as:

> . . . a set of interacting units with relationships among them. The word "set" implies that the units have some common properties. These common properties are essential if the units are to interact or have relationships. The state of each unit is constrained by, conditioned by, or dependent on the state of the other units. The units are coupled. Moreover, there is at least one measure of the sum of its units which is larger than the sum of that measure of its units.

Moreover, systems continually evolve (Heylighen and Joslyn, 1992). Rather than reducing an entity (e.g., the human body) to the properties of its various parts (e.g., cells, organs), systems theory focuses on the relationships and organizations that connect these parts into a whole.

Since evolution of a system is associated with an increase of complexity, it is important to understand what defines something as being complex. According to the *Oxford Dictionary*, something "complex" is "made of (usually several) closely connected parts." Therefore, a system could be characterized as more complex if more parts could be distinguished, and/or if more connections existed between them (Heylighen, 1996a). Edmonds (1996) defines complexity as the midpoint between order and disorder. This definition of complexity also depends on the level of representation: what appears complex on one scale may seem ordered or disordered in a representation at a different scale. Therefore, in this study the magnification at which crystals were viewed may define their relative complexity.

Such views on systems and their intuitive increase in complexity are confirmed by observations in several disciplines. For instance, it is well documented by ecologists and evolutionary biologists that ecosystems tend to become more complex; since the time of Darwin, evolution has been associated with the increase in complexity. Physicists have also cited complex evolution, showing that physical and chemical systems far from thermodynamic equilibrium tend to self-organize by exporting entropy and forming "dissipative structures." Other examples in the sciences that suggest that systems emerge include the "Big Bang" model for the evolution of the universe, studies of fractal geometry, which models the recurrence of similar patterns at different scales, and the field of synergetics that studies collective patterns emerging from interactions as found in chemical reactions and crystal formation (reviewed in Heylighen, 1996b).

Critics to the idea of growing complexity argue that there are evolutionary costs to complexity: a simpler design is preferable to a complex one if it can achieve the same purpose. Another counter-argument, such as that proposed by Gould (1994), is that an increase in complexity implies a preferred direction for evolution, a "progress" or advance towards more sophisticated forms. Observations of evolutionary phenomena seem to indicate that evolution is "largely unpredictable" and "chaotic" (Heylighen, 1996a), though evidence for macro order is emerging (Schwartz and Russek, 1997b). Heylighen (1996a) argues that although evolution appears unpredictable and contingent on numerous uncontrollable factors, which can steer its course in infinite directions, those directions in which complexity increases are preferred. Also, even though systems can evolve towards simpler organization (e.g., internal parasites like viruses), the net effect will be that the entire system, including both the environment and added component, will become more complex.

A new way to understand how complexity grows during evolution is provided by the systemic memory hypothesis. Schwartz and Russek (1997a,b;1998a-c) describe the complex implications of generating dynamic memories using the simple illustration from classical physics: resonance interactions between two tuning forks A and B (see Figure 4 below). When A is struck at time 0, it vibrates with a specific frequency a0. The a0 frequency travels at the speed of sound and reaches B at time 1, at which point B begins to vibrate at some frequency that is a product of a1 (the history of A at time 1) plus B's resting frequency at time 1. The change in B's vibration at time 2 returns a complex sound, a1b2, which interacts with A at time 3, resulting in a1b2a3. At time 4, the first complete A-B cycle, what emerges from A is a1b2a3a4. This pattern reflects (in part) A's response at time 4 to a history of itself from time 0, as it was "perceived" in the past by B at time 1, resulting in a1b2 at time 2, etc. This dynamic interaction continues over time (recurrent/repeated A-B cycles), as the history of the A-B interaction evolves (assuming the system can sustain its organization and wholeness despite possibilities of dilution, dissipation, and decay).

Due to the recurring feedback interactions between A and B, dynamic memory accumulates; it is an inherent requirement for these interactions to take place in a continually dynamical system. Even though dynamic memory occurs to varying degrees at whatever level the systems are interacting, the interactive history of the energy and information should be contained in a complex way.

The growth of new concepts stemming from systems theory, such as advances in information theory, complexity theory, cybernetics, non-equilibrium thermodynamics, deterministic chaos, complex adaptive systems, etc., have led to the awareness that growth in complexity may be much more important than what is typically assumed by classical, reductionistic science. Therefore, both the implications of systems theory and its intrinsic logic, suggest the importance of operationalizing systemic memory predictions and putting them to empirical test.

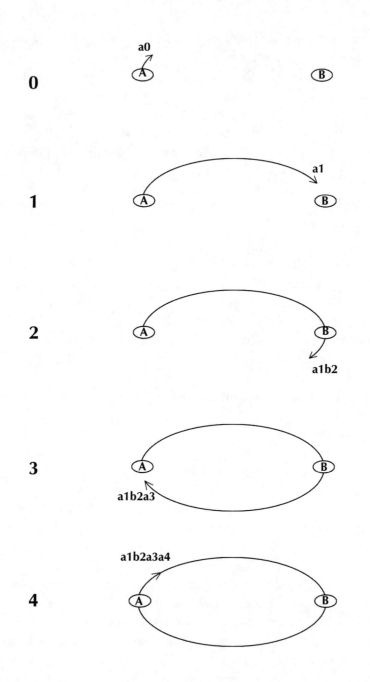

Figure 4
Graphic description of the logic
of the systemic memory mechanism

The Importance of Replication

Seeking validity, or accuracy of scientific findings, is an essential criterion for all research, especially novel and controversial research. Establishing validity involves both determining the extent to which conclusions effectively represent an empirical reality (measuring what is supposed to be measured) and assessing whether the tests and measurements devised by researchers are representative (Wolcott, 1994). An important component of seeking experimental validity is replication, which is "universally accepted as one of the most important criteria for scientifically establishing the existence of a claimed phenomenon" (Radin, 1997). However, despite the high value science places on replication of claimed effects, positive replications are surprisingly rare in science (Collins, 1985). This trend may be a result of the reward system for scientists, such as the editorial guidelines of many professional journals, which places higher value on original work. Also, certain findings are difficult to replicate, such as open systems in the life sciences that change and react as a result of the experiment itself. Some reasons why replications may be difficult to achieve as proposed by Radin (1997) include:

1. The phenomenon may not be replicable.
2. Written experimental procedures may be incomplete.
3. The effect under study may change over time or react to the experimental procedure.
4. Investigators may inadvertently affect the results of their experiments.
5. Experiments sometimes fail for sociological reasons.
6. Psychological factors prevent replications from being easy to conduct.
7. Statistical aspects of replication can be very confusing.
8. Complications in experimental design affect some replications.

Regardless of some of the difficulties in replicating certain phenomenon, based on the existing paradigm for scientific research, replication is necessary for ensuring validity. The number of replications needed to convince scientists that a claimed effect is real, however, depends largely on the claim. For instance, claims not too remote from accepted scientific knowledge can be convincing by just one or two successful studies. For example, the "omega-minus" particle was accepted in physics on the basis of only two events out of a total of nearly 200,000 experimental trials (Barns et al, 1964). The question of where to draw the line as to how many positive results are needed to make it unlikely that results are due to chance is clearly debatable.

The goal of the present research was twofold: to determine whether electrons could carry information, and then to determine if information could be stored within a system (e.g., in a crystal pattern). The first step was an attempt to replicate Reid (1987) with appropriate controls to see if the phenomenon was reproducible. If replicated, many experimental modifications could be made to answer additional questions in future research, such as whether the solutions and circuit components (e.g., the batteries themselves) could have systemic memory properties, and whether other forms of energy could elicit similar results.

METHODS

Materials

The following materials were used in this research:

- 0.15 M NaCl solution (made using powdered NaCl and double-distilled H2O) (beaker B in Experimental (a) and Control (b) paradigms, beakers A and B in control for control paradigms—see figure 5, below)
- albumin/NaCl solutions (using albumin powder-bovine, 99.5% pure added to NaCl solutions) (beaker A in Experimental (a) and Control (b) paradigms).
    1 mg/mL albumin + 0.15 M NaCl
    10 mg/mL albumin + 0.15 M NaCl
- 4 20 mL glass beakers
- several glass pipettes with droppers
- stainless steel wire, insulated
- gold wire (14 K)
- 2 AA battery holders
- 1.5-Volt AA batteries

- microscope slides
- voltmeter and ammeter to measure voltage and current through circuit
- phase contrast light microscope with digital camera

The following circuits were set up (figure 5):

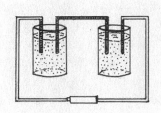   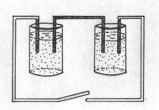

"Experimental (a)"   "Control (b)"

Figure 5
Diagram of circuits. Experimental (a): A 1.5 V dry cell is connected in series using gold wire electrodes with two 20 mL glass beakers. The darker lines signify gold wire. Current flows from the battery to beaker A (albumin/NaCl solution), then to beaker B (NaCl solution), and back to the battery. Control (b): A similar circuit with no inserted battery (open circuit).

Table 1. Summary of experimental trials.			
EXPERIMENT	BEAKER A	BEAKER B	CONTROL
Reid	0.15 M NaCl + 10mg/mL albumin	0.15 M NaCl	Open circuit
Control for current	0.15 M NaCl	0.15 M NaCl	Open circuit

Experimental Trials and Procedures

- **Beaker A (NaCl + albumin), Beaker B (NaCl)**

The above circuit was set up using 15 mL of a 0.15M NaCl + 10 mg/mL albumin solution in beaker A and 15 mL of 0.15M NaCl in beaker B. Because the battery holder was attached to copper wires shown previously to precipitate when submerged in the NaCl solution, gold wire was connected to the battery holder ends (via twisting of the two wires) and placed as electrodes in each solution. To complete the circuit, another gold wire was used to connect the two beakers. Each wire was submerged approximately midway through the 15 mL of solution. (Stainless steel wire was initially used in pilot studies, but was replaced by gold wire to improve current flow and minimize contamination from trace metals.) A new 1.5 V battery was placed in the holder with the positive end in the direction of beaker A, thereby sending current first through beaker A and then through B. A voltmeter was used to measure current flow through the circuit to verify that electrons were moving through both solutions.

Using glass pipettes, two drops of solution were drawn from beaker A and dropped on a glass microscope slide. The pipette was reinserted into the solution, and two drops were dropped on another slide. Using a new pipette, the procedure was repeated for beaker B, placing the drops right below the drops from beaker A on each slide. Drops were drawn every ten minutes for 60 minutes and allowed to dry on the slides. Each time solution was drawn from beaker A first. An effort was made to draw solution close to the submerged electrode without touching it or disrupting the solution. Slides were covered to minimize contamination and were allowed to dry at room temperature overnight before analysis.

- **Beaker A (NaCl), Beaker B (NaCl)**

A similar circuit was set up, except with 15 mL of 0.15 M NaCl solution in both beakers. Solution was drawn out and dropped on slides in a similar manner. This control was used to determine whether electricity itself, rather than albumin, was contributing to the change in NaCl crystal structure.

Control Trials

- **Beaker A (NaCl + albumin), Beaker B (NaCl) – open circuit**

A similar circuit was set up as in the experimental, except without the battery. The wires in the control and in the experimental circuit were connected simultaneously and drops were taken for the same time points. Solutions were sampled in the same order to ensure equal spacing between each ten-minute time point. This was a control for experimental conditions (e.g., contaminated solutions, temperature, effects of submerged wires, etc.).

- **Beaker A (NaCl), Beaker B (NaCl) – open circuit**

Same procedures were used as in the NaCl-NaCl open circuit. Run at the same time as the NaCl-NaCl experiment.

Analyses

Crystals were analyzed using a phase contrast light microscope to determine any changes in pattern associated with electric current and the presence of albumin in the circuit. Each drop on each slide was observed under several different magnifications for both macroscopic and microscopic observations of the crystal patterns. Pictures were taken and patterns were noted.

- Macroscopic (naked eye) level of overall complexity; wholeness of circular pattern of crystallized drop; evidence of haze.
- Microscopic (200X and 400X magnification) patterns within crystals and surrounding haze.

RESULTS

Based on the experimental trials, there was evidence that information from albumin could be transferred and stored, as NaCl crystal patterns, when connected to a NaCl + albumin solution, and show signs of the albumin present via accumulation of a fern pattern (figures 6, 7, 8 and table 2). This result was confirmed by a series of controls: an open circuit (table 3) and passing current through

NaCl in both beakers (tables 3,4). Both these control trials showed no evidence of a fern pattern in the NaCl (figures 9, 10, 11). Therefore, they demonstrated that the evidence of a fern pattern in NaCl was probably not due to experimental conditions (contamination, temperature, way solutions were crystallized) or the electric current in absence of albumin.

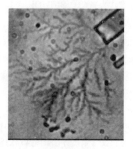

Figure 6
Reid Replication. Photomicrograph of 0.15M NaCl crystals after being in circuit with 0.15 M NaCl + 10 mg/mL albumin for 10 minutes. Fern pattern. 400X magnification.

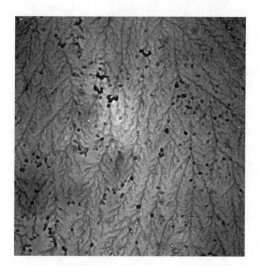

Figure 7
Reid Replication. Photomicrograph of 0.15M NaCl crystals after being in circuit with 0.15 M NaCl + 10 mg/mL albumin for 40 minutes. Fern pattern. 400X magnification.

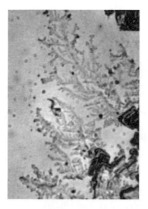

Figure 8
Reid Replication. Photomicrograph of 0.15M NaCl crystals after
being in a circuit with 0.15 M NaCl + 10 mg/mL albumin for
50 minutes. Fern pattern. 400X magnification.

	Reid Replication		
Time (min)	Macroscopic Observations of Crystal Structure (naked eye)	Microscopic Observations of Crystal Structure (400X magnification)	Photo-micro-graph Figures
0	filled in circular ring; same throughout	Albumin- intricate branching; fern-like pattern; no intact NaCl crystals; no observable change throughout	
0	single dot	NaCl- 1 large cubic crystal with surrounding haze on edges	
10	partial circular haze around edges of drop	NaCl- 2 complex, cubic crystals; within haze light branching fern pattern	6
20, 30	no haze	NaCl- large cubic crystals	
40	thicker circular haze	NaCl- within haze see fern pattern in certain locations	7
50, 60	circular haze partially filled in	NaCl- lots of fern patterns within haze; more defined at edge	8

Table 2. Summary of observations from a successful Reid
replication with beaker A (0.15 M NaCl)
and beaker B (0.15 M NaCl + 10 mg/mL albumin).
See figures for evidence of albumin pattern in NaCl crystals.

Reid Replication Control			
Time (min)	Macroscopic Observations of Crystal Structure (naked eye)	Microscopic Observations of Crystal Structure (400X magnification)	Photo-micro-graph Figures
0	Filled in circle	Albumin- same intricate fern pattern	
0	Single dot	NaCl- large, cubic, complex crystal with surrounding haze	
10, 20, 30	Single crystal; no haze	NaCl- same	9
40, 50, 60	Circular haze	NaCl- haze appears to have pattern but not branched; cubic crystals within	10, 11

Table 3. Summary of observations from control for Reid replication. Open circuit. No evidence of fern pattern in NaCl crystals.

NaCl-NaCl Control			
Time (min)	Macroscopic Observations of Crystal Structure (naked eye)	Microscopic Observations of Crystal Structure (400X magnification)	Photomi-crograph Figures
0	half circular haze	NaCl (Beaker B)- complex, cubic crystals within haze; no fern in haze	
10-60	Circular haze; par-tially filled in	NaCl (Beaker B)- lots of haze; cubic crystals and pieces, patterned haze but no fern	

Table 4. Summary of observations for electricity control for Reid replication. NaCl in both beakers. More haze, but no evidence of fern pattern in NaCl crystals.

Control for NaCl-NaCl Control			
Time (min)	Macroscopic Observations of Crystal Structure (naked eye)	Microscopic Observations of Crystal Structure (400X magnification)	Photo-micro-graph Figures
0	Circular haze	NaCl (Beaker B)- complex, cubic crystals within haze; no fern in haze	
10-60	Circular haze; partially filled in	NaCl (Beaker B)- lots of haze; cubic crystals and pieces, patterned haze but no fern	13

Table 5. Summary of observations for open circuit control for electricity control. NaCl in both beakers; open circuit. Haze, but no evidence of fern pattern in NaCl crystals.

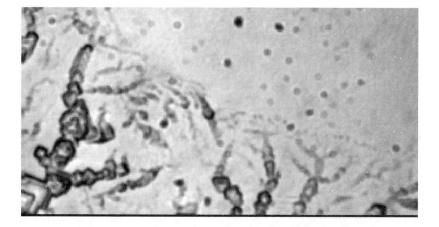

Figure 9
Reid Replication Control. Photomicrograph of 0.15M NaCl crystals after being in open circuit (no battery) with 0.15 M NaCl + 10 mg/mL albumin for 40 minutes. No fern pattern. 400X magnification.

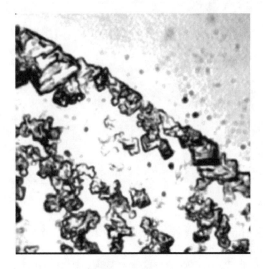

Figure 10
Reid Replication Control. Photomicrograph of 0.15M NaCl
crystals after being in open circuit (no battery) with 0.15 M
NaCl + 10 mg/mL albumin for 50 minutes. No fern pattern.
400X magnification

Figure 11
NaCl-NaCl Control. Photomicrograph of 0.15 M NaCl after
being in a circuit with another beaker of 0.15 M NaCl for 50
minutes. No fern pattern. 400X magnification.

The Reid effect ultimately "disappeared" using gold wire and 0.15 M NaCl with 10 mg/mL albumin. A branching fern pattern was found in the control NaCl solutions at time 0, implying that contamination of the solution, either through the beakers, wires, or pipettes was possible. We report this observation to point out the care that must be taken in conducting research of this sort, including the requirement for rigorous control conditions to rule out potential contamination.

DISCUSSION

It appears that the Reid experiment could be replicated to show that NaCl crystal patterns become more ornate (similar to a form found when albumin is present in NaCl solution) when in a circuit with a solution of NaCl and added albumin. This finding implies that electrons carry information and convey this information in patterns of crystal growth that are stored over time. However, in order to support the conclusion that the Reid effect was replicated, careful consideration of potential courses of contamination need to be considered in future research. It should be noted that Reid (1987) was well aware of possible sources of contamination and addressed many of them in his original paper.

Potential Effects of "Haze"

An important observation seen both macroscopically and microscopically in the NaCl crystal patterns was the occasional production of "haze" usually surrounding cubic NaCl crystals. The observations of the fern pattern in the Reid replication were seen *within* the haze produced by the crystallized NaCl. Therefore, some level of "haze" was probably necessary for elucidating (expressing) the transfer of information and conveying the effect of albumin. For instance, in our initial replication attempts, no haze was seen surrounding the NaCl crystals, so there was no "medium" from which to observe the fern pattern. When haze patterns were seen in later trials, the Reid experiment was replicated.

What caused the haze was not determined, although similar haze patterns observed in both the open circuit and NaCl-NaCl controls, suggested that something in the NaCl solutions themselves or in the experimental components was causing the haze. New stock solutions of NaCl were made that still produced haze when crystallized. Also, the beakers, pipettes, and wires were individually tested in several NaCl crystallization trials, but none were demonstrated to cause the haze.

Double Blind Scoring of the Photomicrographs

Though not typically employed in biophysical studies, double blind scoring of experimental and control photomicrographs is desirable. Since we were interested in replicating crystallization effects that were presumably visible to the naked eye, we would not accept as a replication "subtle" differences that might be statistically reliable (e.g. comparing pairs of control and experimental pictures, and having blind judges sort them into relatively increased degrees of complexity). Instead, we required that the experiment produce findings that were immediately and obviously discriminable to the naked eye.

Hence, when figures 7 and 9 are paired blindly, and figures 8 and 10 are paired blindly, and subjects are asked simply to indicate which figure in each pair has more of a fern pattern, the discrimination is universal–figures 7 and 8 clearly have more fern patterns than figures 9 and 10.

Ideally, future research can employ computer analyses of digitized micrographs using pattern recognition and expert systems to precisely quantify degrees of fern pattern and complexity. This is especially important to measure the kinds of phenomena and predictions outlined below.

Integration with Systemic Memory

Viewed in terms of systemic memory, the accumulation of haze can conceivably be explained by an accumulation of memory in the system. Except for the battery (which was continually replaced), the other components of the experimental system were used repeatedly for all the trials (e.g., the beakers, battery holders, and gold wire). Although they were "cleaned" and did not have traces of material contamination as verified by the open circuit controls, according to systemic memory, the experimental components could have built up a dynamic history with time. Therefore, the dynamical interactions between each component could have been stored within the system, leading to increased complexity of the crystal patterns and the haze. This build up of information in the system may also explain the apparent contamination in the haze and fern-like branching patterns observed in later NaCl control solutions regardless of current (for example, at time 0).

Another interesting observation that ties in with systemic memory was the change in patterns within cubic NaCl crystals when in a circuit. Although it was not analyzed specifically, there appeared to be an overall trend in increasing complexity of the NaCl crystal pattern over time when it received electric current from other NaCl molecules with or without albumin. In terms of systemic memory, the more rapidly that recurrent feedback interactions occur in a system, the more rapidly a "holistic history" should emerge. Therefore, due to the recurrent interactions between NaCl and water molecules, a NaCl solution may accumulate memory with time such that its crystals increase in complexity. The systemic memory hypothesis predicts that passing an electric current through the solutions should speed up this process.

Another possible explanation that could discount the finding of electrons conveying information is that the change in NaCl crystal pattern was due to chance. Also, one could argue that there were flaws in the experiment setup itself. For instance, the circuit could be polarizing solutions rather than sending current through, or the current could be causing electrolysis of the solutions. However, most of these explanations were discounted experimentally by running the trials simultaneously in an open circuit control and observing the effects of the current through NaCl solutions without albumin.

Future Research

To further verify that electrons can store and convey information, additional trials should be run, using the lower concentration of albumin (1 mg/mL) to see if the fingerprint pattern can be replicated in the NaCl crystals. Moreover, replications should be done at different temperatures, using different amounts of current, and with different salt/protein combinations to further demonstrate the effect of information flow through electrons. Also, the direction of current should be changed to see if the effect is still observed.

Based on the evidence suggesting that electrons carried the information of albumin, which altered NaCl crystal structure, further studies can be done to specifically test the thesis of systemic memory. For instance, it is possible to determine if the battery can retain its capacity to induce ornate, fern-like crystal patterns in NaCl after being in a circuit with NaCl and albumin (Reid, 1987, suggested this possibility himself, and claimed to have observed it in his research). The same battery could be placed in a circuit with only NaCl to see if fern patterns developed upon crystallization. Systemic memory would also predict that a single beaker of NaCl solution should produce salt crystals of increasing complexity when set up in a circuit that allowed recurrent flow of electrons and information. If one beaker of NaCl solution were connected to a beaker of water in a circuit for a given amount of time, information of the NaCl should be stored in the water. Dissolving pure NaCl powder in this water to see if more complex crystals are produced could test this storage of dynamic energy.

Some Possible Implications for Alternative and Complementary Medicine

The essence of science, its highest virtue, can be said to reflect a passion for knowledge—the search for "veritas" (the motto of Harvard University)—"the relentless search for truth . . ." (Newton, 1997). The scientific pursuit of truth requires that one always be open to new information—that one have a devotion for data.

However, science and its applications to medicine do not always embody this primary value. As Jobst (1998) recently phrased the problem in his editorial "The truth and nothing but the truth":

> *"What is perhaps most important of all to try to understand is the reticence of the scientist or clinician, orthodox or alternative, to apply with integrity and passionate discipline the tools of his or her trade to discover the veracity of phenomena."*

Following Jobst's (1998) call for integrity in science and medicine, we include a brief discussion of some of the implications of the systemic memory hypothesis for potentially understanding, and investigating, a number of controversial phenomena and claims in alternative and complementary medicine, not only homeopathy, but cellular memory, and distant healing through intentionality and prayer, as well (reviewed in Schwartz and Russek, 1997a).

We recognize, as one anonymous reviewer put it, that "the extrapolation to humans is not solid"—we offer these speculations as theoretical possibilities potentially worthy of empirical investigation.

Organ transplants, especially heart transplants, have sometimes been accompanied by changes in the recipient's perceptions and behavior that are consistent with the donor's preferences and personalities (Sylvia, 1997; Pearsall, 1998). According to Russek and Schwartz (1996), the heart can be viewed as a dynamical energy generating system due to its central location, rich circulatory connections to all cells of the body, and intensity of electromagnetic transmission. In fact, the electromagnetic energy emitted by the heart has been measured to be 1000 to 5000 times the electromagnetic energy emitted by the brain, and these patterns of energy reach every cell in the body through volume conduction.

Systemic memory predicts that all cells (not just neurons and immune cells) store information and energy to various degrees. Therefore, the personal history of a given individual should, to various degrees, be implicitly stored in his or her peripheral organ systems as well. This history could then be accessible by especially sensitive recipients of organ donations, leading to changes in the recipient's preferences that match those of the donor.

For example, Claire Sylvia, a former dancer and recipient of a heart-lung transplant, describes how after her transplant operation, when she left the hospital she drove to a Kentucky Fried Chicken, a place she had never been before, and ordered chicken nuggets. She later found out that her eighteen-year-old donor had a fondness for chicken nuggets and that at the time of the young man's death, un-eaten chicken nuggets were found inside the pocket of his jacket (Sylvia, 1997).

Although claims such as this are typically explained by conventional medicine as side-effects of the immunosuppresant drugs, the stress of the surgery, or statistical coincidence, cellular memory via the systemic memory hypothesis is also plausible and deserves systematic investigation.

Another implication relates to the idea of consciousness and memory extending outside the body (just as energy and information extend outside a system). Within the realm of consciousness research is the concept of intentionality where person A can exert some control over the physiology of person B (at some distance from person A) through conscious intent (Benor, 1996; Schlitz, 1996). In terms of dynamical energy systems theory, intention may focus biophysical energy in a way that it is synchronized and organized (Schwartz and Russek, 1997a). The result of this dynamically organized energy could be large bursts of focused energy that are stronger at further distances than is typically expected. For example, experiments have been conducted in which healers were able to change the absorption spectrum of DNA (modulating the helix coil conformation) according to their intention (reviewed in Benor, 1996).

If future research confirms and extends the Reid (1987) findings, the integration of classical and quantum physics with contemporary systems theory (including complexity, chaos, and dynamical energy systems) may pave the way for advancing the understanding of alternative and complementary medicine, and providing additional support for emerging new models of homeopathy, non-contact therapeutic touch, and other alternative healing practices.

As Singer and Reid (1998) phrased the general question concerning homeopathy, and by extension, concerning systemic memory in general, "Is it too much to hope that this will be the case?"

References

Barns, V. E., et al. 1964. Confirmation of the existence of the omega-minus hyperon. *Physics Letters.* 12:134-35.

Benor, D. J. 1996. Intention: An experimental focus. *Advances.* 12(3):4-13.

Capra, F. 1996. *The Web of Life: A New Scientific Understanding of Living Systems.* New York: Anchor Books.

Collins, H. H. 1985. *Changing Order: Replication and Induction in Scientific Practice.* Beverly Hills: Sage.

Edmonds, B. 1996. What is complexity? In *The Evolution of Complexity*; ed. F. Heylighen, and D. Aerts. Kluwer Academic Publishers.

Flint, E. 1971. *Essentials of Crystallography.* Moscow: Mir Publishers.

Gould, S. J. 1994. The evolution of life on earth. *Sci. American.* 271(4):62-69.

Halle, B., and B. Lindman. 1978. Chloride ion binding to human plasma albumin from chlorine-35 quadrupole relaxation. *Biochem.* 17:3774-3781.

Heylighen, F., and C. Joslyn. 1992. What is systems theory? Available from *Principia Cybernetica* http://pespmc1.vub.ac.be.; Internet.

Heylighen, F. 1996a. The growth of structural and functional complexity during evolution. Kluwer Academic Publishers. Available from *Principia Cybernetica* http://pespmc1.vub.ac.be; Internet.

———. **1996b.** Self-organization and complexity in the natural sciences. Available from *Principia Cybernetica* http://pespmc1.vub.ac.be; Internet.

Jobst, K. A. 1998. The truth and nothing but the truth: Objectivity in alternative and orthodox biomedicine? *J. Alt. Comp. Med.* 4,7:1-4.

Kauffman, S. A. 1993. *The Origins of Order.* New York: Oxford University Press.

Miller, J. G. 1978. *Living Systems.* New York: McGraw-Hill.

Newton, R. G. 1997. *The Truth of Science: Physical Theories and Reality*. Cambridge: Harvard University Press.

Pearsall, P. 1998. *The Heart's Code*. New York: Broadway Books.

Peters, T. 1996. *All about Albumin: Biochemistry, Genetics, and Medical Applications*. San Diego: Academic Press.

Radin, D. I. 1997. *The Conscious Universe*. New York: HarperCollins.

Reid, B. L. 1987. The ability of an electric current to carry information for crystal growth patterns. *J. Bio. Physics*. 15(2):33-35.

———. 1989. On the nature of growth and new growth based on experiments designed to reveal a structure and function for laboratory space: Part I. *Med. Hypotheses*. 29(2):105-26.

———. 1995. Aspects of intelligible energy function in biosystems. *Med. Hypotheses*. 44:527-536.

Russek, L. G., and G. E. Schwartz. 1996. Energy cardiology: A dynamical energy systems approach for integrating conventional and alternative medicine. *Advances*. 12(4):36-45.

Schlitz, M. J. 1996. Intentionality and intuition and their clinical applications: A challenge for science and medicine. *Advances*. 12(2):58-66.

Schwartz, G. E., and L. G. Russek. 1997a. Dynamical energy systems and modern physics: Fostering the science and spirit of complementary and alternative medicine. *Alt. Ther. Health Med*. 3(3):46-56.

———. 1997b. The challenge of one medicine: Theories of Health and 'Eight World Hypotheses.' *Advances*. 13(3):7-23.

———. 1998c. Do all dynamical systems have memory? Implications of the systemic memory hypothesis for science and society. In *Brain and Values: Is a Biological Science of Values Possible*; ed. K.H. Pribram, 249-76. Hillsdale, NJ: Lawrence Erlbaum Associates.

Schwartz, G. E. R., and L. G. S. Russek. 1998b. The plausibility of homeopathy: The systemic memory mechanism. *Integrative Med*. 1:53-59.

———. 1998d. The origin of holism and memory in nature: The systemic memory hypothesis. *Frontier Perspectives*. 7(2):23-30.

Singer, A., and B. Reid. 1998. Can physics and physical chemistry explain the workings of homeopathy? A clinician's view. *J. Alt. Comp. Med*. 4:132-135.

Sylvia, C., with W. Novak. 1997. *A Change of Heart*. New York: Little, Brown.

Wolcott, H. F. 1994. *Transforming Qualitative Data: Description, Analysis, and Interpretation*. Thousand Oaks, CA: Sage.

Index

Authors' Note

When we are ready to listen with our heart, we are transformed.
Dr. James Levin

After *The Living Energy Universe* was completed, Linda and I realized that a Sony digital video camera with frame by frame slow-motion recording could be used to demonstrate the creation and evolution of systemic memory over time. The dynamic images are often dramatic and beautiful, a new form of video feedback art. If you have a regular camcorder and TV, or video digitizer and computer monitor, you too can learn how to create your own systemic memory art and witness the theory become real.

We subsequently discovered that video feedback had been used in the introductory chapter of a textbook on fractals to demonstrate how feedback works. Paraphrasing the authors, feedback is the "backbone" of systemic memory.

Linda and I rapidly wrote an epilogue that unfortunately could not be included in the first printing of this book. However, the complete epilogue is now available at www.livingenergyuniverse.com. There you can see actual pictures of video feedback in action, visit the Human Energy Systems Laboratory, and find references to additional books such as *Earthmind*, in which one of the authors, John Steele, applied systemic memory to the Earth. The story continues, and there's so much more for all of us to see.

About the Authors

Gary E. R. Schwartz is a professor of psychology, medicine, neurology, and psychiatry at the University of Arizona; director of the Human Energy Systems Laboratory; co-facilitator in energy medicine and senior research advisor for Andrew Weil's program in integrative medicine. He is also director of the Bioenergy Core, The Pediatric Alternative Medicine Center at the University of Arizona. He received his Ph.D. from Harvard University in 1971 and was an assistant professor at Harvard. He was a professor of psychology and psychiatry at Yale University, director of the Yale Psychophysiology Center, and co-director of the Yale Behavioral Medicine Clinic from 1976–1988.

Linda G. S. Russek is clinical assistant professor of medicine, co-director of the Human Energy Systems Laboratory, and co-facilitator of the energy medicine program in integrative medicine at the University of Arizona. She is also president of the Family Love and Health Foundation, and director of the Elayne and Henry Russek Center. She received her M.A. from Columbia University in 1973 and her Ph.D. from United States International University in 1978. For 20 years she was director of the Harvard Mastery of Stress follow-up study.

Hampton Roads Publishing Company

. . . for the evolving human spirit

Hampton Roads Publishing Company
publishes books on a variety of subjects including
metaphysics, health, complementary medicine,
visionary fiction, and other related topics.

For a copy of our latest catalog,
call toll-free, 800-766-8009,
or send your name and address to:

Hampton Roads Publishing Company, Inc.
134 Burgess Lane
Charlottesville, VA 22902

E-mail: hrpc@hrpub.com
www.hrpub.com